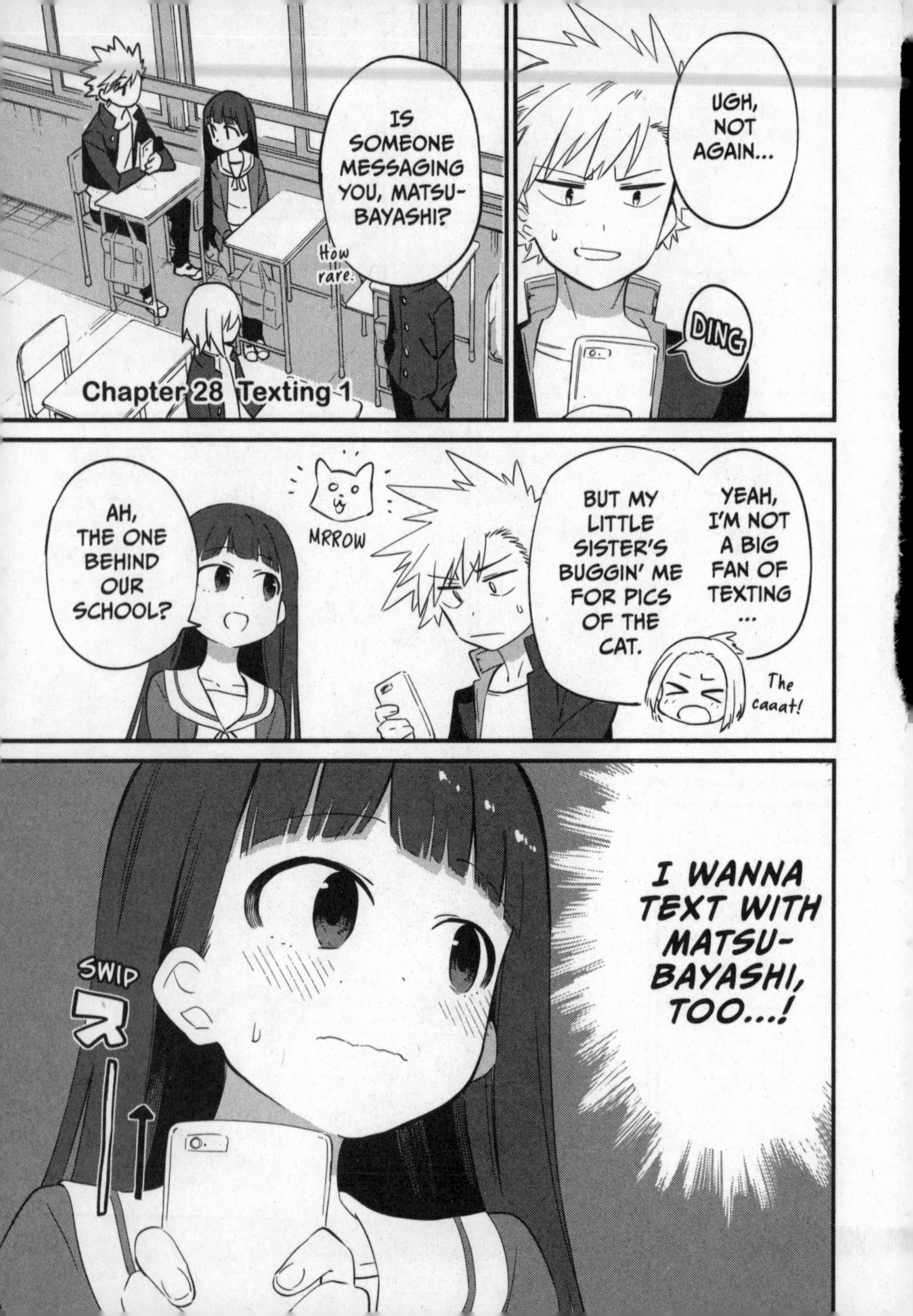
UGH, NOT AGAIN...
DING
IS SOMEONE MESSAGING YOU, MATSU-BAYASHI?
How rare.
Chapter 28 Texting 1
YEAH, I'M NOT A BIG FAN OF TEXTING ...
The caaat!
BUT MY LITTLE SISTER'S BUGGIN' ME FOR PICS OF THE CAT.
MRROW
AH, THE ONE BEHIND OUR SCHOOL?
I WANNA TEXT WITH MATSU-BAYASHI, TOO...!
SWIP

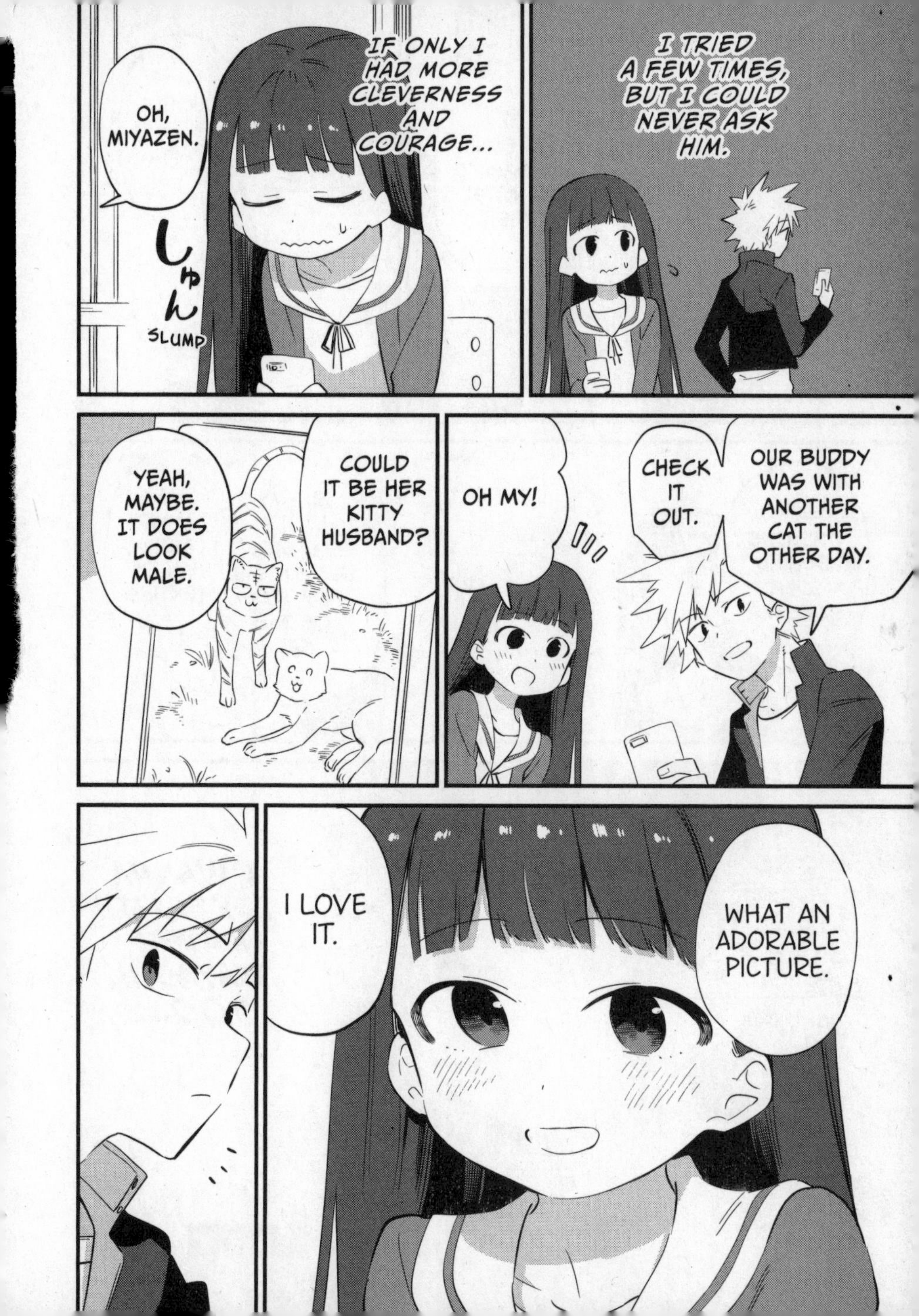
I TRIED A FEW TIMES, BUT I COULD NEVER ASK HIM.
IF ONLY I HAD MORE CLEVERNESS AND COURAGE...
OH, MIYAZEN.
しゅん
SLUMP
OUR BUDDY WAS WITH ANOTHER CAT THE OTHER DAY.
CHECK IT OUT.
OH MY!
COULD IT BE HER KITTY HUSBAND?
YEAH, MAYBE. IT DOES LOOK MALE.
WHAT AN ADORABLE PICTURE.
I LOVE IT.

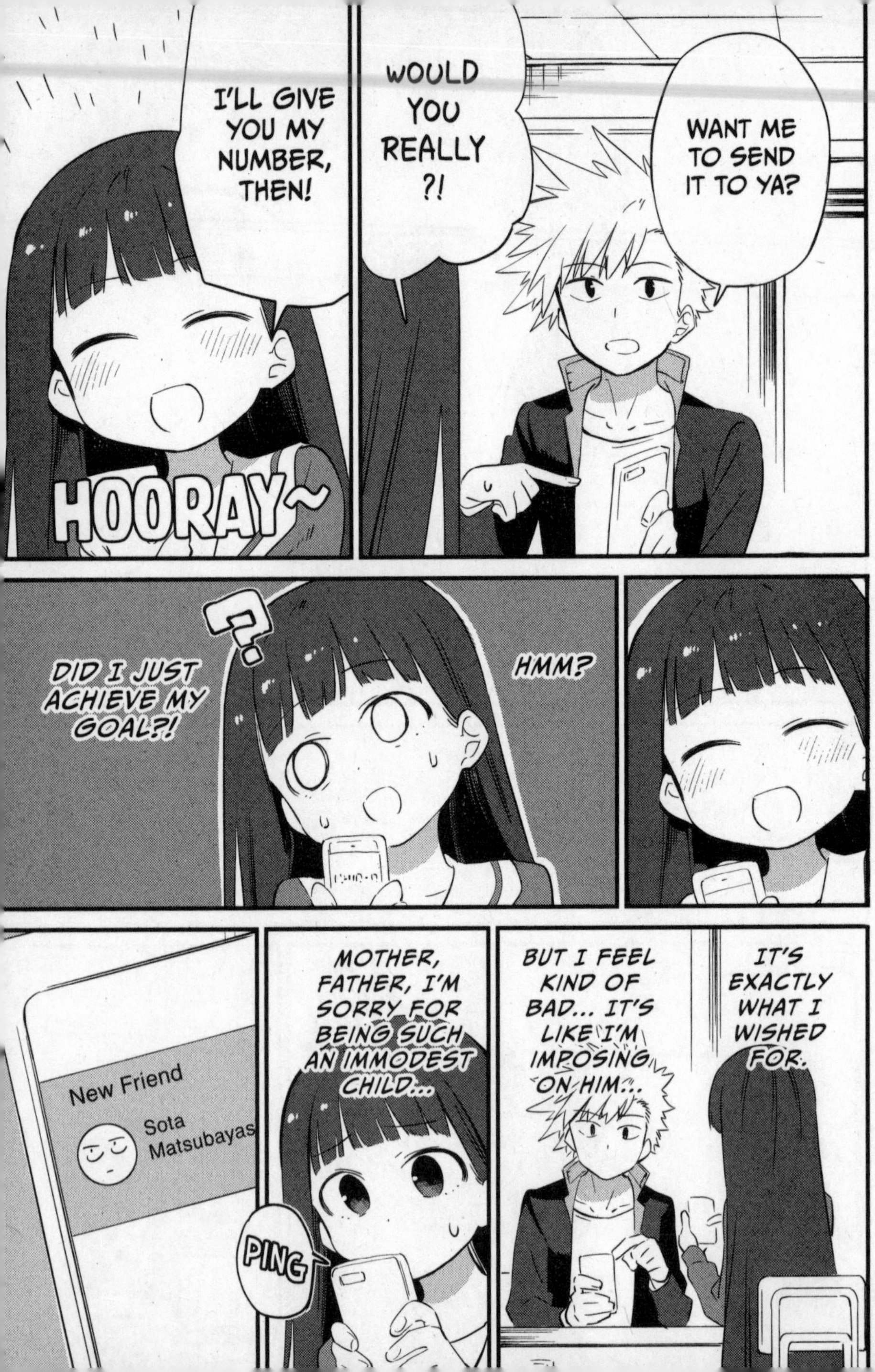
WANT ME TO SEND IT TO YA?
WOULD YOU REALLY ?!
I'LL GIVE YOU MY NUMBER, THEN!
HOORAY~
HMM?
?
DID I JUST ACHIEVE MY GOAL?!
IT'S EXACTLY WHAT I WISHED FOR.
BUT I FEEL KIND OF BAD... IT'S LIKE I'M IMPOSING ON HIM...
MOTHER, FATHER, I'M SORRY FOR BEING SUCH AN IMMODEST CHILD...
PING
New Friend
Sota Matsubayas

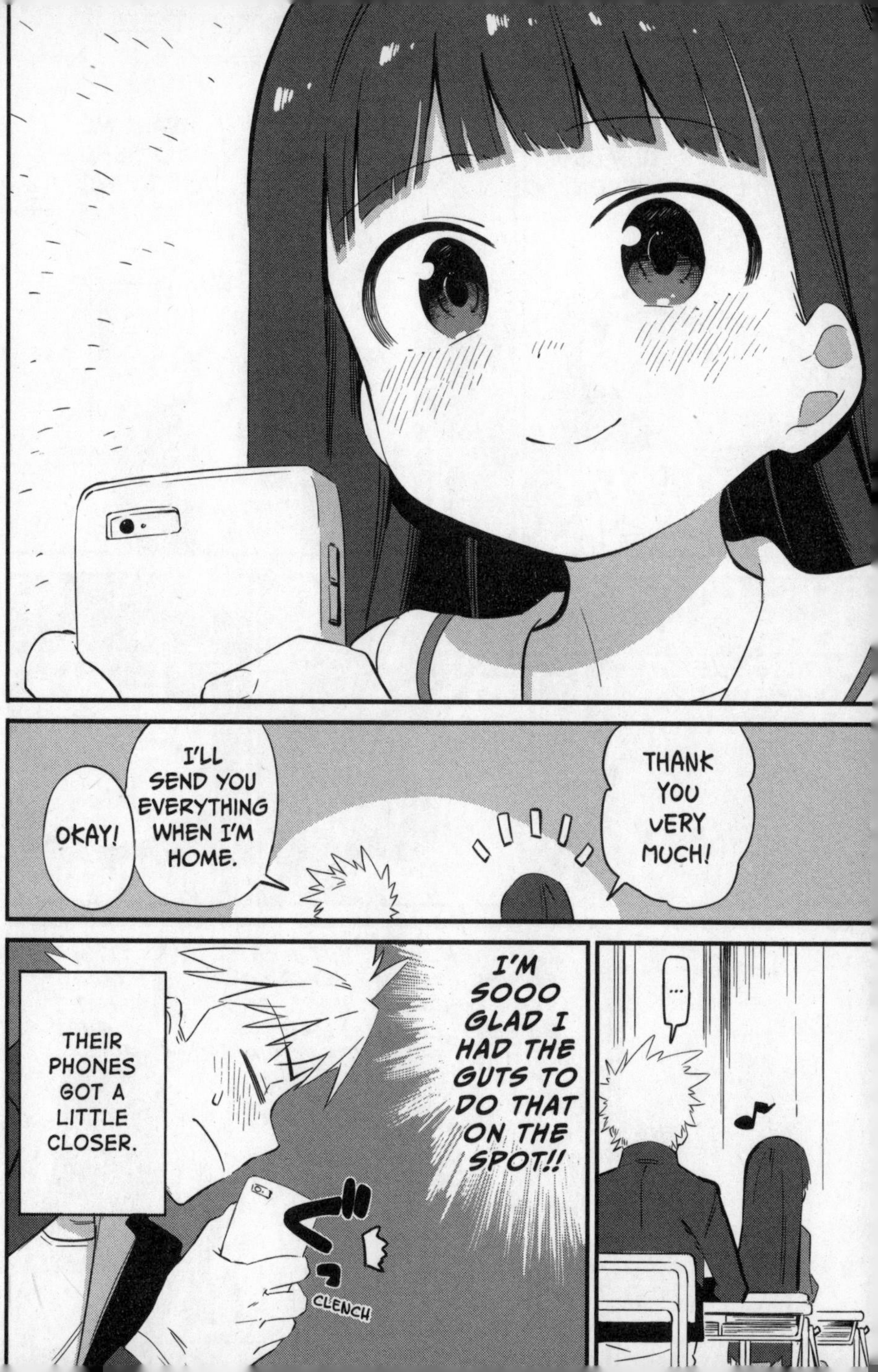
THANK YOU VERY MUCH!
I'LL SEND YOU EVERYTHING WHEN I'M HOME.
OKAY!
...
I'M SOOO GLAD I HAD THE GUTS TO DO THAT ON THE SPOT!!
THEIR PHONES GOT A LITTLE CLOSER.
CLENCH

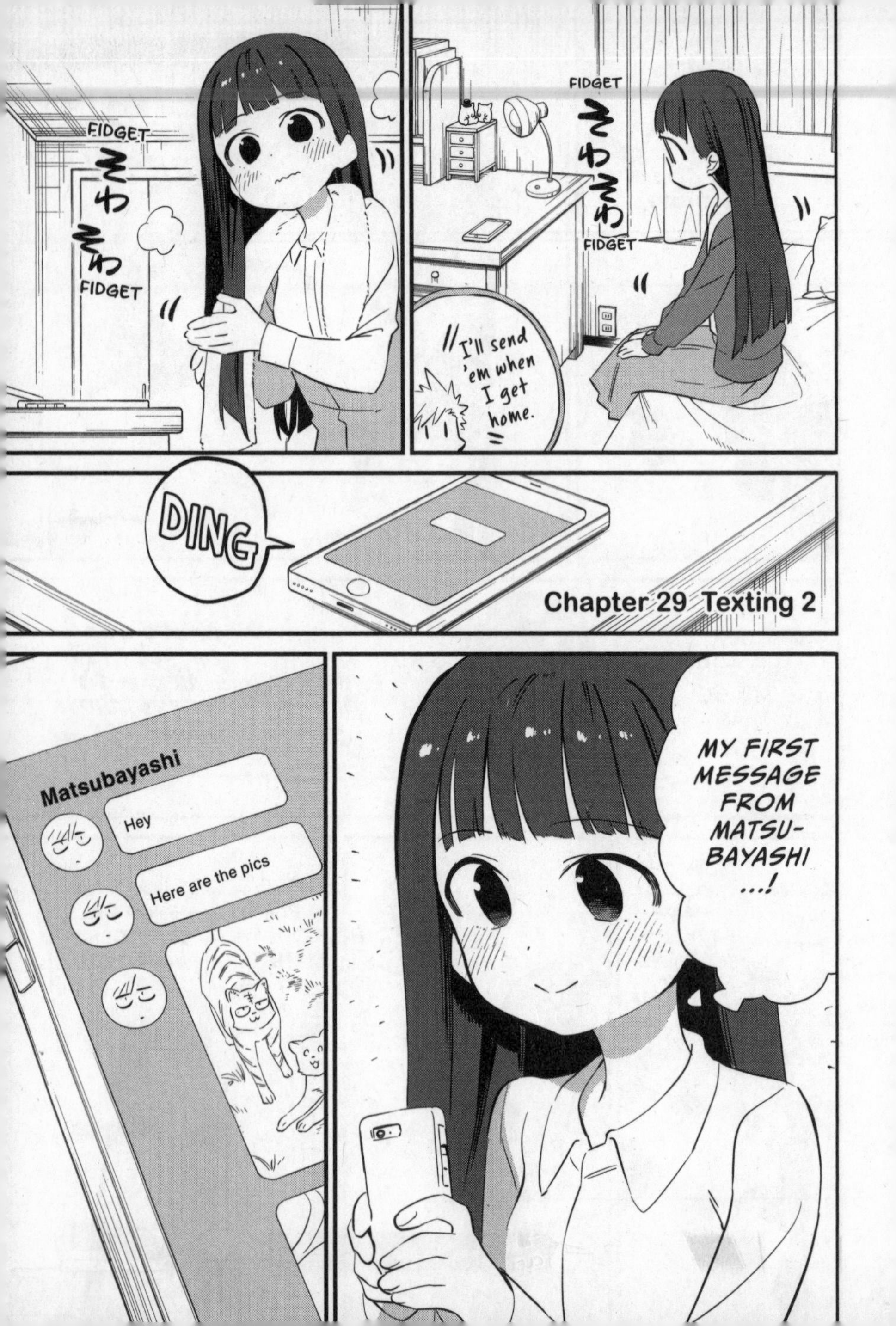
FIDGET
そわそわ
FIDGET
I'll send 'em when I get home.
FIDGET
そわ
そわ
FIDGET
DING
Chapter 29 Texting 2
MY FIRST MESSAGE FROM MATSU-BAYASHI ...!
Matsubayashi
Hey
Here are the pics

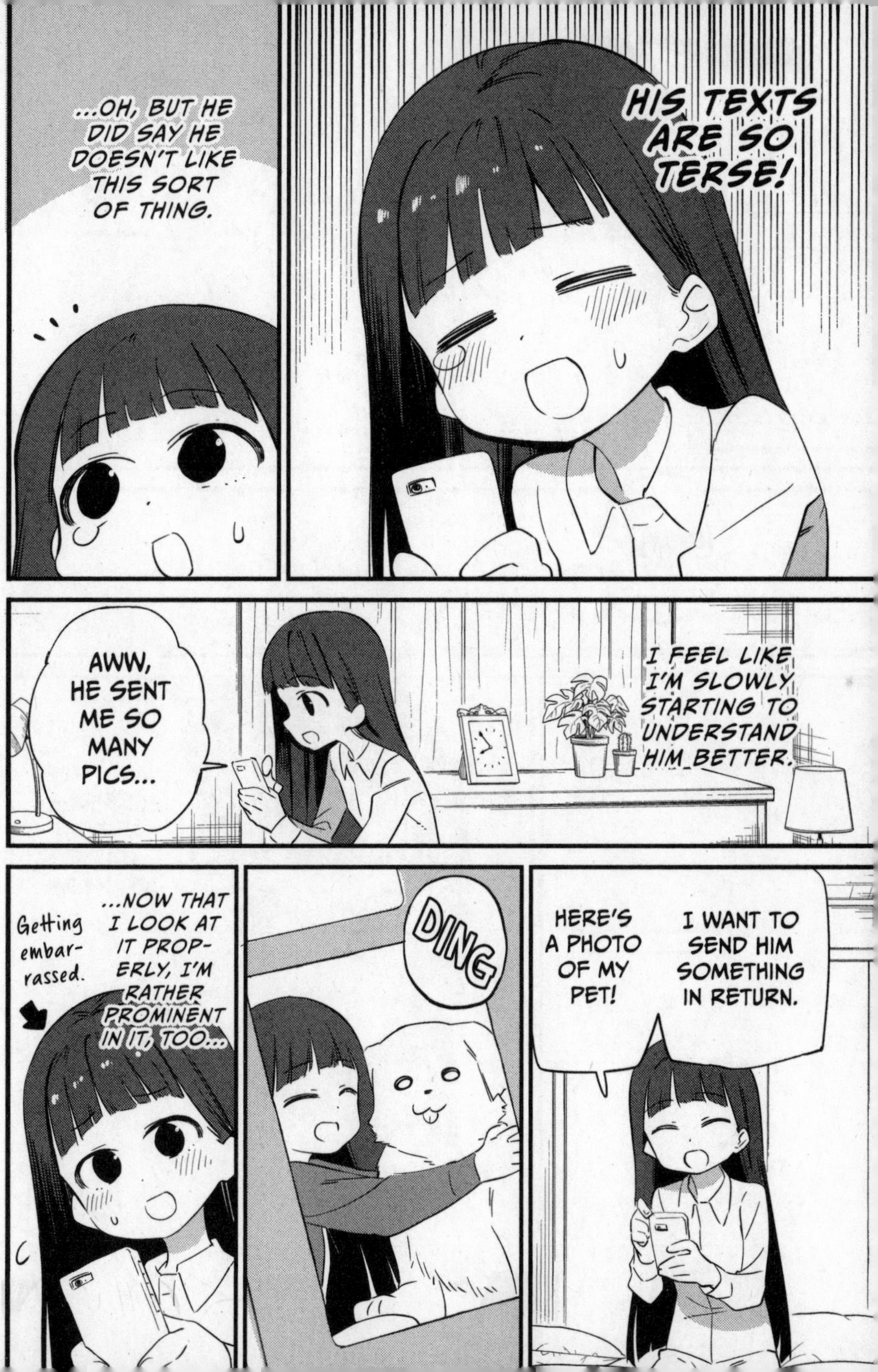
HIS TEXTS ARE SO TERSE!
...OH, BUT HE DID SAY HE DOESN'T LIKE THIS SORT OF THING.
I FEEL LIKE I'M SLOWLY STARTING TO UNDERSTAND HIM BETTER.
AWW, HE SENT ME SO MANY PICS...
I WANT TO SEND HIM SOMETHING IN RETURN.
HERE'S A PHOTO OF MY PET!
DING
...NOW THAT I LOOK AT IT PROP-ERLY, I'M RATHER PROMINENT IN IT, TOO...
Getting embar-rassed.

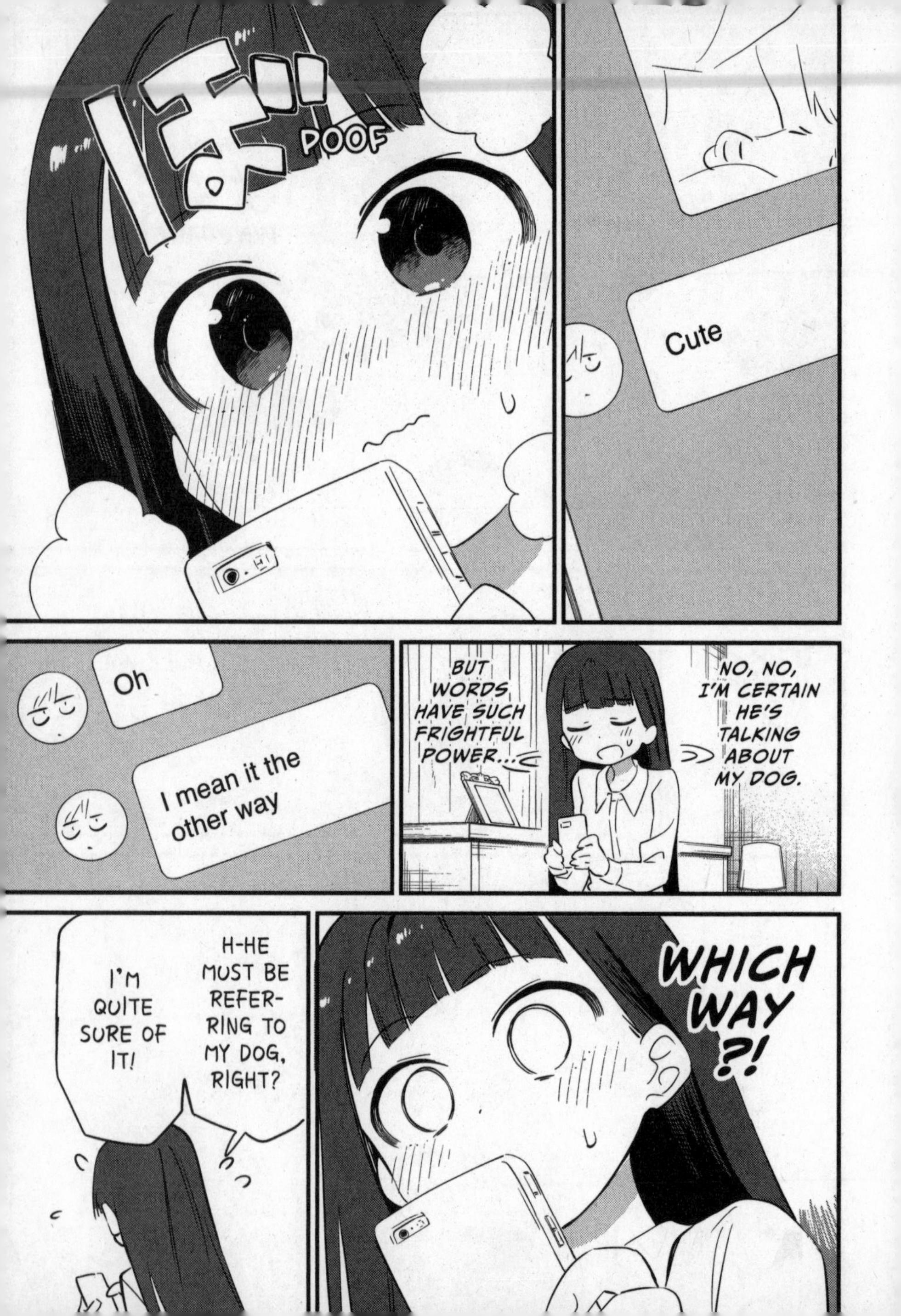
Cute
POOF
NO, NO, I'M CERTAIN HE'S TALKING ABOUT MY DOG.
BUT WORDS HAVE SUCH FRIGHTFUL POWER...
Oh
I mean it the other way
WHICH WAY ?!
H-HE MUST BE REFER-RING TO MY DOG, RIGHT?
I'M QUITE SURE OF IT!

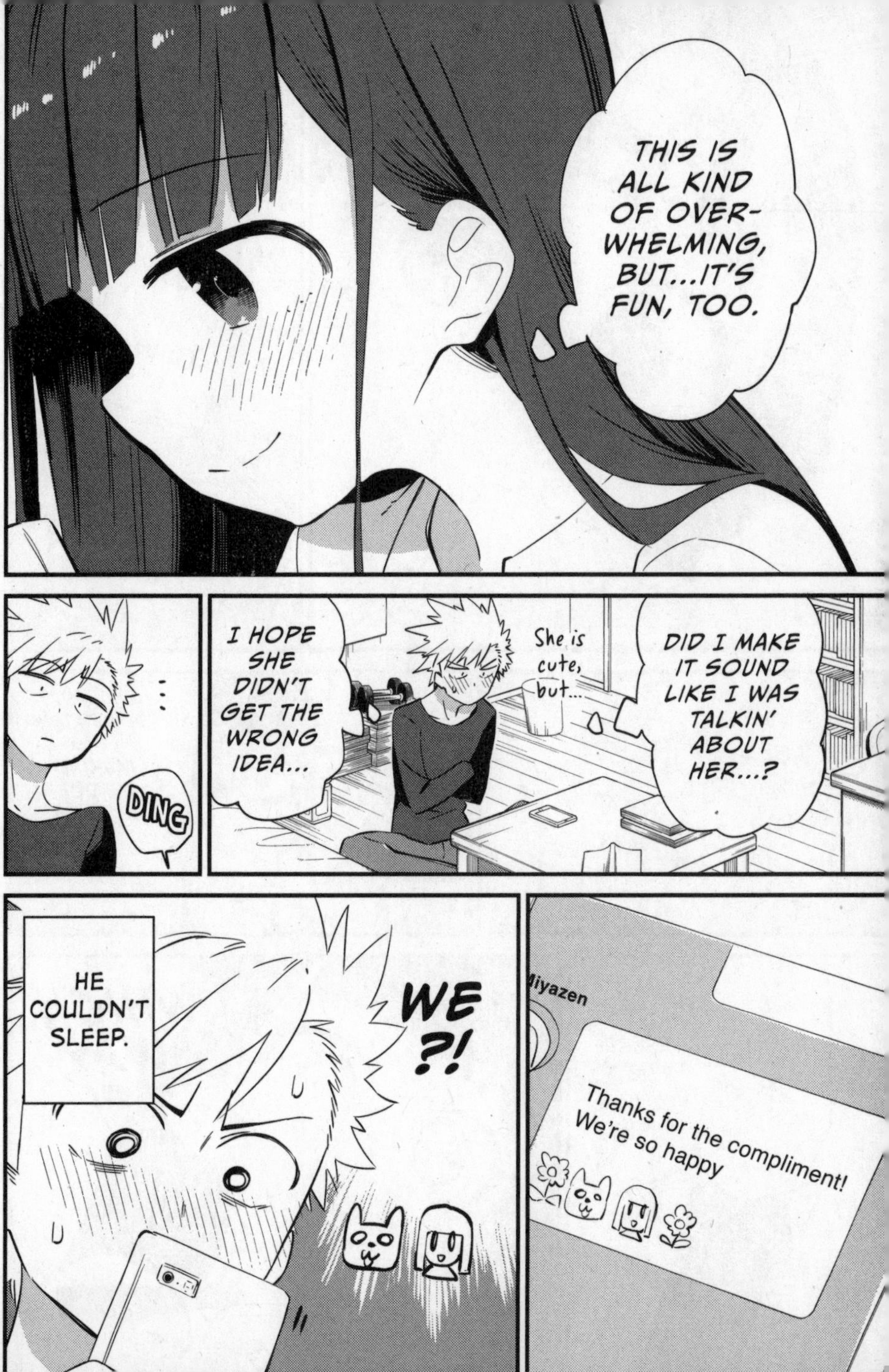
THIS IS ALL KIND OF OVER-WHELMING, BUT...IT'S FUN, TOO.
DID I MAKE IT SOUND LIKE I WAS TALKIN' ABOUT HER...?
She is cute, but...
I HOPE SHE DIDN'T GET THE WRONG IDEA...
...
DING
Miyazen
Thanks for the compliment! We're so happy
WE ?!
HE COULDN'T SLEEP.

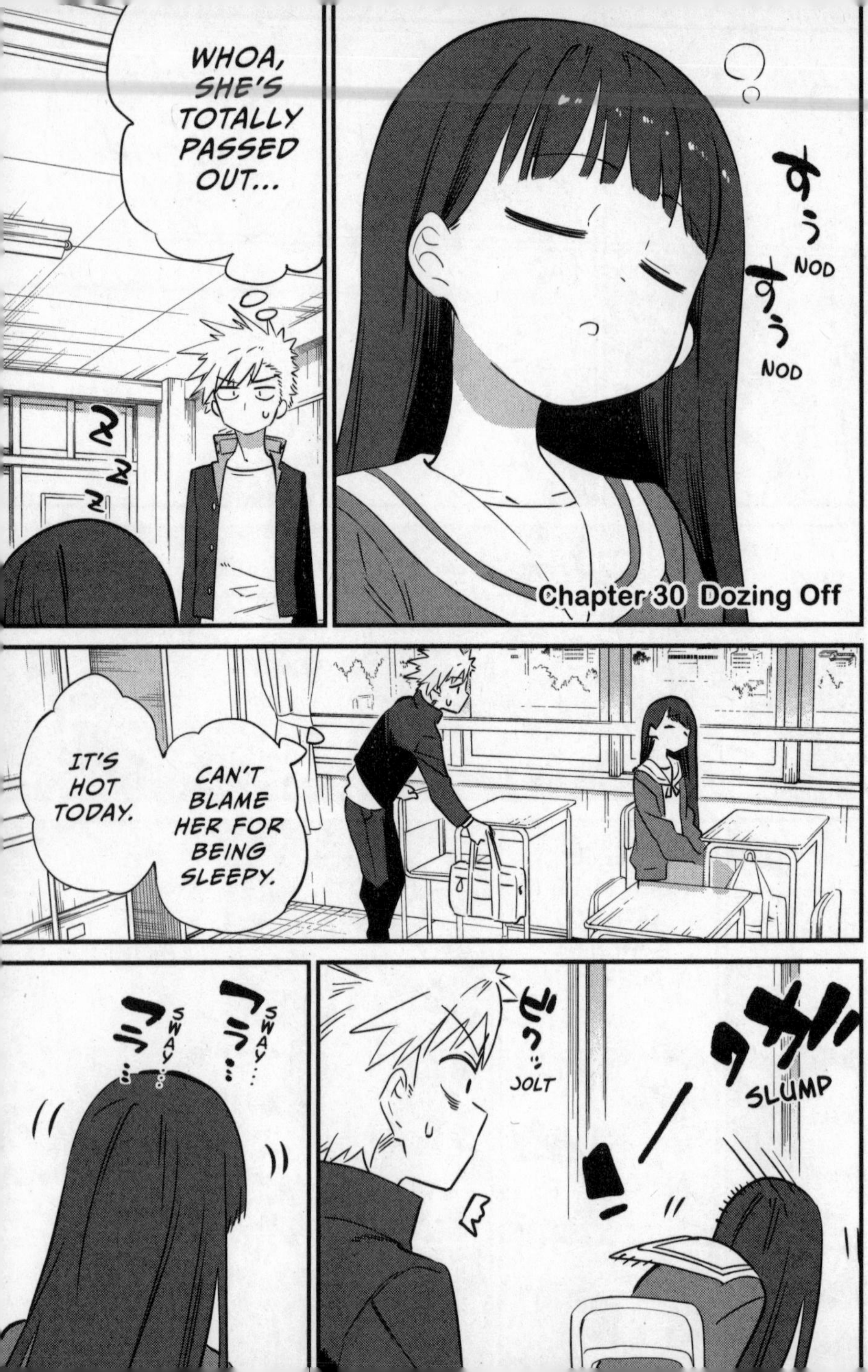
すう
NOD
すう
NOD
Chapter 30 Dozing Off
WHOA, SHE'S TOTALLY PASSED OUT...
ZZZ
IT'S HOT TODAY. CAN'T BLAME HER FOR BEING SLEEPY.
ガクッ
SLUMP
ビクッ
JOLT
フラ
SWAY...
フラ...
SWAY...

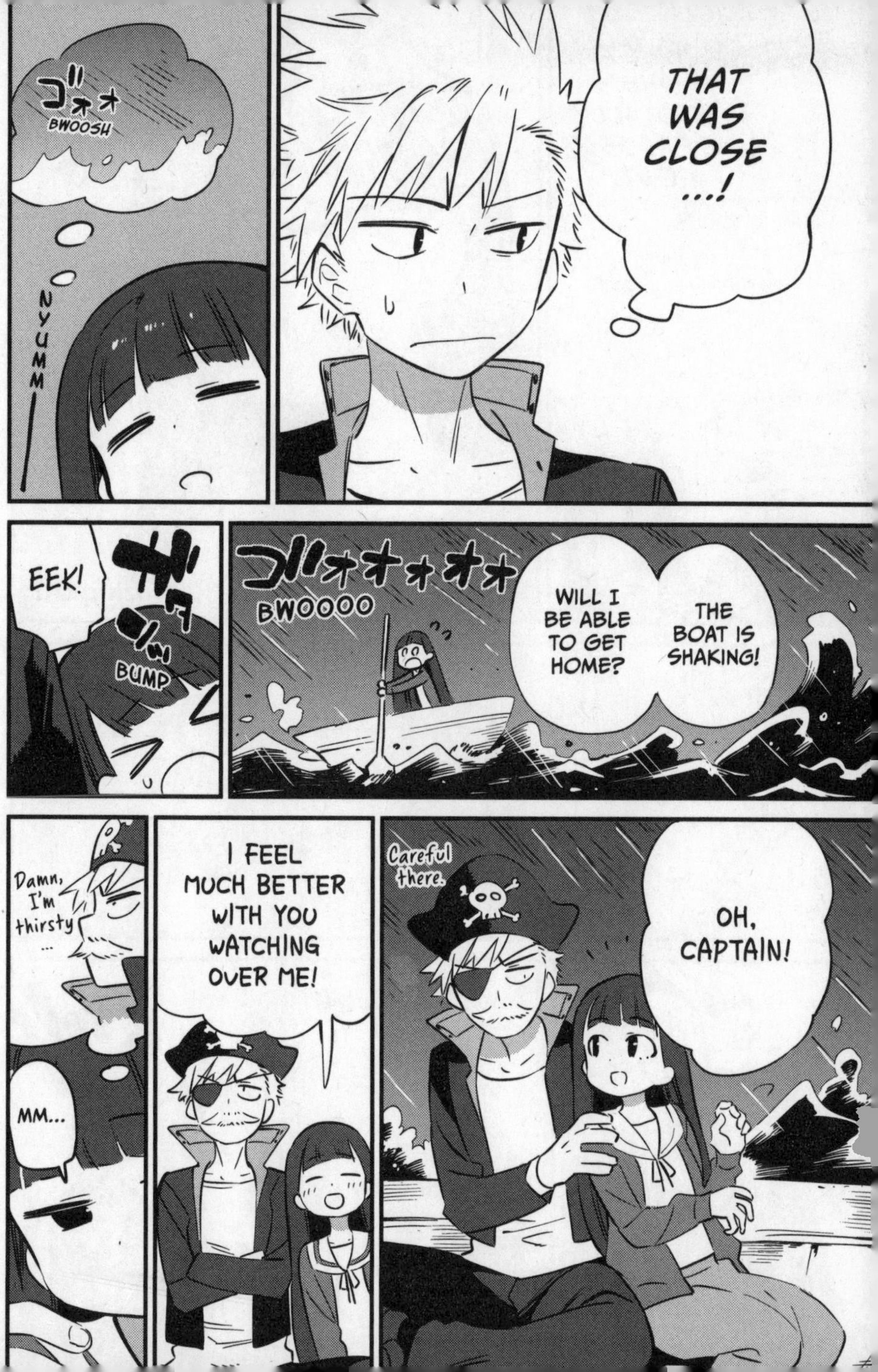
THAT WAS CLOSE ...!
ゴォォ
BWOOSH
NYUMM
ゴォォォォォ
BWOOOO
THE BOAT IS SHAKING!
WILL I BE ABLE TO GET HOME?
BUMP
EEK!
OH, CAPTAIN!
Careful there.
I FEEL MUCH BETTER WITH YOU WATCHING OVER ME!
Damn, I'm thirsty ...
MM...

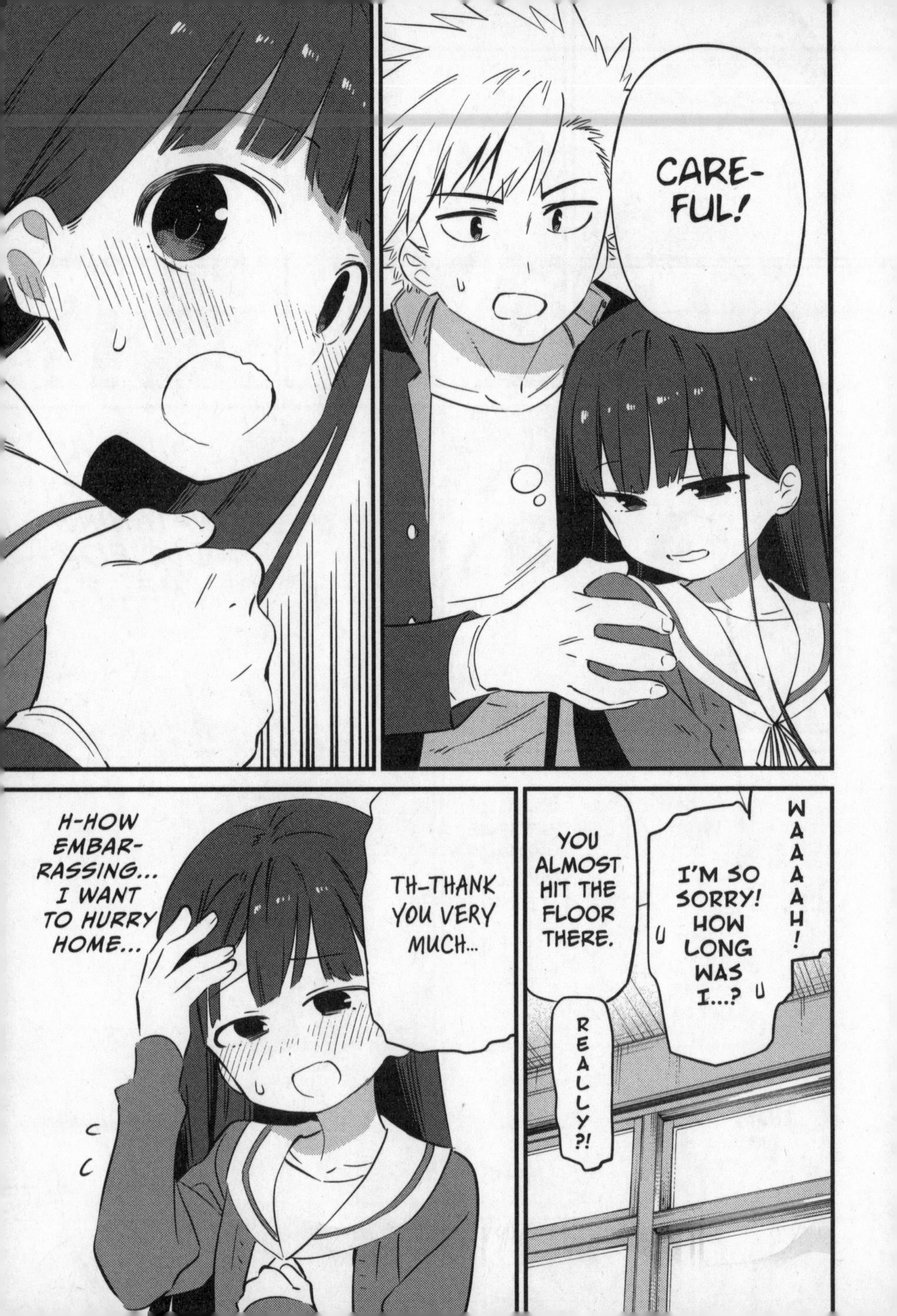
CARE-FUL!
WAAAAAH!
I'M SO SORRY! HOW LONG WAS I...?
YOU ALMOST HIT THE FLOOR THERE.
REALLY?!
TH-THANK YOU VERY MUCH...
H-HOW EMBARRASSING... I WANT TO HURRY HOME...

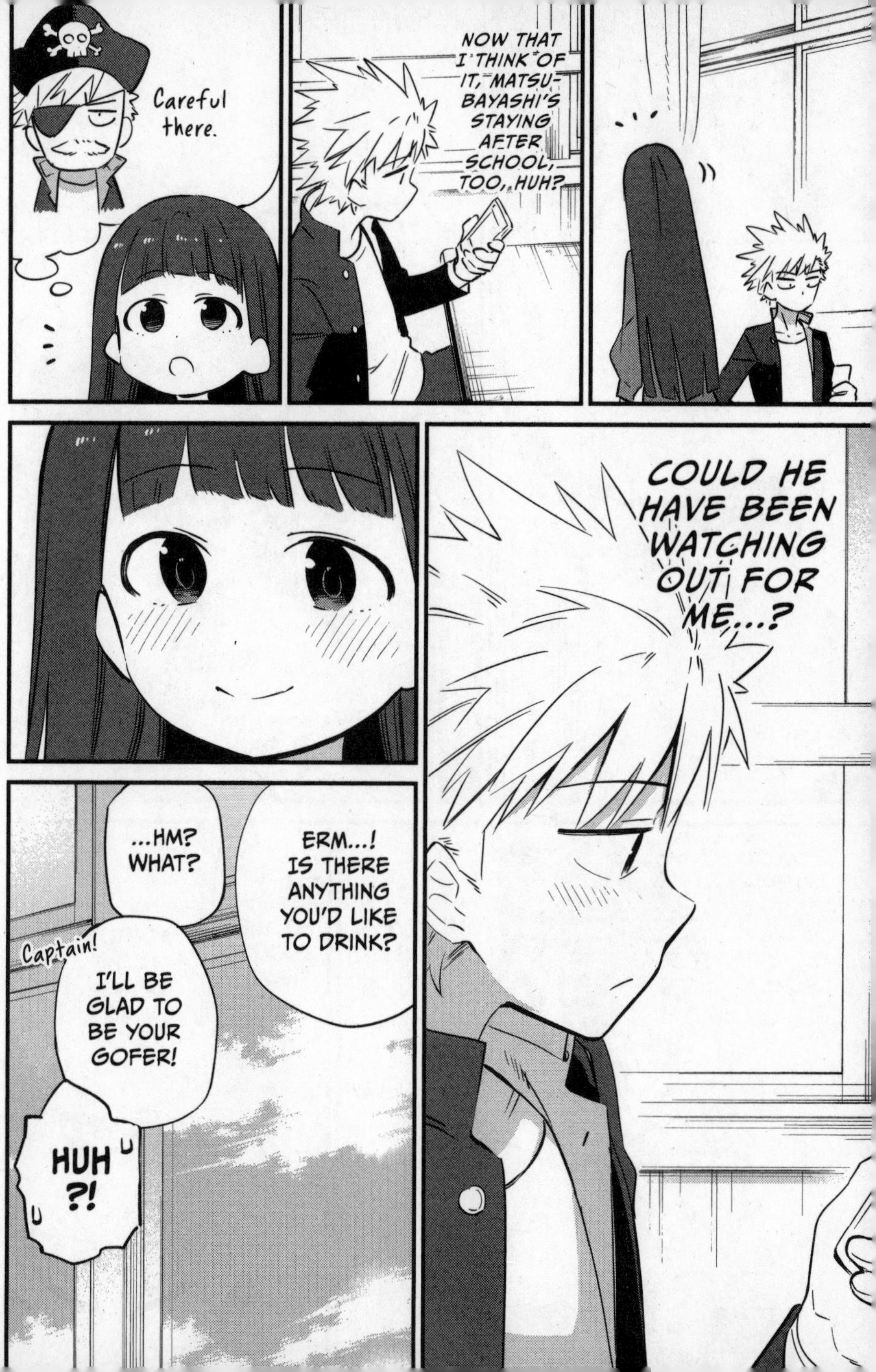
NOW THAT I THINK OF IT, MATSU-BAYASHI'S STAYING AFTER SCHOOL, TOO, HUH?
Careful there.
COULD HE HAVE BEEN WATCHING OUT FOR ME...?
ERM...! IS THERE ANYTHING YOU'D LIKE TO DRINK?
...HM? WHAT?
Captain!
I'LL BE GLAD TO BE YOUR GOFER!
HUH ?!

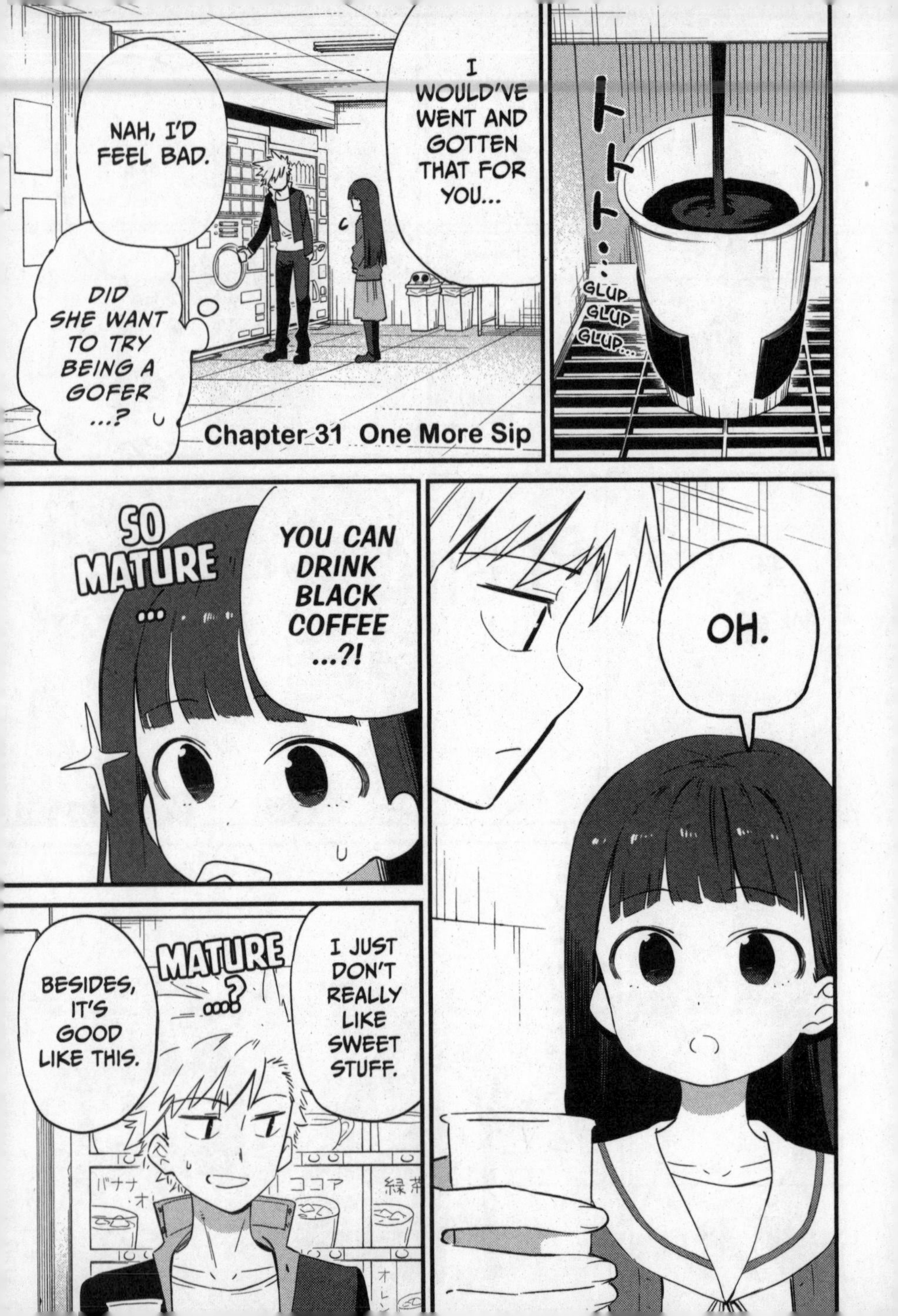
トトト…
GLUP GLUP GLUP...
I WOULD'VE WENT AND GOTTEN THAT FOR YOU...
NAH, I'D FEEL BAD.
DID SHE WANT TO TRY BEING A GOFER ...?
Chapter 31 One More Sip
OH.
YOU CAN DRINK BLACK COFFEE ...?!
SO MATURE
...
I JUST DON'T REALLY LIKE SWEET STUFF.
MATURE ...?
BESIDES, IT'S GOOD LIKE THIS.
バナナ
ココア

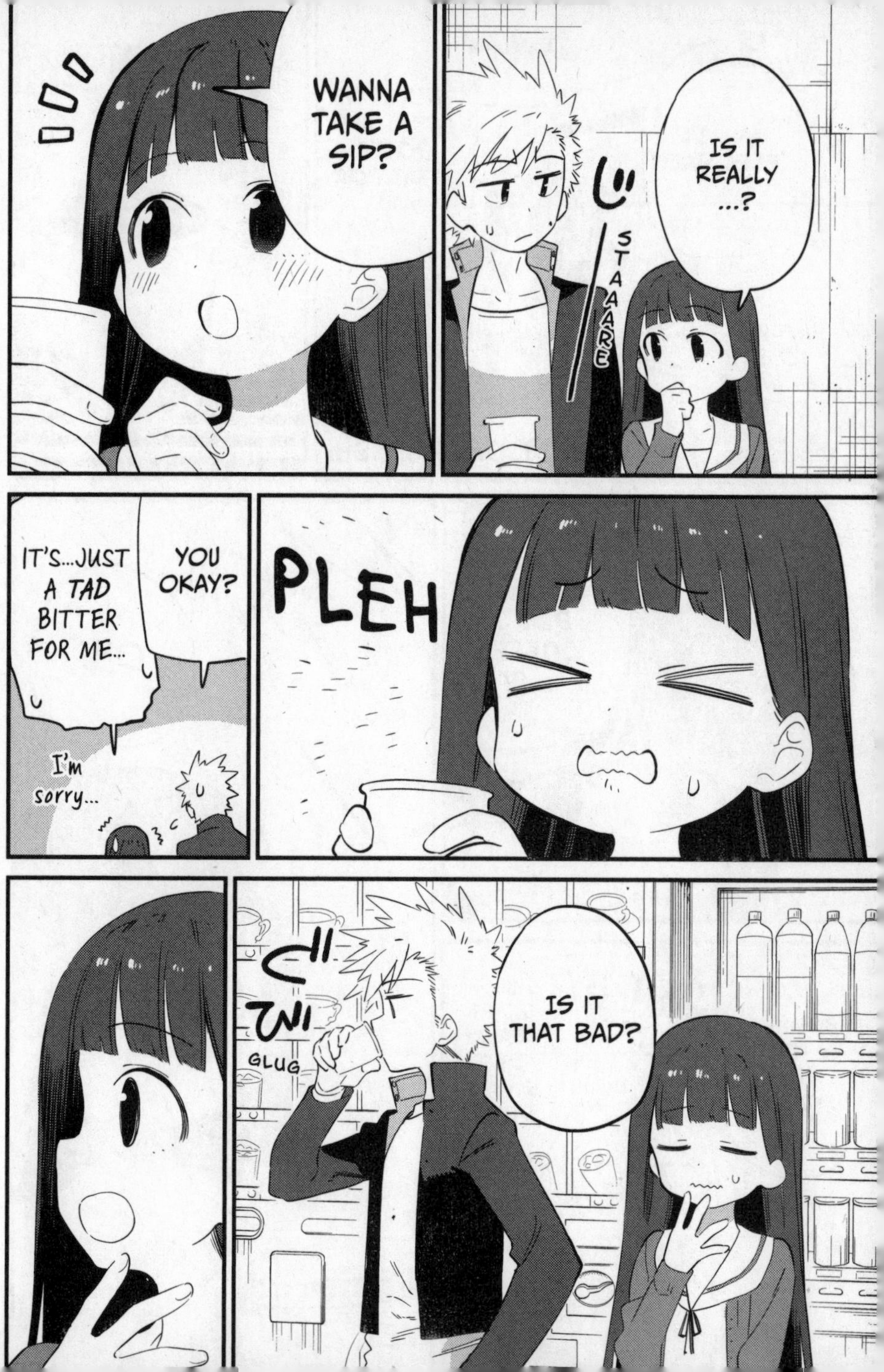
IS IT REALLY ...?
STAAAARE
WANNA TAKE A SIP?
PLEH
YOU OKAY?
IT'S...JUST A TAD BITTER FOR ME...
I'm sorry...
IS IT THAT BAD?
GLUG

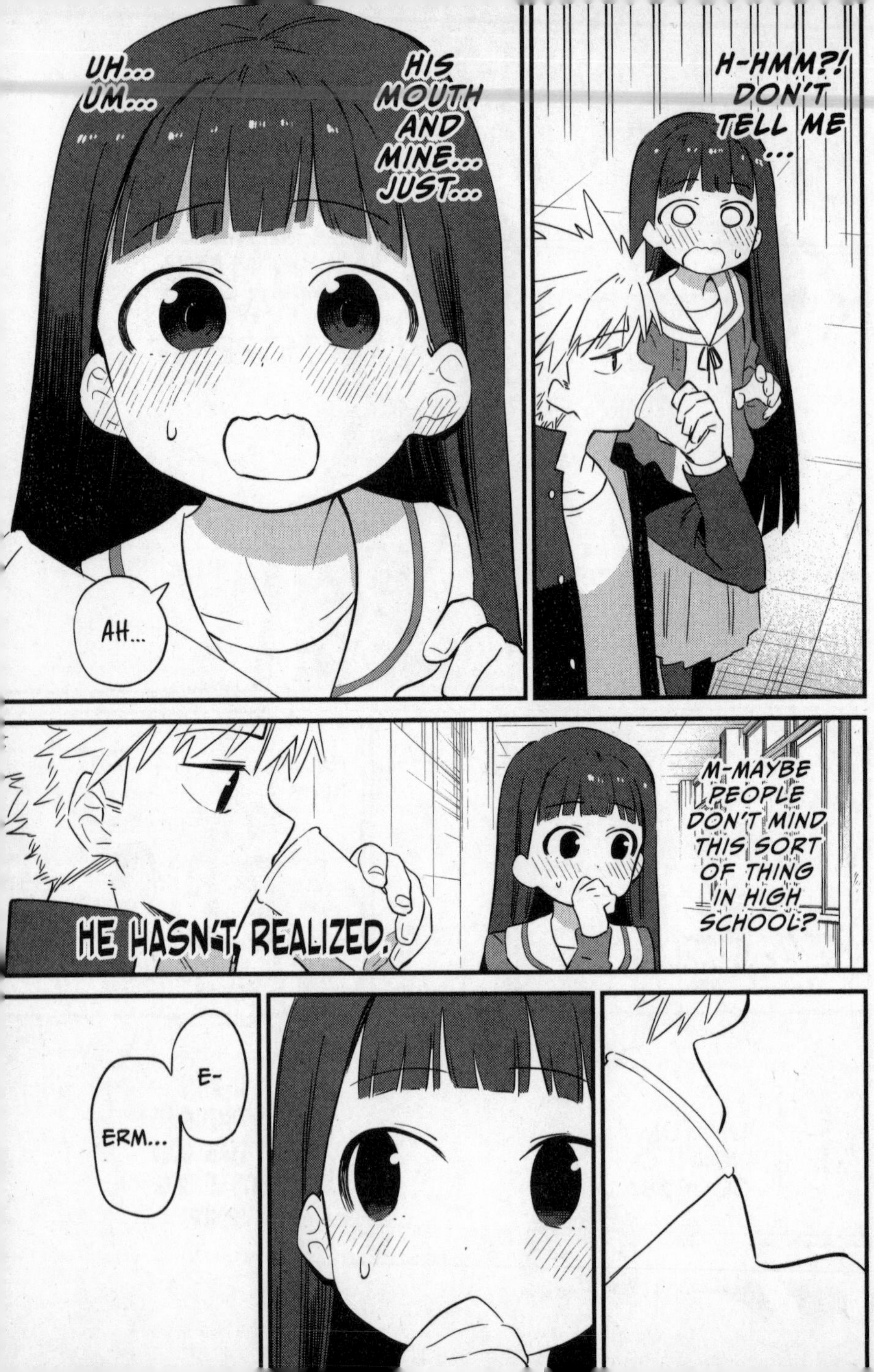
H-HMM?! DON'T TELL ME ...
HIS MOUTH AND MINE... JUST...
UH... UM...
AH...
M-MAYBE PEOPLE DON'T MIND THIS SORT OF THING IN HIGH SCHOOL?
HE HASN'T REALIZED.
E- ERM...

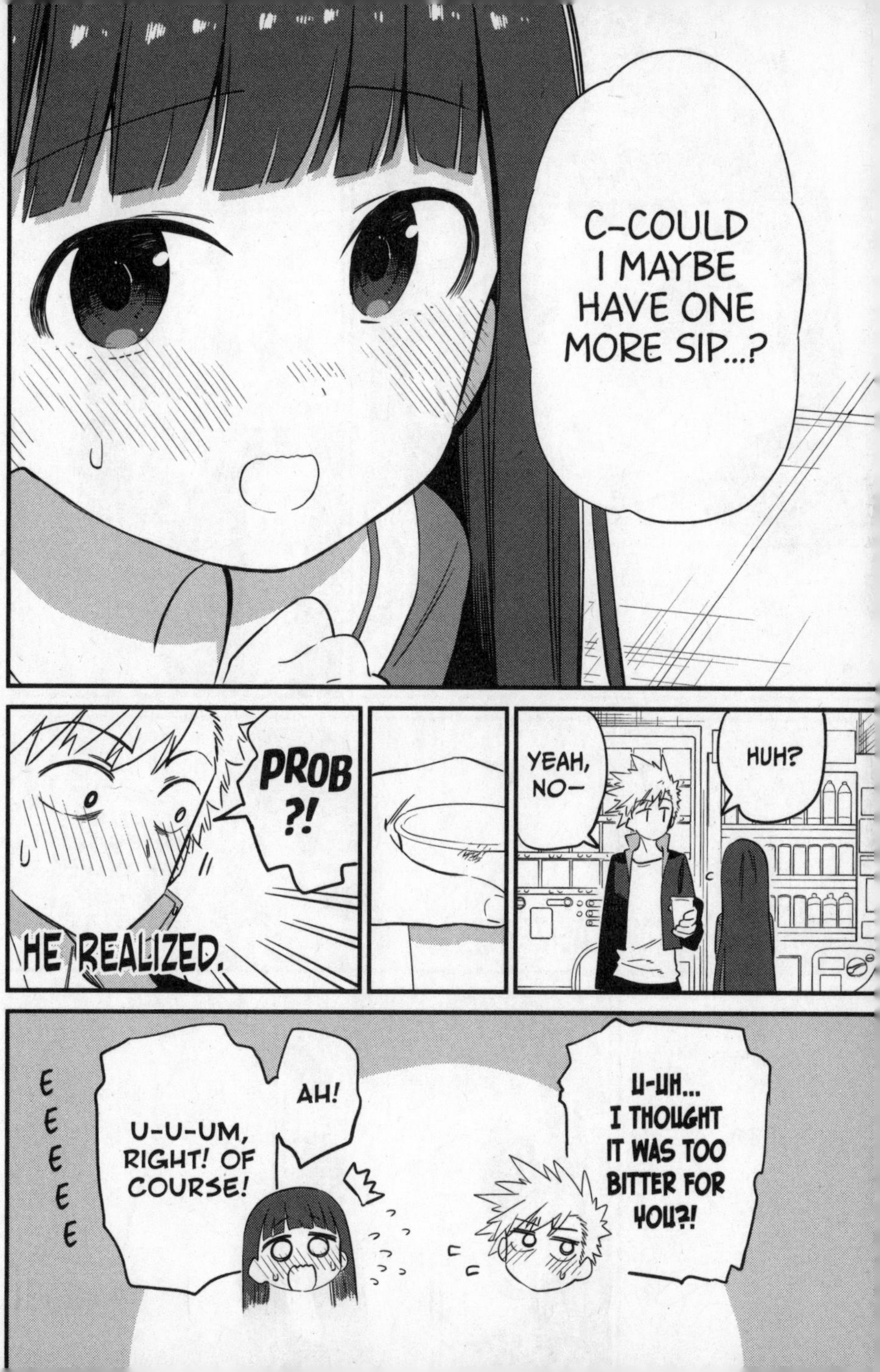
C-COULD I MAYBE HAVE ONE MORE SIP...?
HUH?
YEAH, NO—
PROB ?!
HE REALIZED.
U-UH... I THOUGHT IT WAS TOO BITTER FOR YOU?!
AH!
U-U-UM, RIGHT! OF COURSE!
EEEEE

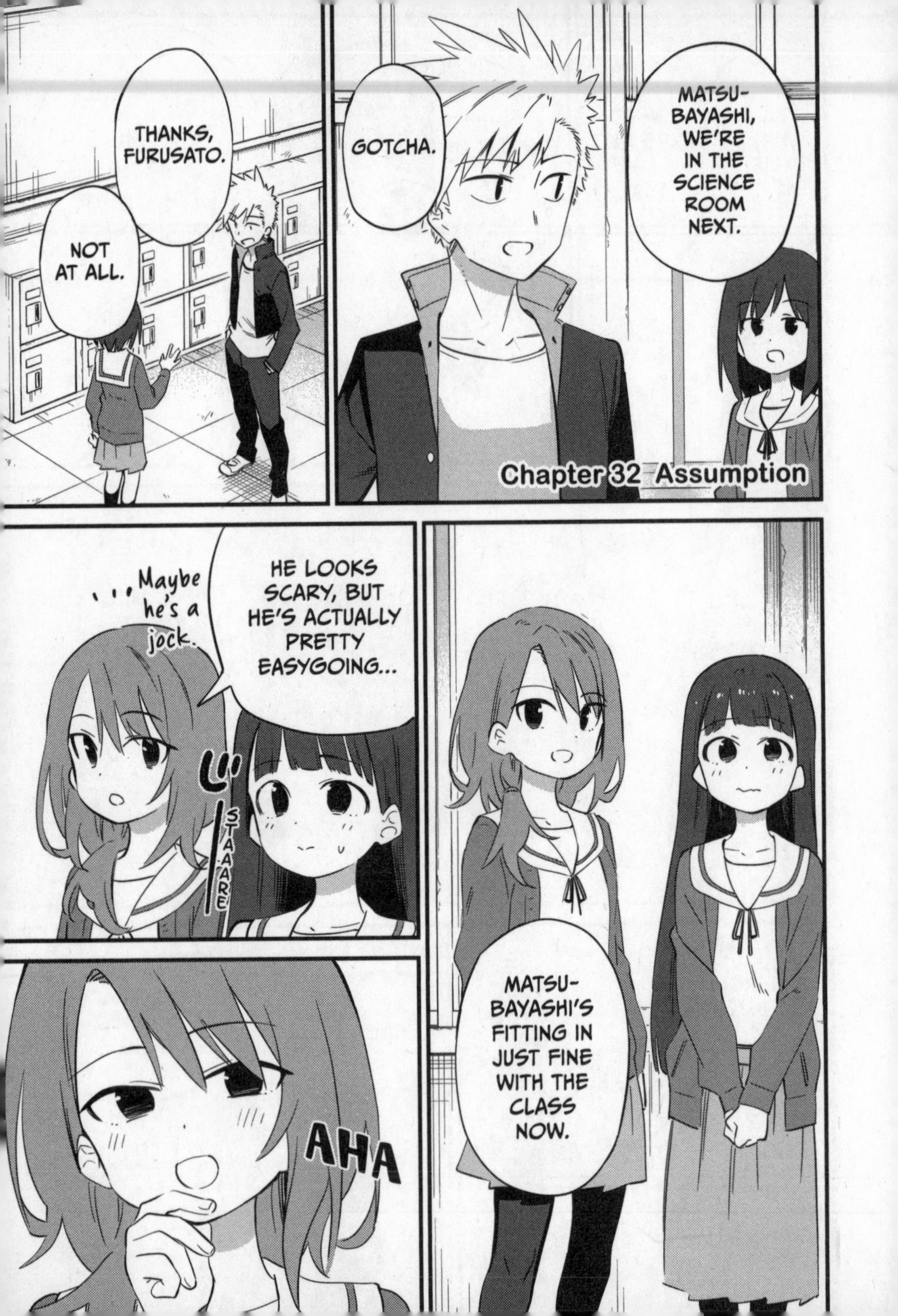
MATSU-BAYASHI, WE'RE IN THE SCIENCE ROOM NEXT.
GOTCHA.
Chapter 32 Assumption
THANKS, FURUSATO.
NOT AT ALL.
MATSU-BAYASHI'S FITTING IN JUST FINE WITH THE CLASS NOW.
HE LOOKS SCARY, BUT HE'S ACTUALLY PRETTY EASYGOING...
...Maybe he's a jock.
JI
STAAARE
AHA

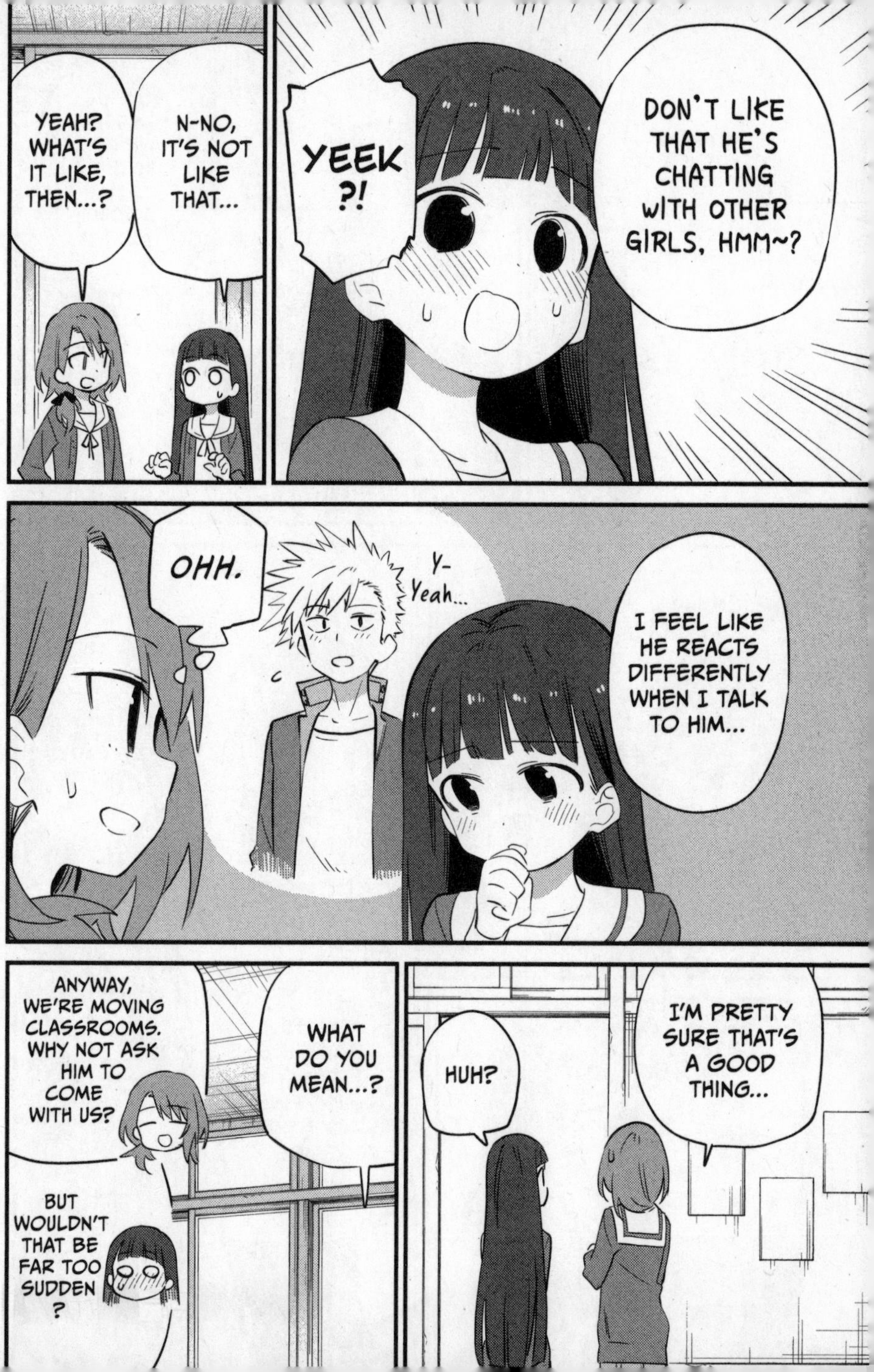
DON'T LIKE THAT HE'S CHATTING WITH OTHER GIRLS, HMM~?
YEEK ?!
N-NO, IT'S NOT LIKE THAT...
YEAH? WHAT'S IT LIKE, THEN...?
I FEEL LIKE HE REACTS DIFFERENTLY WHEN I TALK TO HIM...
Y- Yeah...
OHH.
I'M PRETTY SURE THAT'S A GOOD THING...
HUH?
WHAT DO YOU MEAN...?
ANYWAY, WE'RE MOVING CLASSROOMS. WHY NOT ASK HIM TO COME WITH US?
BUT WOULDN'T THAT BE FAR TOO SUDDEN ?

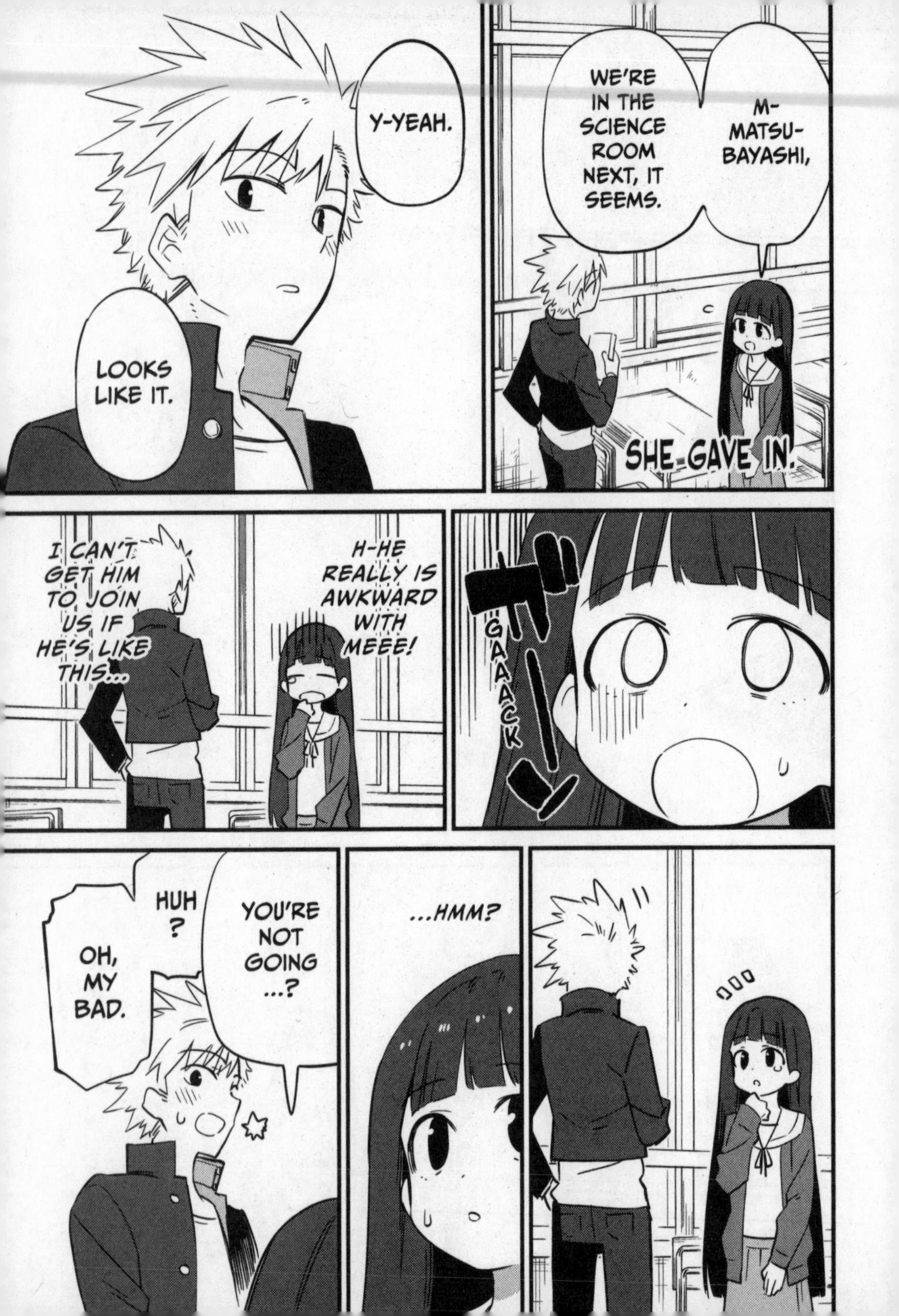
M-MATSU-BAYASHI,
WE'RE IN THE SCIENCE ROOM NEXT, IT SEEMS.
SHE GAVE IN.
Y-YEAH.
LOOKS LIKE IT.
GAAACK
H-HE REALLY IS AWKWARD WITH MEEE!
I CAN'T GET HIM TO JOIN US IF HE'S LIKE THIS...
...HMM?
YOU'RE NOT GOING...?
HUH?
OH, MY BAD.

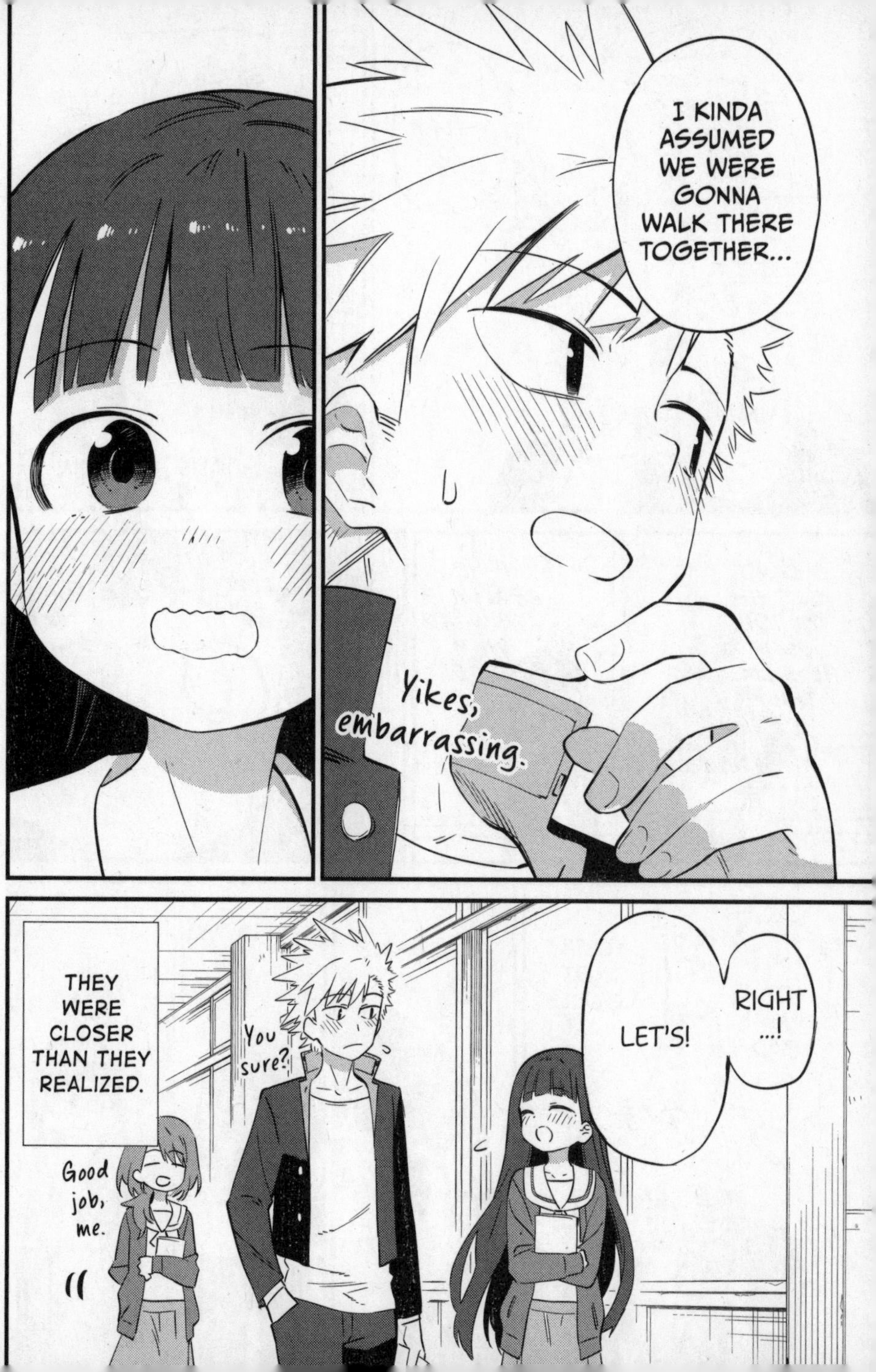
I KINDA ASSUMED WE WERE GONNA WALK THERE TOGETHER...
Yikes, embarrassing.
RIGHT ...!
LET'S!
You sure?
THEY WERE CLOSER THAN THEY REALIZED.
Good job, me.

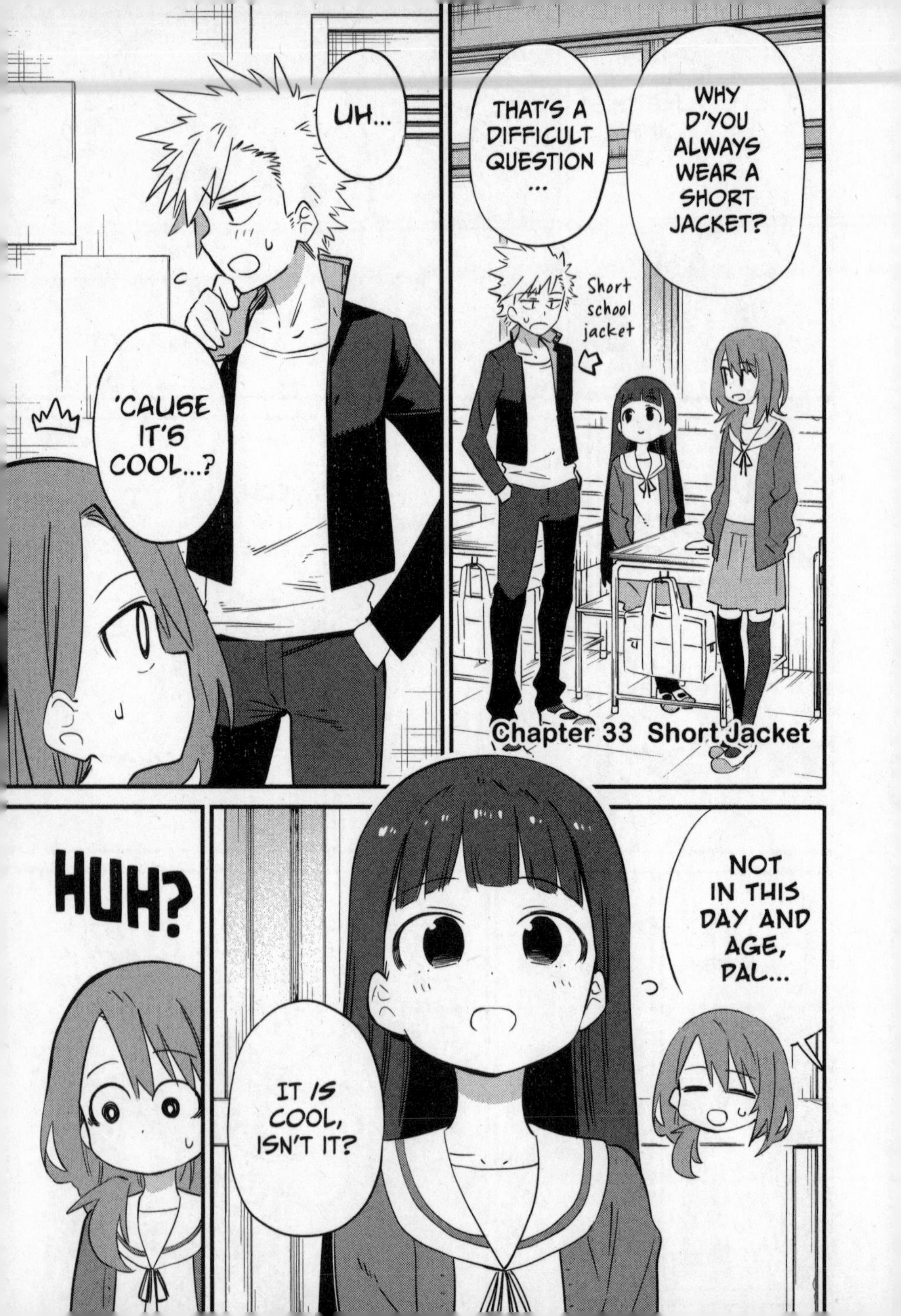
WHY D'YOU ALWAYS WEAR A SHORT JACKET?
THAT'S A DIFFICULT QUESTION ...
Short school jacket
Chapter 33 Short Jacket
UH...
'CAUSE IT'S COOL...?
NOT IN THIS DAY AND AGE, PAL...
IT IS COOL, ISN'T IT?
HUH?

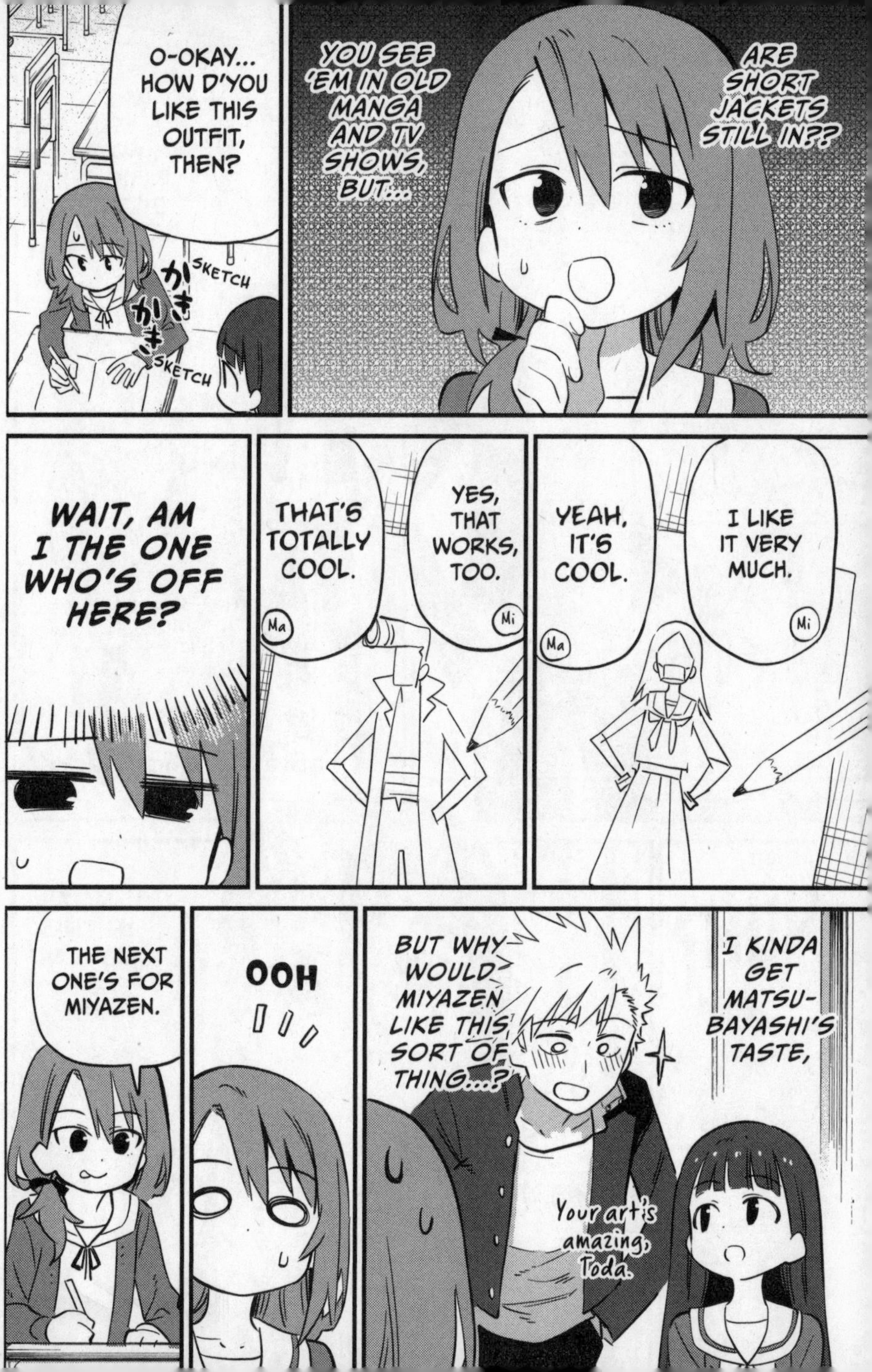
ARE SHORT JACKETS STILL IN??
YOU SEE 'EM IN OLD MANGA AND TV SHOWS, BUT...
O-OKAY... HOW D'YOU LIKE THIS OUTFIT, THEN?
かき
かき
SKETCH
SKETCH
I LIKE IT VERY MUCH.
Mi
YEAH, IT'S COOL.
Ma
YES, THAT WORKS, TOO.
Mi
THAT'S TOTALLY COOL.
Ma
WAIT, AM I THE ONE WHO'S OFF HERE?
I KINDA GET MATSU-BAYASHI'S TASTE,
BUT WHY WOULD MIYAZEN LIKE THIS SORT OF THING...?
Your art's amazing, Toda.
OOH
THE NEXT ONE'S FOR MIYAZEN.

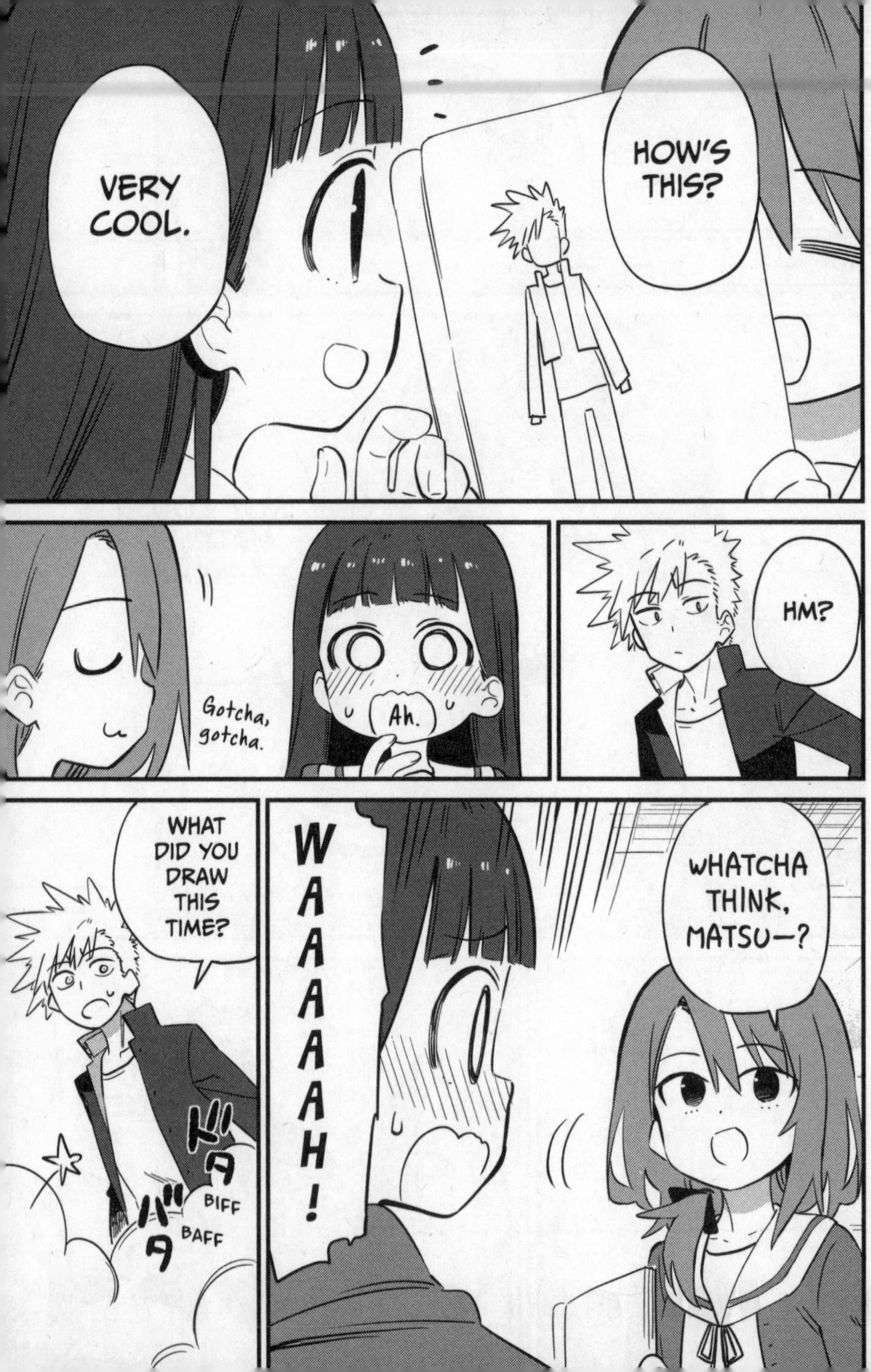
HOW'S THIS?
VERY COOL.
HM?
Ah.
Gotcha, gotcha.
WHATCHA THINK, MATSU—?
WAAAAAAAH!
WHAT DID YOU DRAW THIS TIME?
ドタ
BIFF
バタ
BAFF

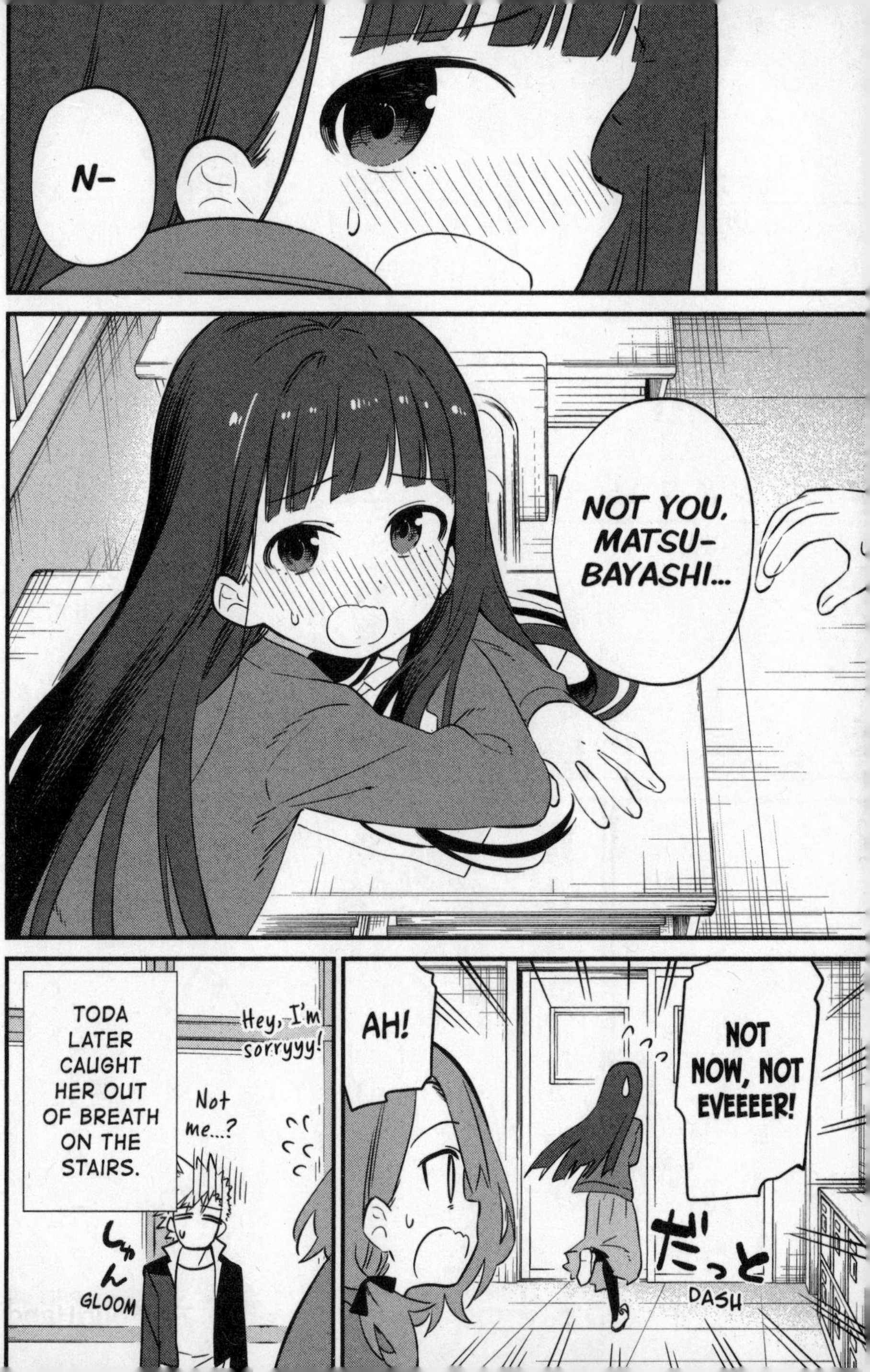
N-
NOT YOU, MATSU-BAYASHI...
NOT NOW, NOT EVEEEER!
AH!
だっと
DASH
Hey, I'm sorryyy!
TODA LATER CAUGHT HER OUT OF BREATH ON THE STAIRS.
Not me...?
しゅん
GLOOM

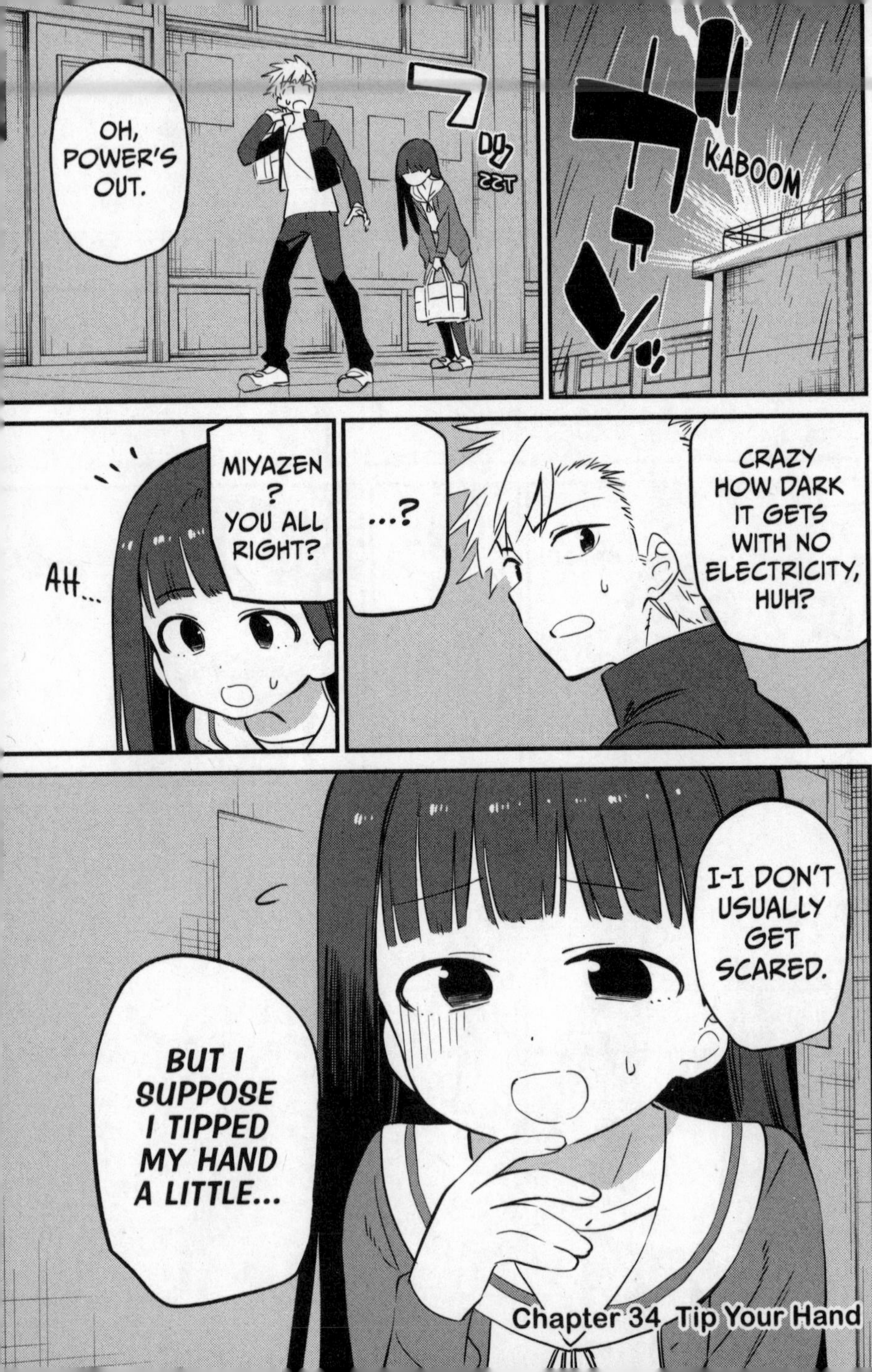
KABOOM
OH, POWER'S OUT.
CRAZY HOW DARK IT GETS WITH NO ELECTRICITY, HUH?
...?
MIYAZEN? YOU ALL RIGHT?
AH...
I-I DON'T USUALLY GET SCARED.
BUT I SUPPOSE I TIPPED MY HAND A LITTLE...
Chapter 34 Tip Your Hand

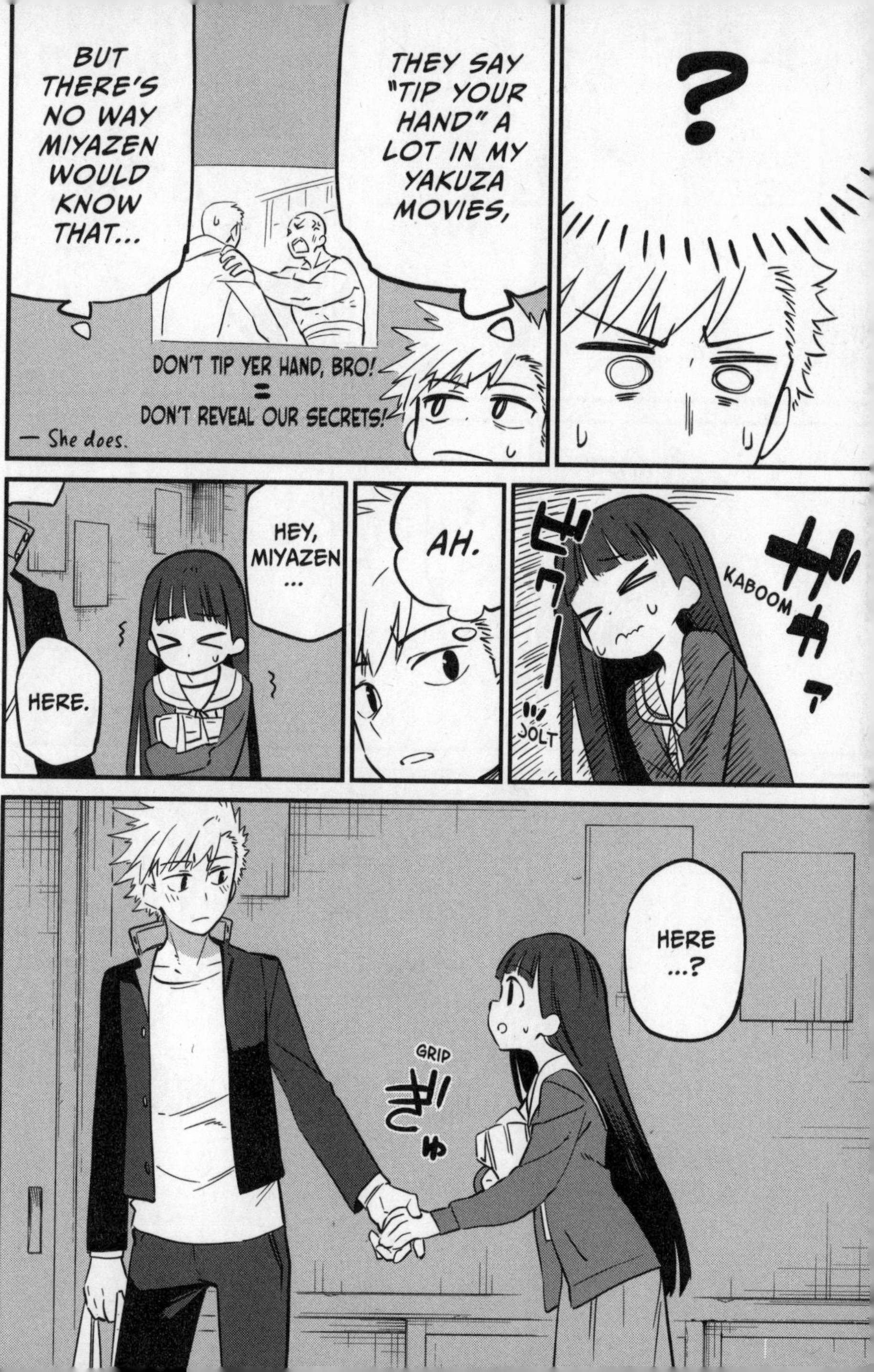
?
THEY SAY "TIP YOUR HAND" A LOT IN MY YAKUZA MOVIES,
BUT THERE'S NO WAY MIYAZEN WOULD KNOW THAT...
DON'T TIP YER HAND, BRO!
=
DON'T REVEAL OUR SECRETS!
— She does.
KABOOM
JOLT
AH.
HEY, MIYAZEN ...
HERE.
HERE ...?
GRIP

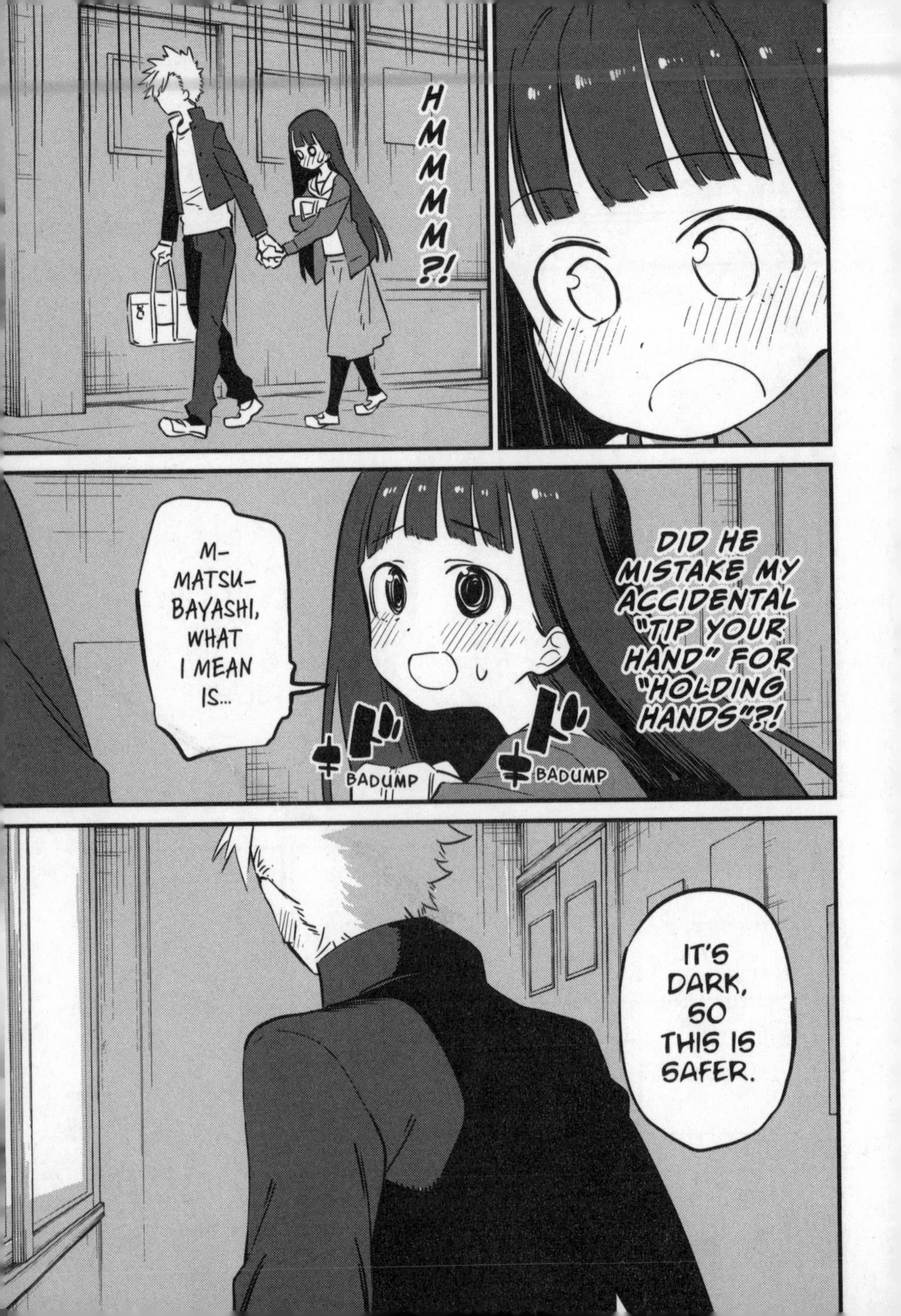
HMMMMM?!
DID HE MISTAKE MY ACCIDENTAL "TIP YOUR HAND" FOR "HOLDING HANDS"?!
M-MATSU-BAYASHI, WHAT I MEAN IS...
BADUMP
BADUMP
IT'S DARK, SO THIS IS SAFER.

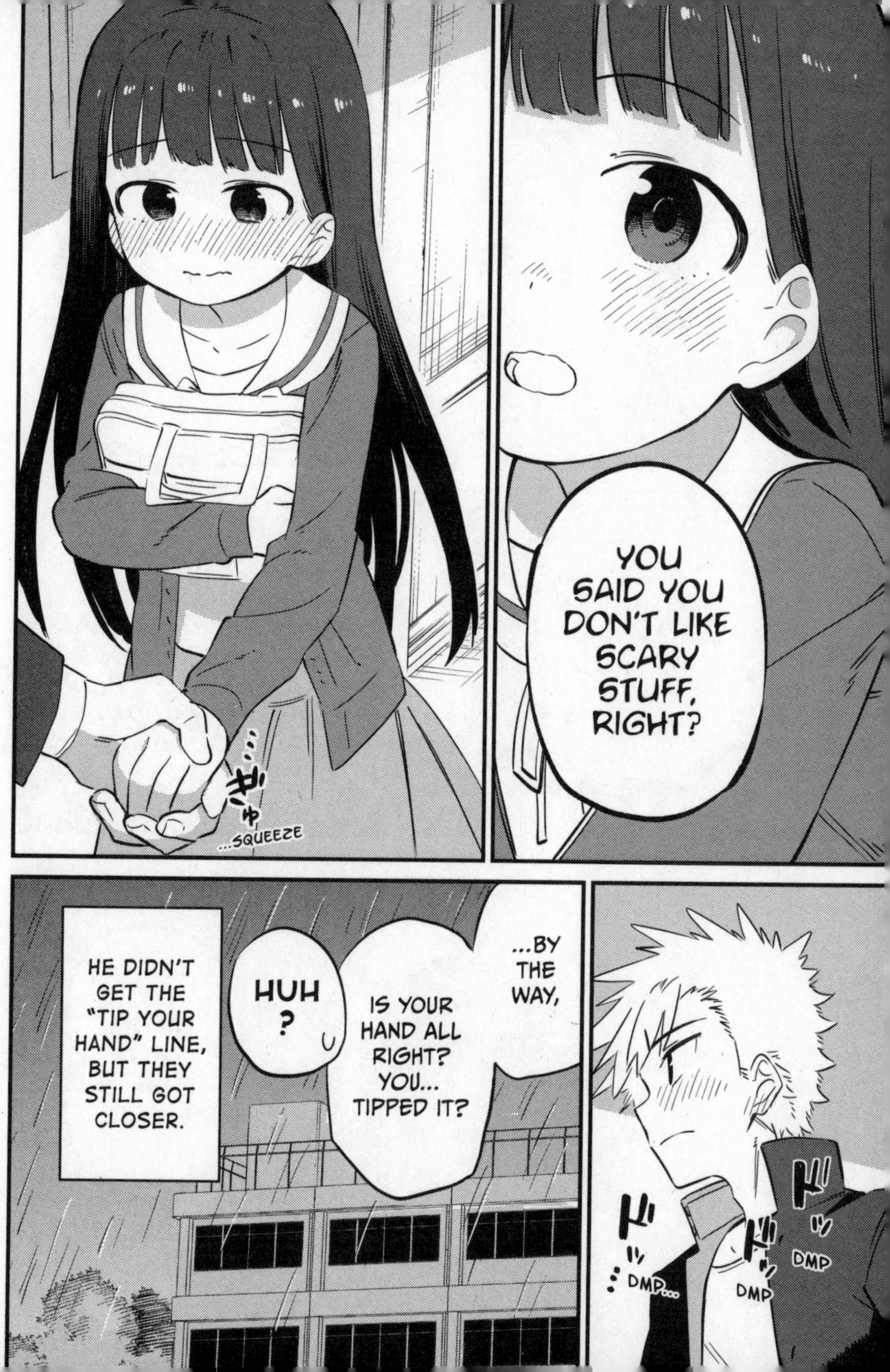
YOU SAID YOU DON'T LIKE SCARY STUFF, RIGHT?
...SQUEEZE
DMP
DMP
DMP...
...BY THE WAY,
IS YOUR HAND ALL RIGHT? YOU... TIPPED IT?
HUH?
HE DIDN'T GET THE "TIP YOUR HAND" LINE, BUT THEY STILL GOT CLOSER.

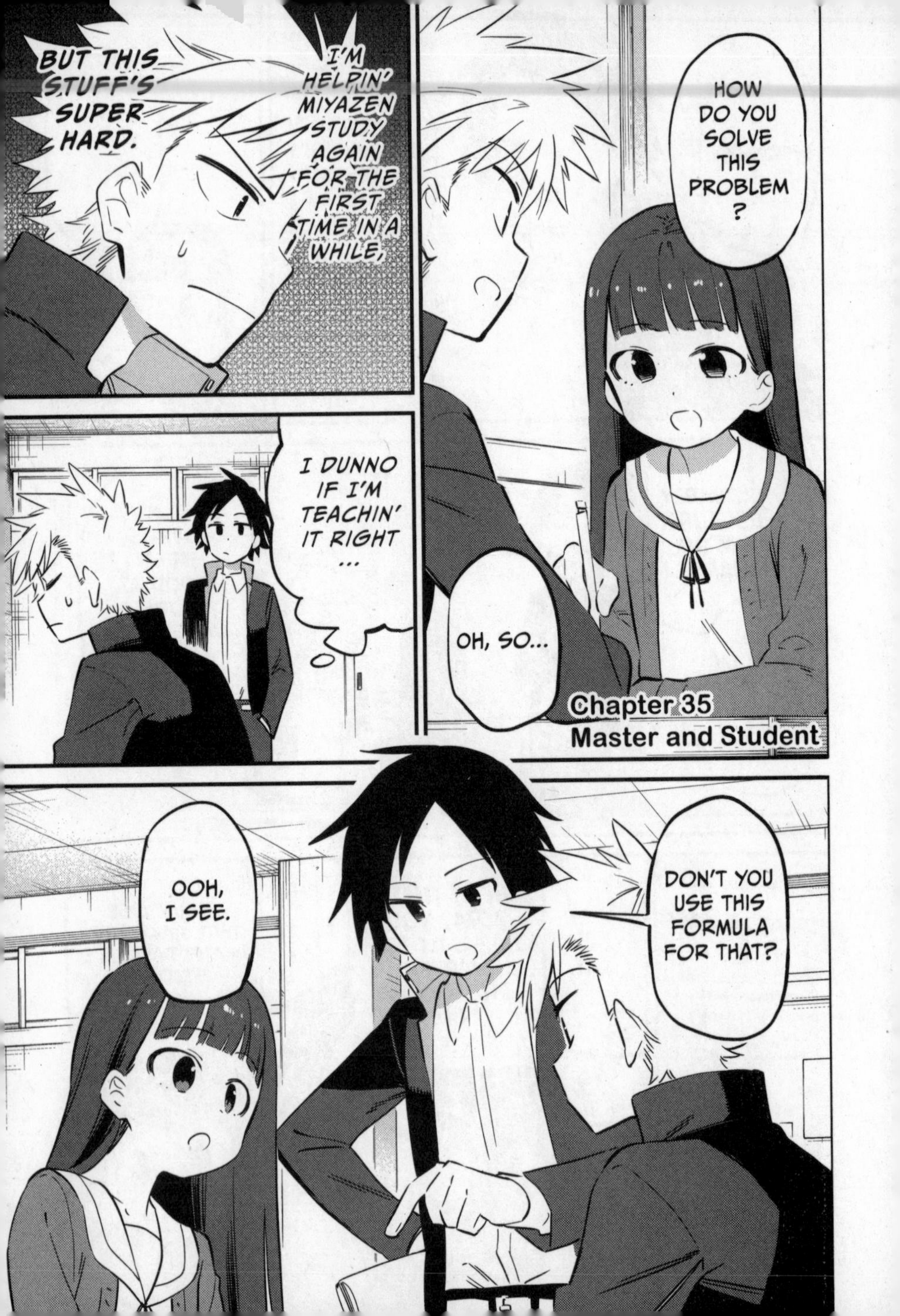
HOW DO YOU SOLVE THIS PROBLEM?
OH, SO...
Chapter 35
Master and Student
I'M HELPIN' MIYAZEN STUDY AGAIN FOR THE FIRST TIME IN A WHILE,
BUT THIS STUFF'S SUPER HARD.
I DUNNO IF I'M TEACHIN' IT RIGHT...
DON'T YOU USE THIS FORMULA FOR THAT?
OOH, I SEE.

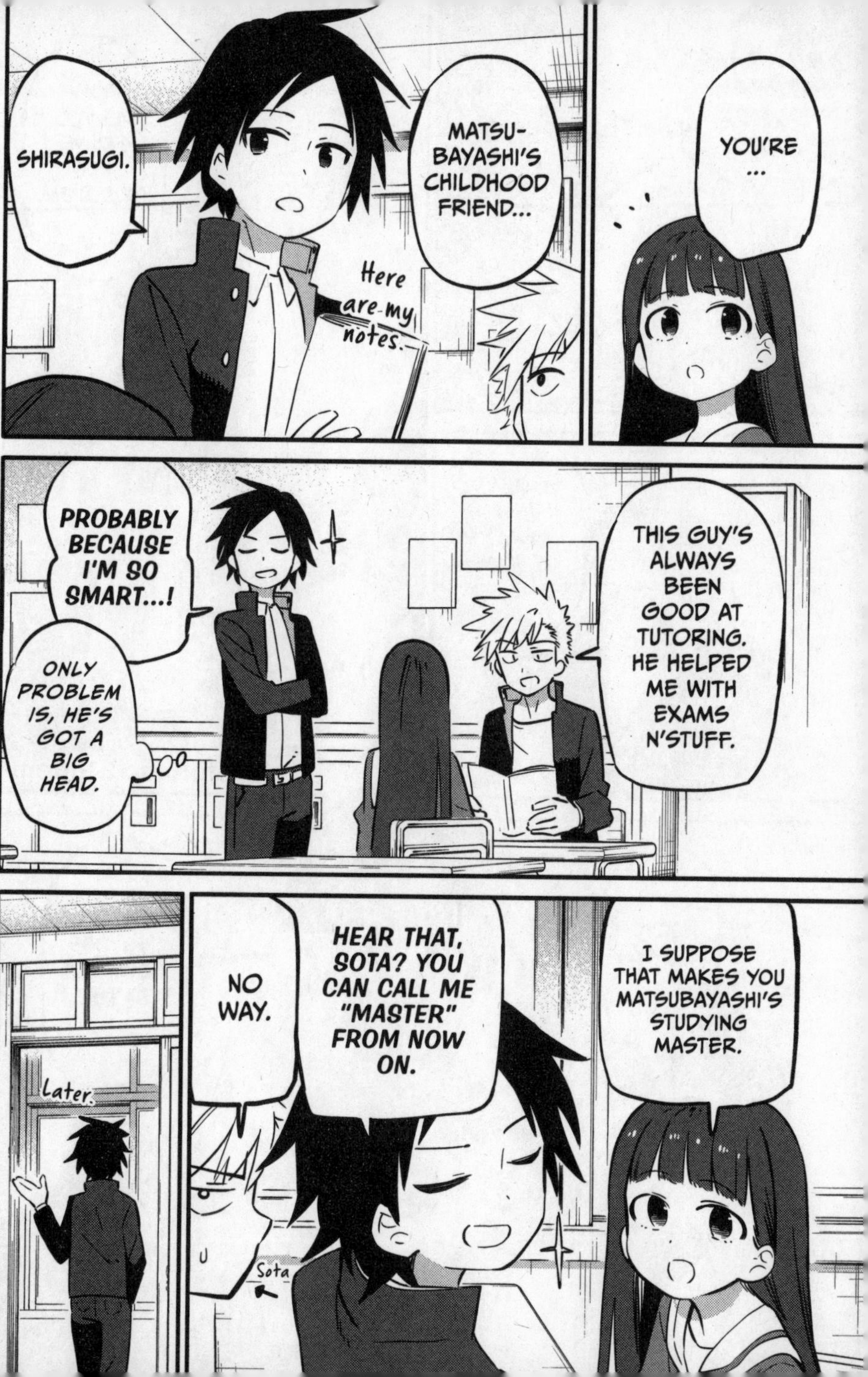
YOU'RE ...
MATSU-BAYASHI'S CHILDHOOD FRIEND...
SHIRASUGI.
Here are my notes.
THIS GUY'S ALWAYS BEEN GOOD AT TUTORING. HE HELPED ME WITH EXAMS N'STUFF.
PROBABLY BECAUSE I'M SO SMART...!
ONLY PROBLEM IS, HE'S GOT A BIG HEAD.
I SUPPOSE THAT MAKES YOU MATSUBAYASHI'S STUDYING MASTER.
HEAR THAT, SOTA? YOU CAN CALL ME "MASTER" FROM NOW ON.
NO WAY.
Sota
Later.

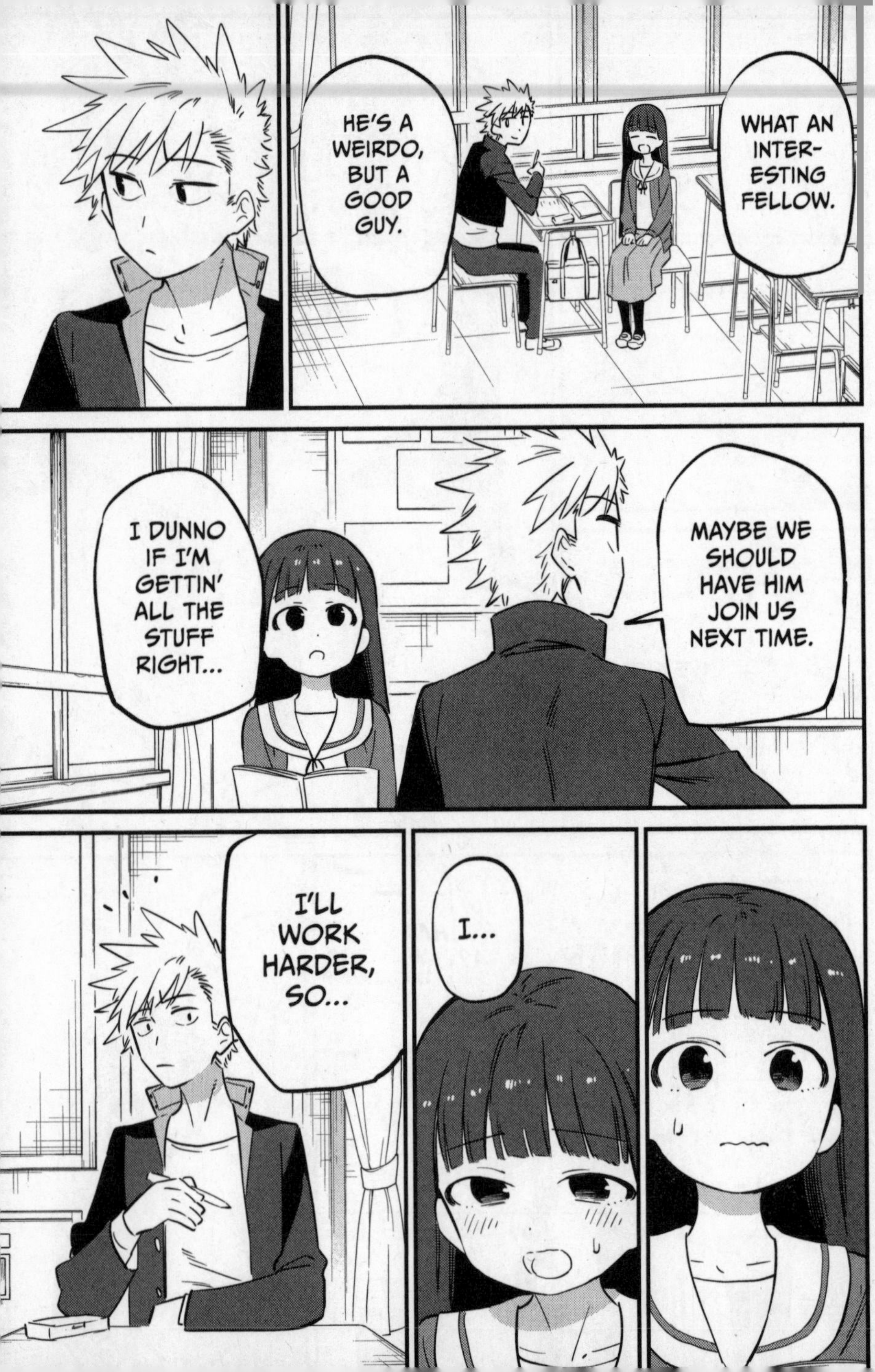
WHAT AN INTER-ESTING FELLOW.
HE'S A WEIRDO, BUT A GOOD GUY.
MAYBE WE SHOULD HAVE HIM JOIN US NEXT TIME.
I DUNNO IF I'M GETTIN' ALL THE STUFF RIGHT...
I...
I'LL WORK HARDER, SO...

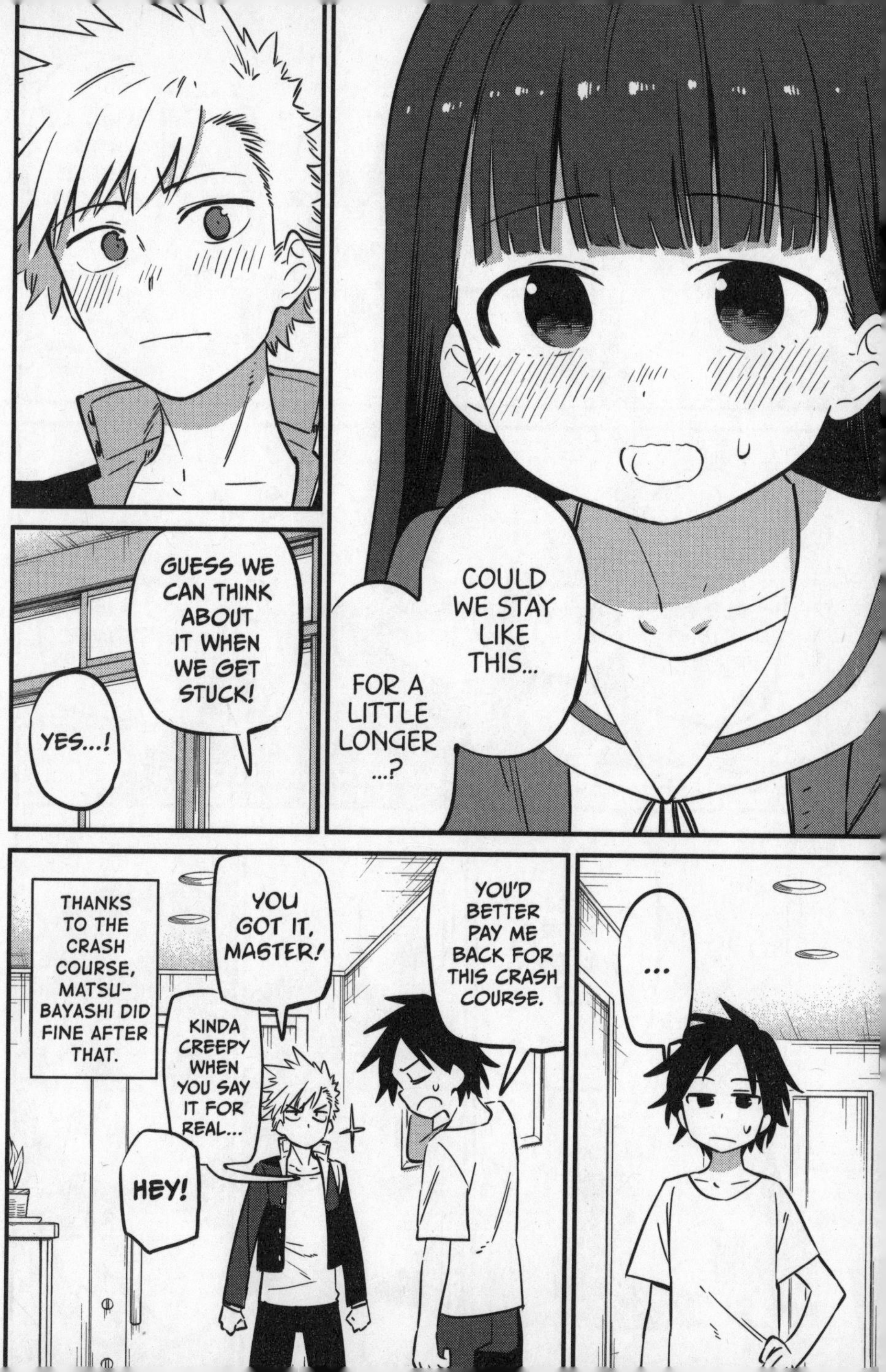
COULD WE STAY LIKE THIS...
FOR A LITTLE LONGER ...?
GUESS WE CAN THINK ABOUT IT WHEN WE GET STUCK!
YES...!
...
YOU'D BETTER PAY ME BACK FOR THIS CRASH COURSE.
YOU GOT IT, MASTER!
THANKS TO THE CRASH COURSE, MATSU-BAYASHI DID FINE AFTER THAT.
KINDA CREEPY WHEN YOU SAY IT FOR REAL...
HEY!

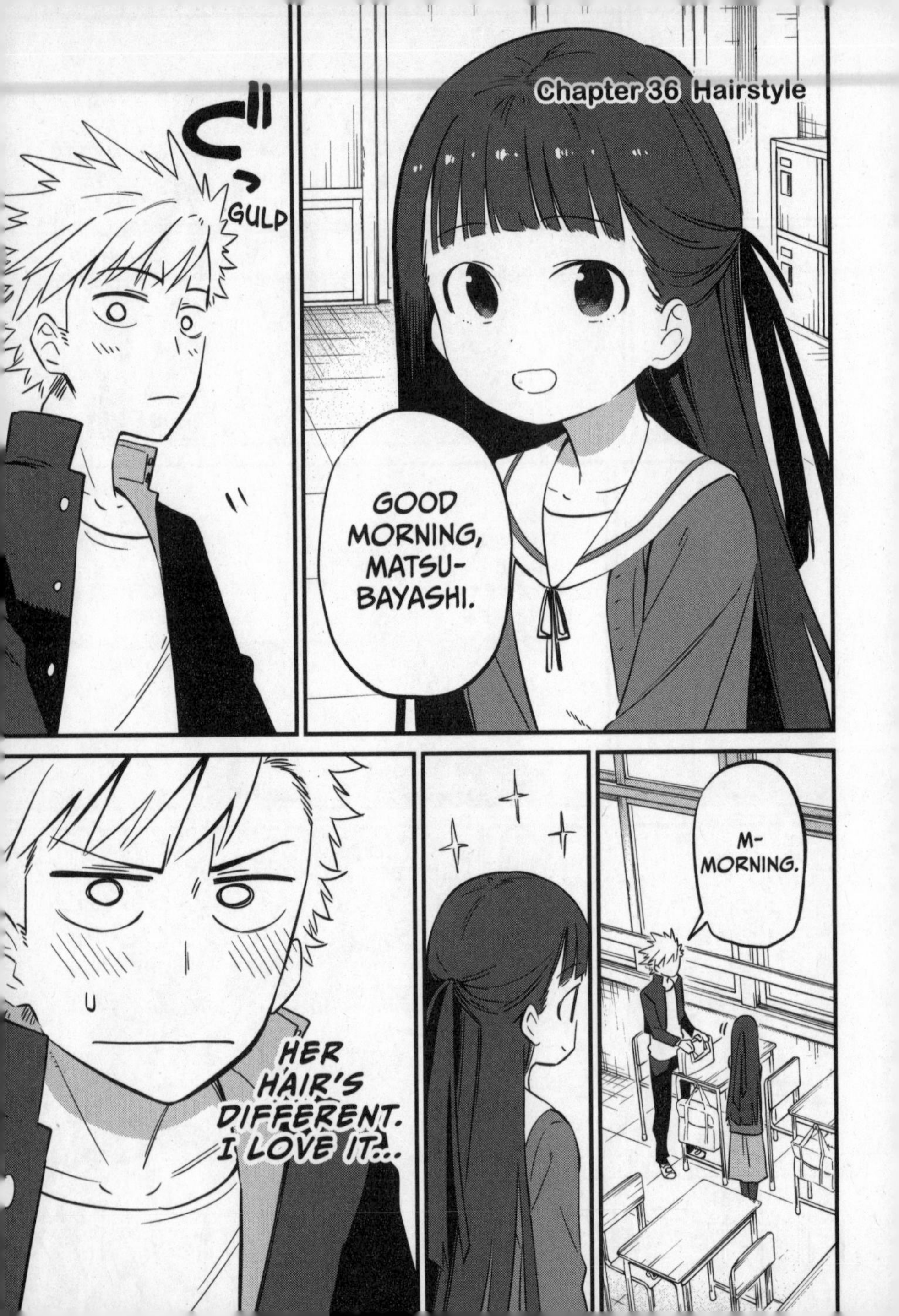
Chapter 36 Hairstyle
GOOD MORNING, MATSU-BAYASHI.
GULP
M-MORNING.
HER HAIR'S DIFFERENT. I LOVE IT...

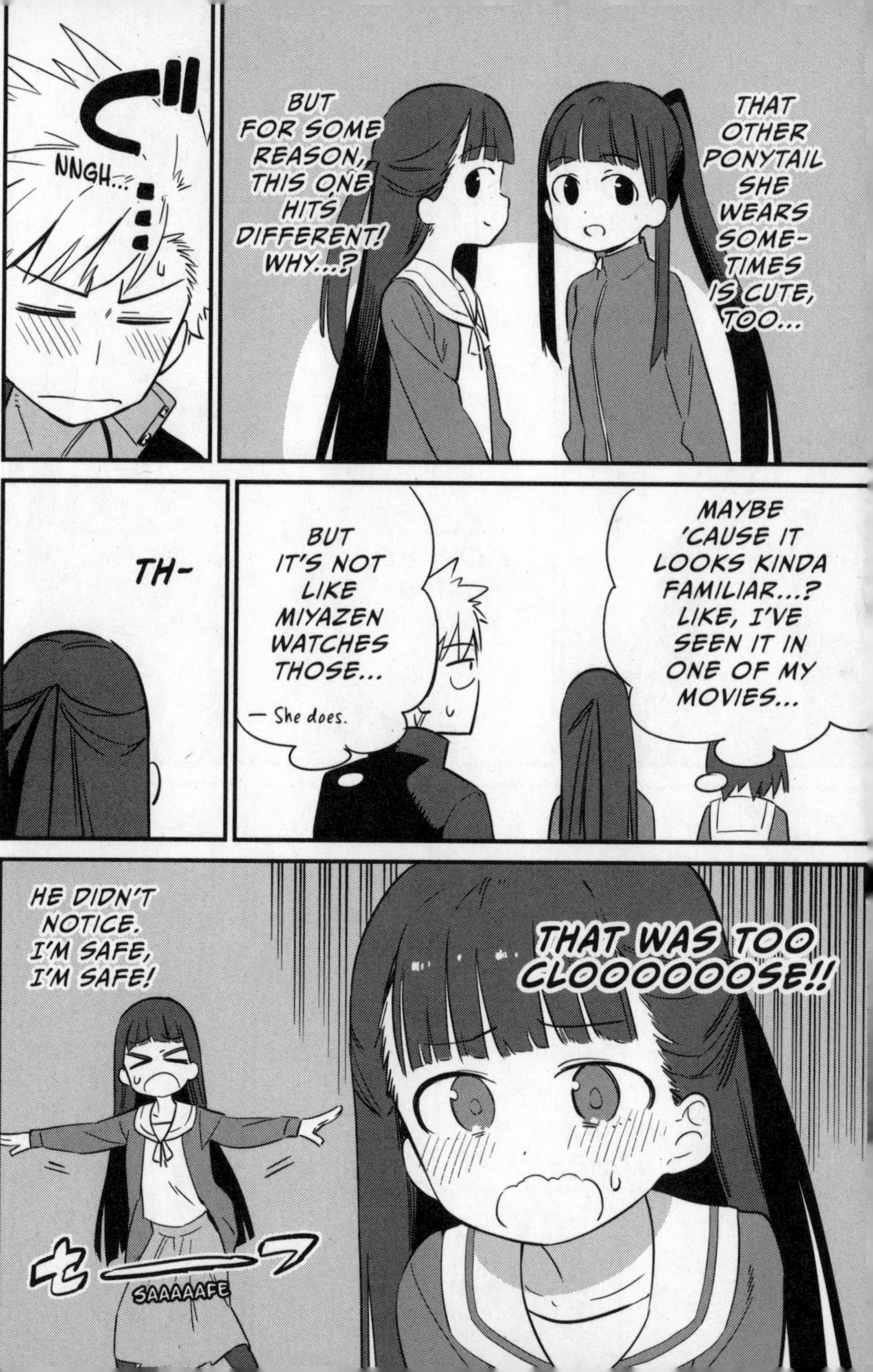
THAT OTHER PONYTAIL SHE WEARS SOMETIMES IS CUTE, TOO...
BUT FOR SOME REASON, THIS ONE HITS DIFFERENT! WHY...?
ぐ
NNGH...
MAYBE 'CAUSE IT LOOKS KINDA FAMILIAR...? LIKE, I'VE SEEN IT IN ONE OF MY MOVIES...
BUT IT'S NOT LIKE MIYAZEN WATCHES THOSE...
— She does.
TH-
THAT WAS TOO CLOOOOOOOSE!!
HE DIDN'T NOTICE. I'M SAFE, I'M SAFE!
セーフ
SAAAAAFE

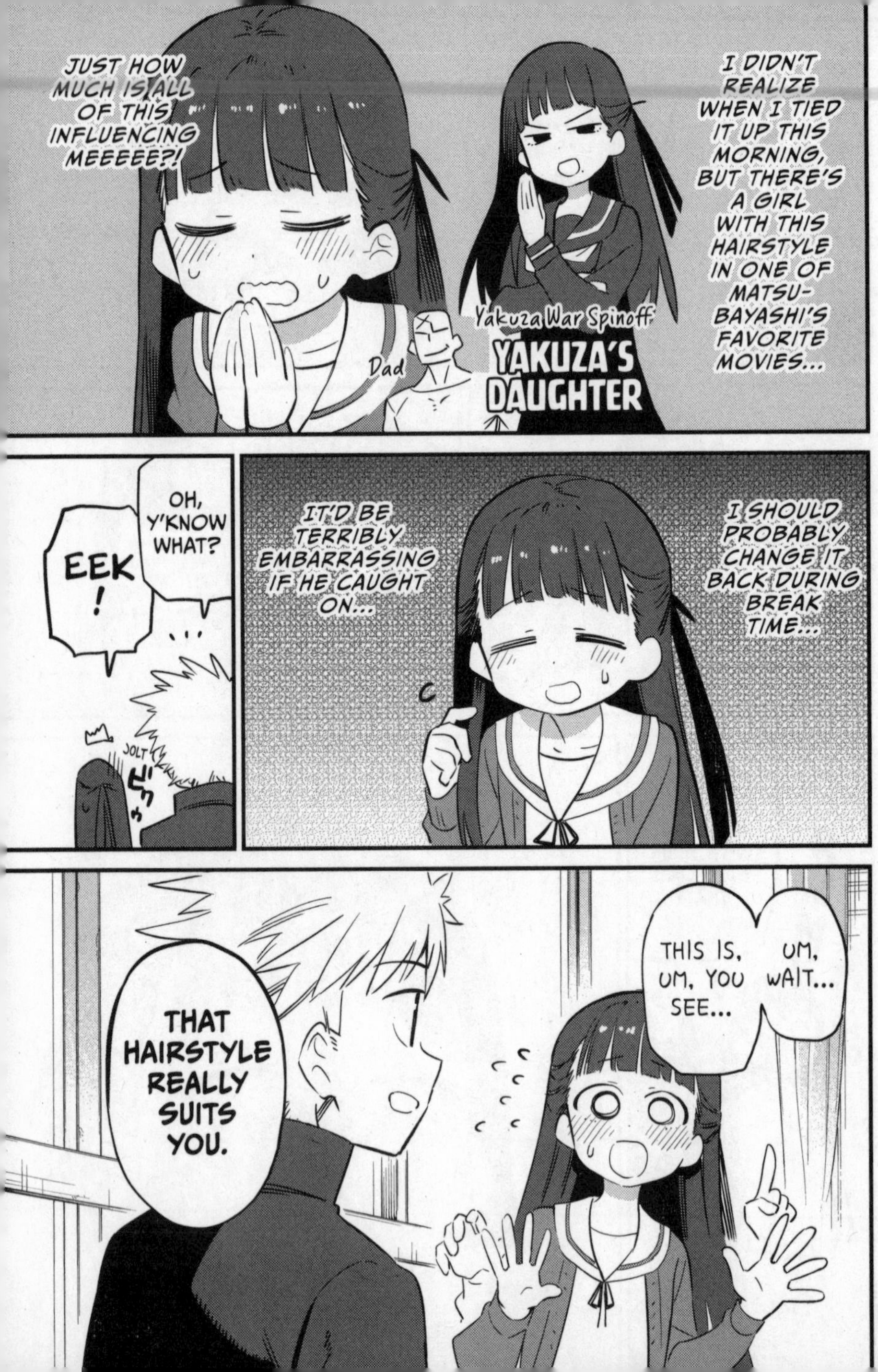
I DIDN'T REALIZE WHEN I TIED IT UP THIS MORNING, BUT THERE'S A GIRL WITH THIS HAIRSTYLE IN ONE OF MATSU-BAYASHI'S FAVORITE MOVIES...
JUST HOW MUCH IS ALL OF THIS INFLUENCING MEEEEEE?!
Yakuza War Spinoff
YAKUZA'S DAUGHTER
Dad
I SHOULD PROBABLY CHANGE IT BACK DURING BREAK TIME...
IT'D BE TERRIBLY EMBARRASSING IF HE CAUGHT ON...
OH, Y'KNOW WHAT?
EEK!
JOLT
THIS IS, UM, YOU SEE... UM, WAIT...
THAT HAIRSTYLE REALLY SUITS YOU.

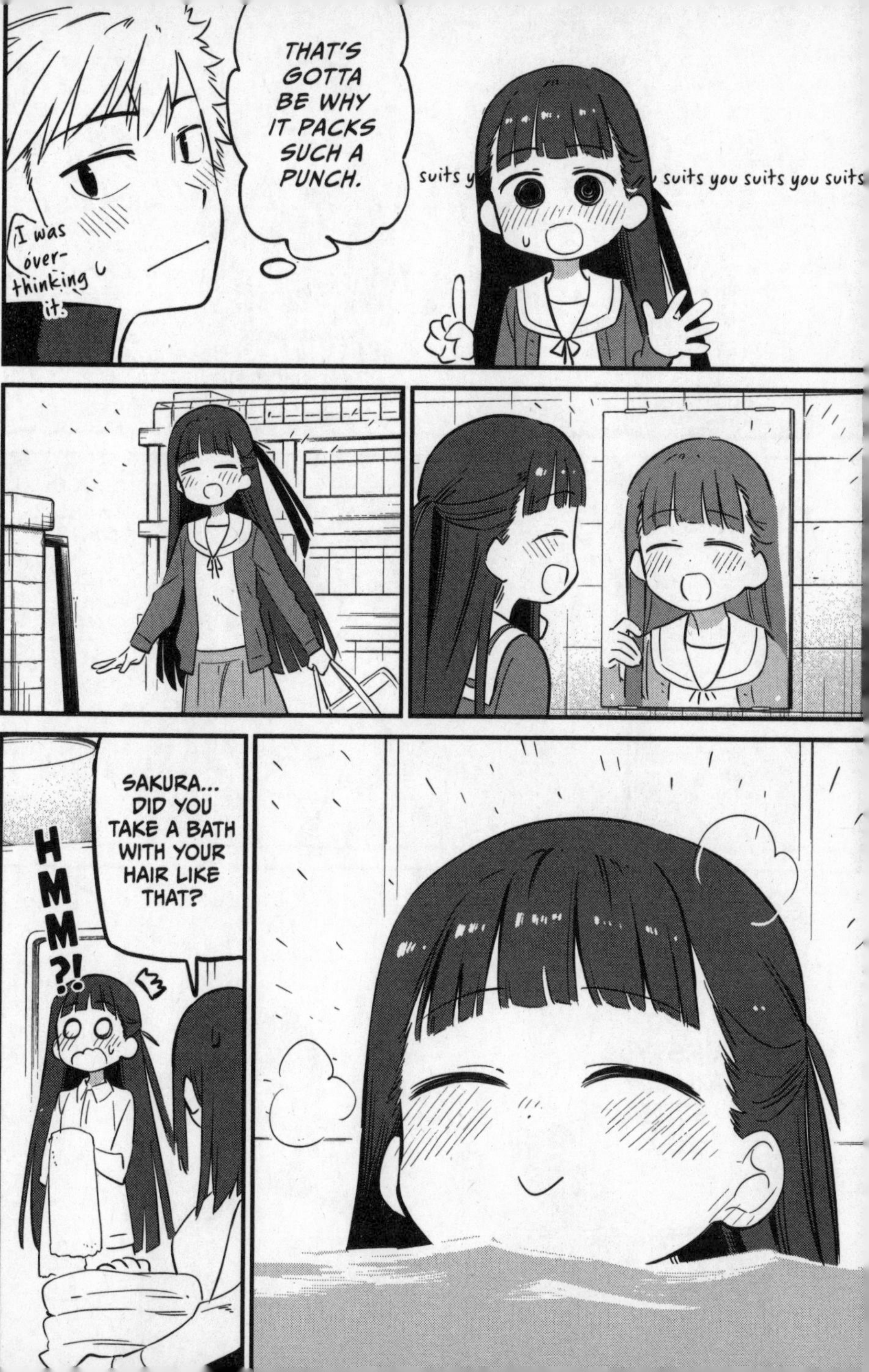
suits y
u suits you suits you suits
THAT'S GOTTA BE WHY IT PACKS SUCH A PUNCH.
I was over-thinking it.
SAKURA... DID YOU TAKE A BATH WITH YOUR HAIR LIKE THAT?
HMM?!

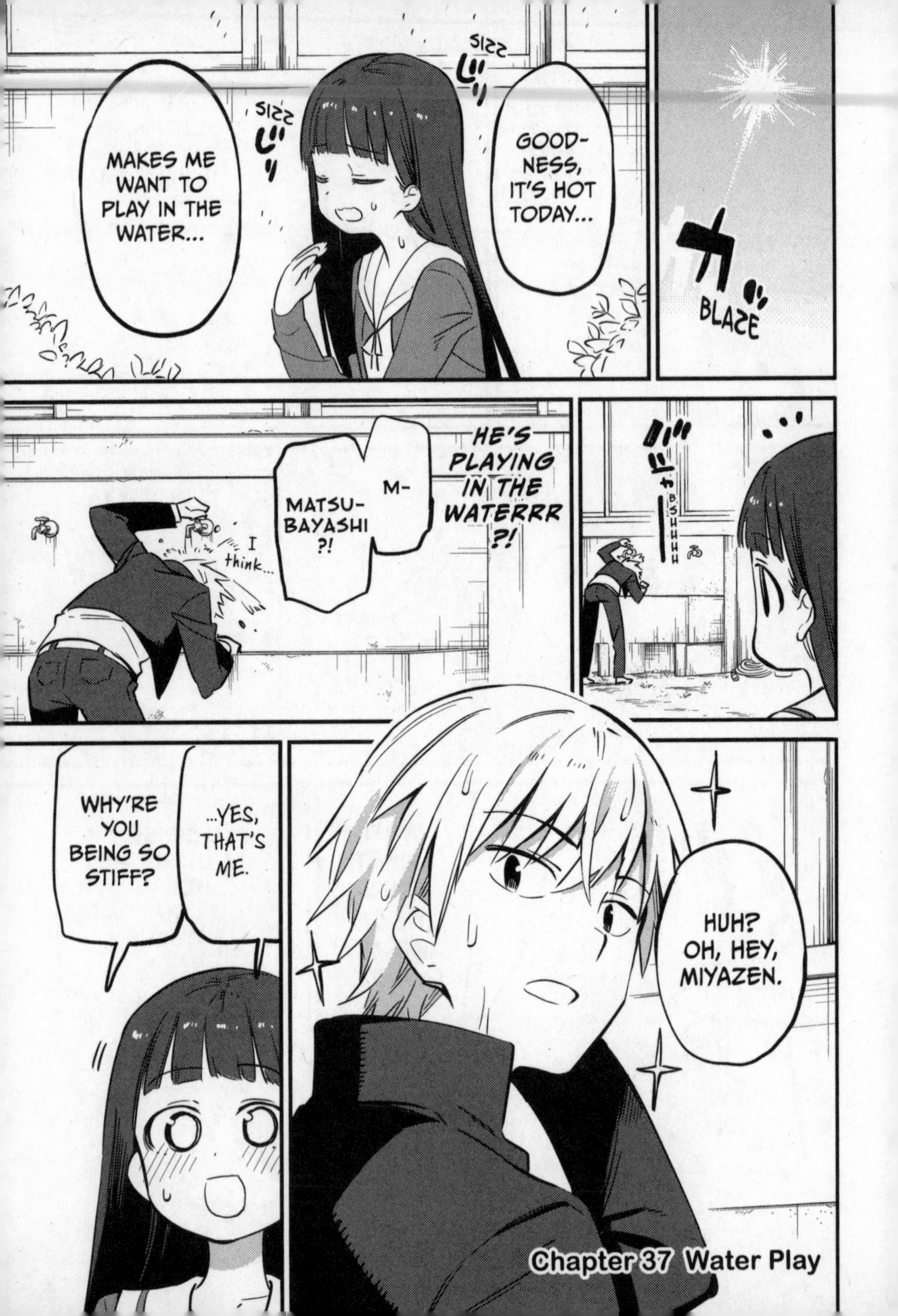
BLAZE
SIZZ
GOODNESS, IT'S HOT TODAY...
SIZZ
MAKES ME WANT TO PLAY IN THE WATER...
...
BSHHHH
HE'S PLAYING IN THE WATERRR?!
M- MATSUBAYASHI?!
I think...
HUH? OH, HEY, MIYAZEN.
...YES, THAT'S ME.
WHY'RE YOU BEING SO STIFF?

Chapter 37 Water Play

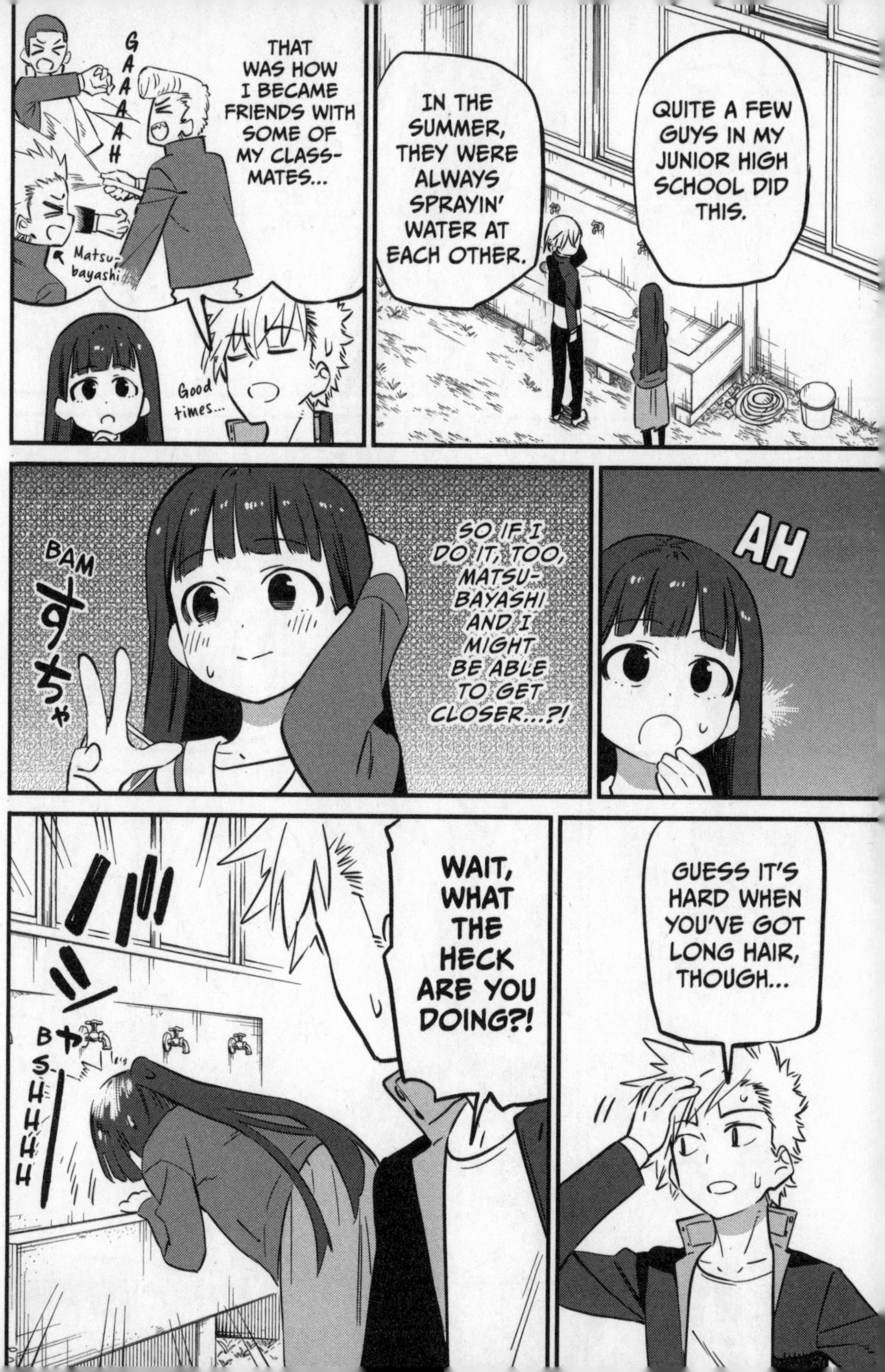
QUITE A FEW GUYS IN MY JUNIOR HIGH SCHOOL DID THIS.
IN THE SUMMER, THEY WERE ALWAYS SPRAYIN' WATER AT EACH OTHER.
THAT WAS HOW I BECAME FRIENDS WITH SOME OF MY CLASS-MATES...
GAAAAAH
Matsu-bayashi
Good times...
AH
SO IF I DO IT, TOO, MATSU-BAYASHI AND I MIGHT BE ABLE TO GET CLOSER...?!
BAM
すちゃ
GUESS IT'S HARD WHEN YOU'VE GOT LONG HAIR, THOUGH...
WAIT, WHAT THE HECK ARE YOU DOING?!
BS-HHHHHH
や

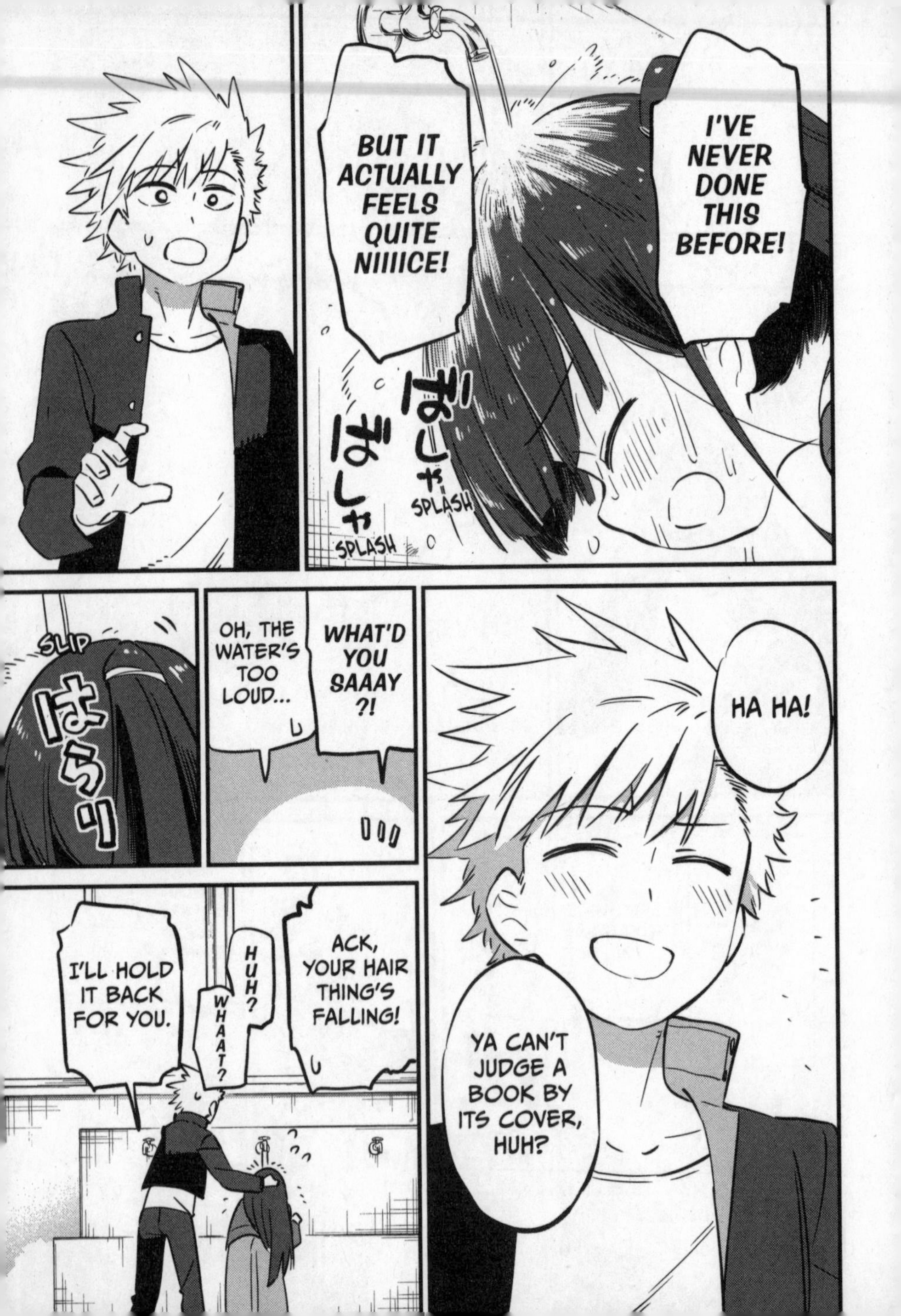
I'VE NEVER DONE THIS BEFORE!
BUT IT ACTUALLY FEELS QUITE NIIIICE!
ばしゃ
SPLASH
ばしゃ
SPLASH
HA HA!
YA CAN'T JUDGE A BOOK BY ITS COVER, HUH?
WHAT'D YOU SAAAY?!
OH, THE WATER'S TOO LOUD...
SLIP
はらり
ACK, YOUR HAIR THING'S FALLING!
HUH?
WHAAAT?
I'LL HOLD IT BACK FOR YOU.

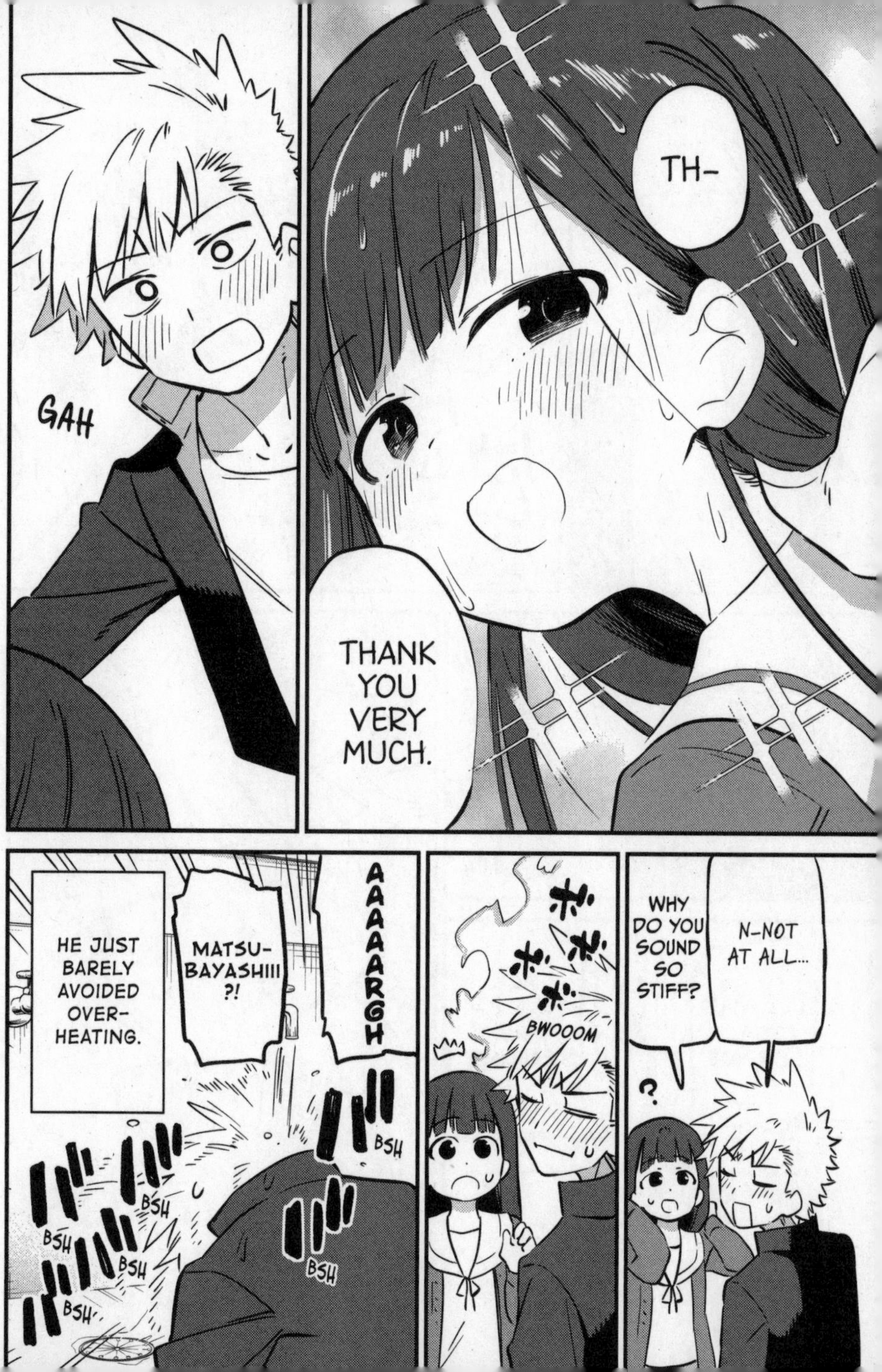
TH-
THANK YOU VERY MUCH.
GAH
N-NOT AT ALL...
WHY DO YOU SOUND SO STIFF?
ボ ボ ボ ボ
BWOOOM
AAAAARGH
MATSU-BAYASHIII?!
HE JUST BARELY AVOIDED OVER-HEATING.
BSH
BSH
BSH
BSH
BSH
BSH

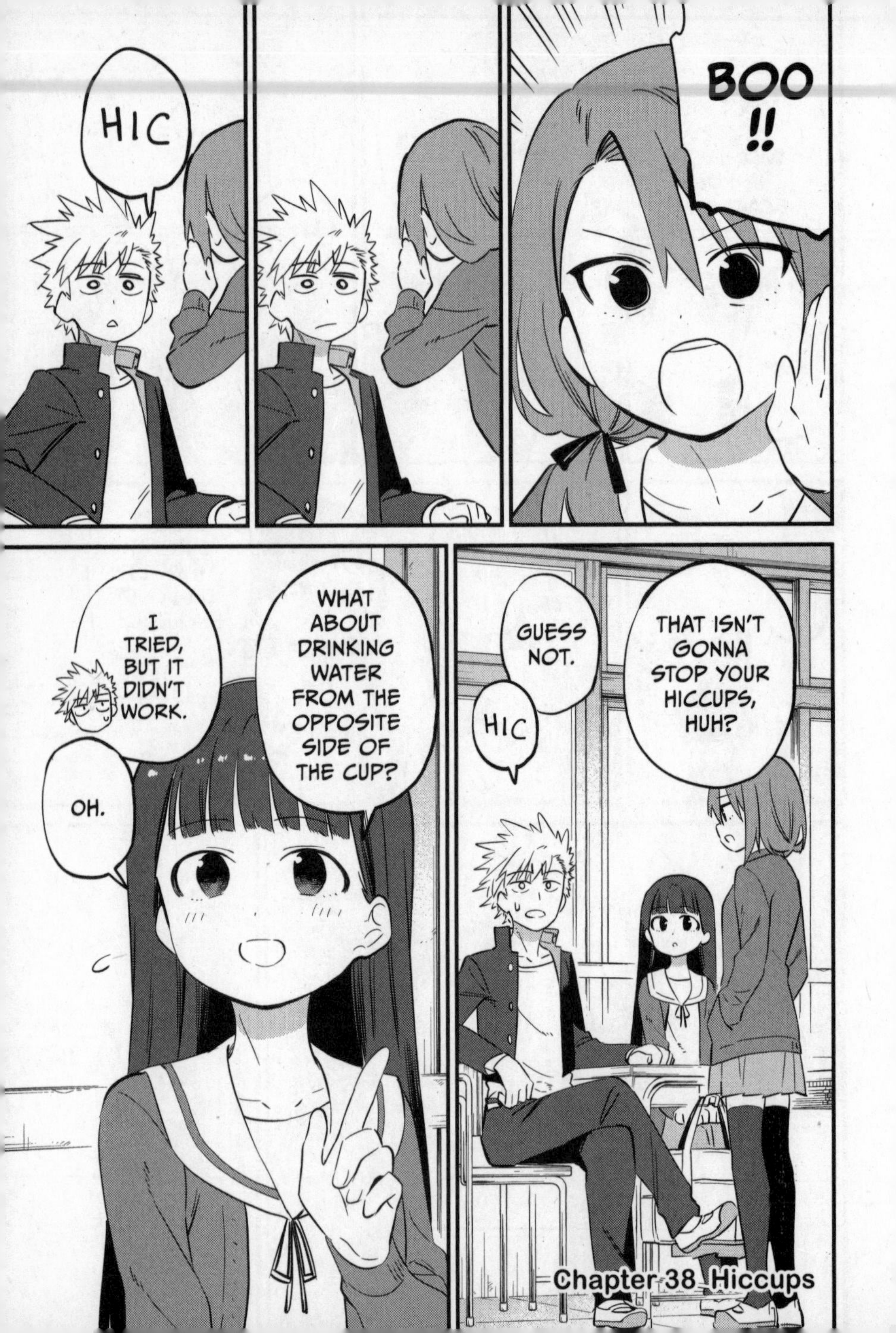
HIC
BOO!!
WHAT ABOUT DRINKING WATER FROM THE OPPOSITE SIDE OF THE CUP?
I TRIED, BUT IT DIDN'T WORK.
OH.
THAT ISN'T GONNA STOP YOUR HICCUPS, HUH?
GUESS NOT.
HIC
Chapter 38 Hiccups

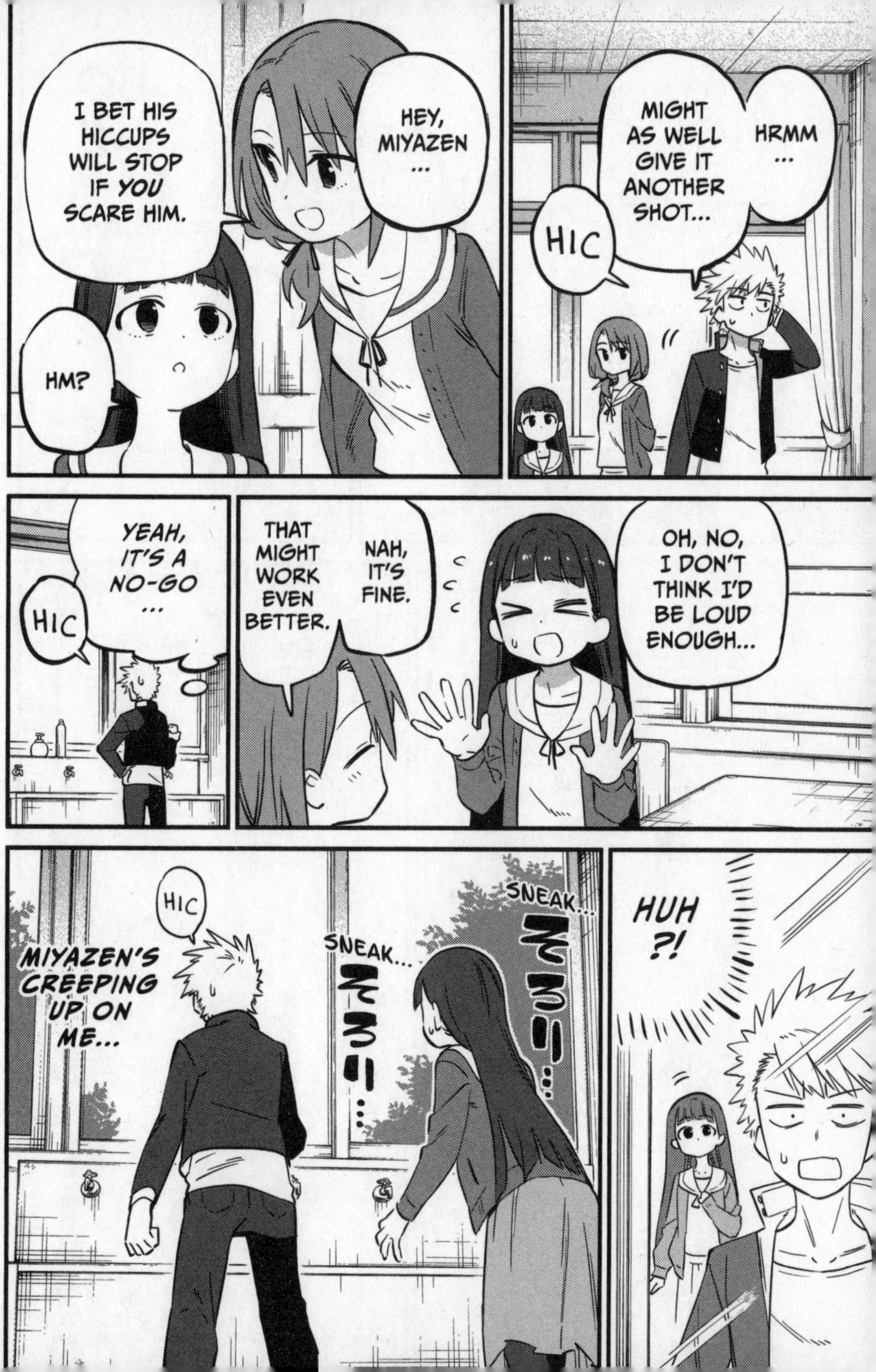
HRMM ...
MIGHT AS WELL GIVE IT ANOTHER SHOT...
HIC
HEY, MIYAZEN ...
I BET HIS HICCUPS WILL STOP IF YOU SCARE HIM.
HM?
OH, NO, I DON'T THINK I'D BE LOUD ENOUGH...
NAH, IT'S FINE.
THAT MIGHT WORK EVEN BETTER.
YEAH, IT'S A NO-GO ...
HIC
HUH ?!
SNEAK...
そろーり...
SNEAK...
そろり...
HIC
MIYAZEN'S CREEPING UP ON ME...

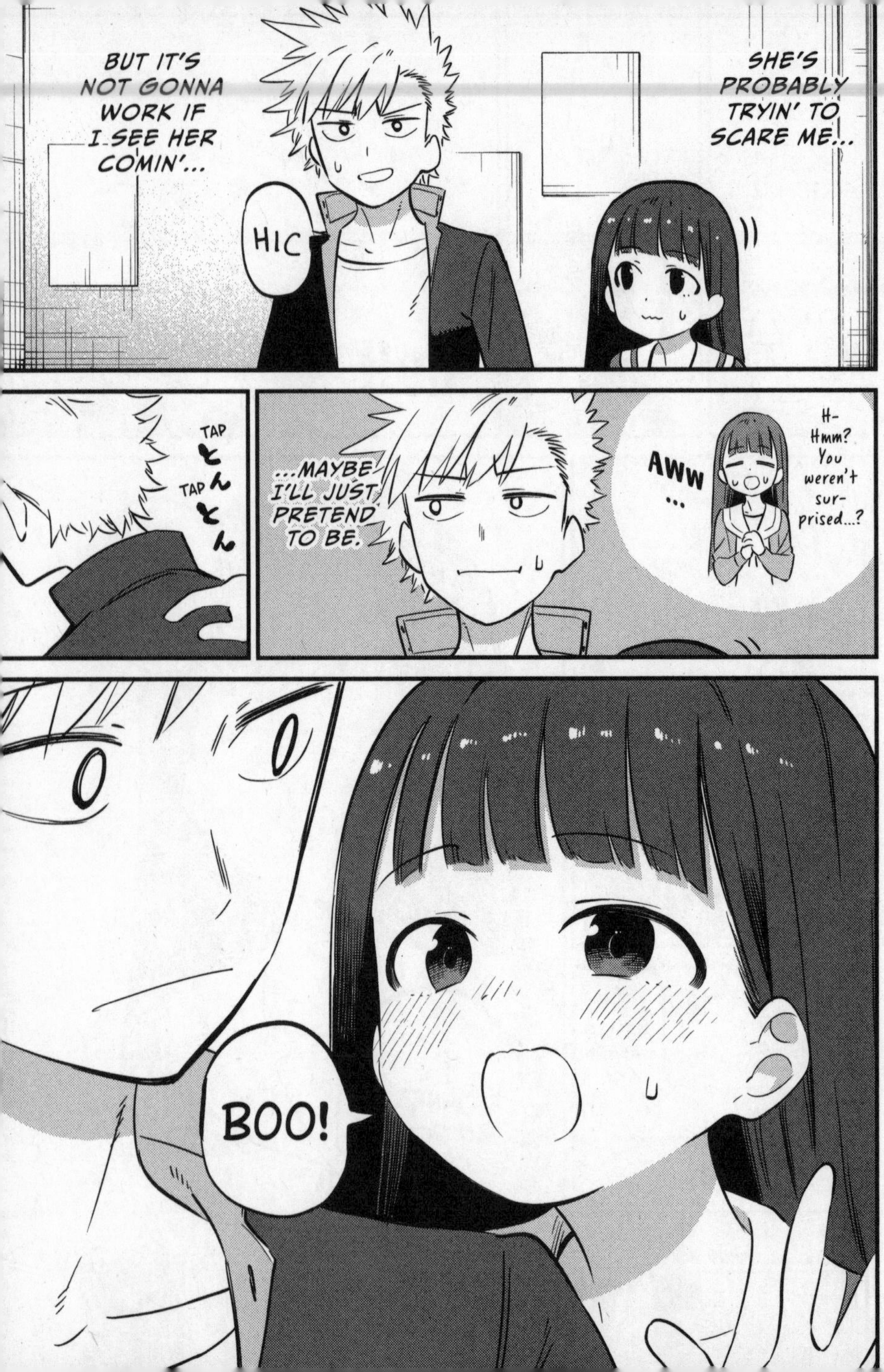
SHE'S PROBABLY TRYIN' TO SCARE ME...
BUT IT'S NOT GONNA WORK IF I SEE HER COMIN'...
HIC
H-Hmm? You weren't sur-prised...?
AWW...
...MAYBE I'LL JUST PRETEND TO BE.
TAP とん
TAP とん
BOO!

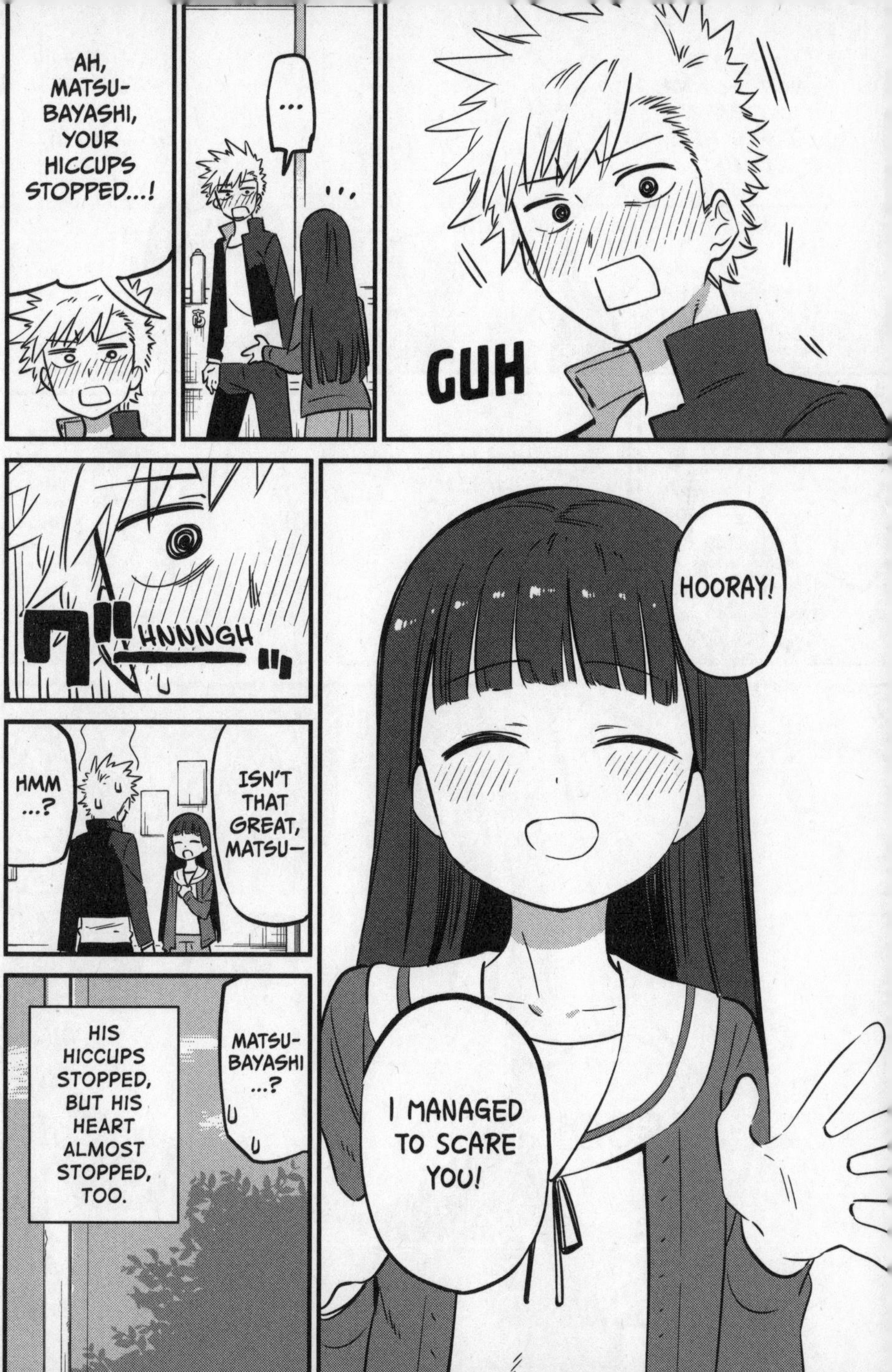
GUH
...
AH, MATSUBAYASHI, YOUR HICCUPS STOPPED...!
HOORAY!
I MANAGED TO SCARE YOU!
HNNNGH
ISN'T THAT GREAT, MATSU—
HMM ...?
MATSUBAYASHI ...?
HIS HICCUPS STOPPED, BUT HIS HEART ALMOST STOPPED, TOO.

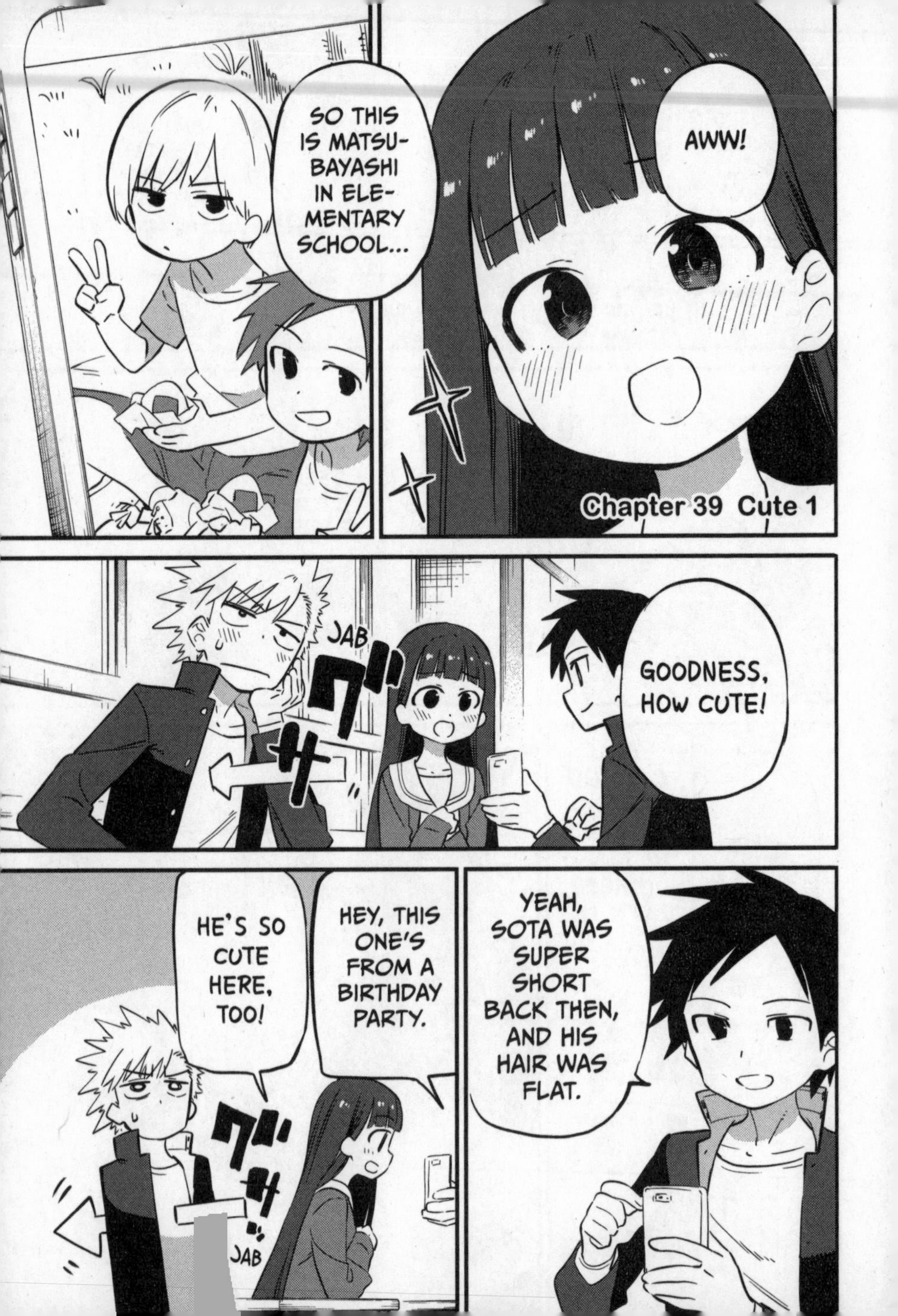
AWW!
Chapter 39 Cute 1
SO THIS IS MATSU-BAYASHI IN ELE-MENTARY SCHOOL...
GOODNESS, HOW CUTE!
JAB
グサ
YEAH, SOTA WAS SUPER SHORT BACK THEN, AND HIS HAIR WAS FLAT.
HEY, THIS ONE'S FROM A BIRTHDAY PARTY.
HE'S SO CUTE HERE, TOO!
グサ
JAB

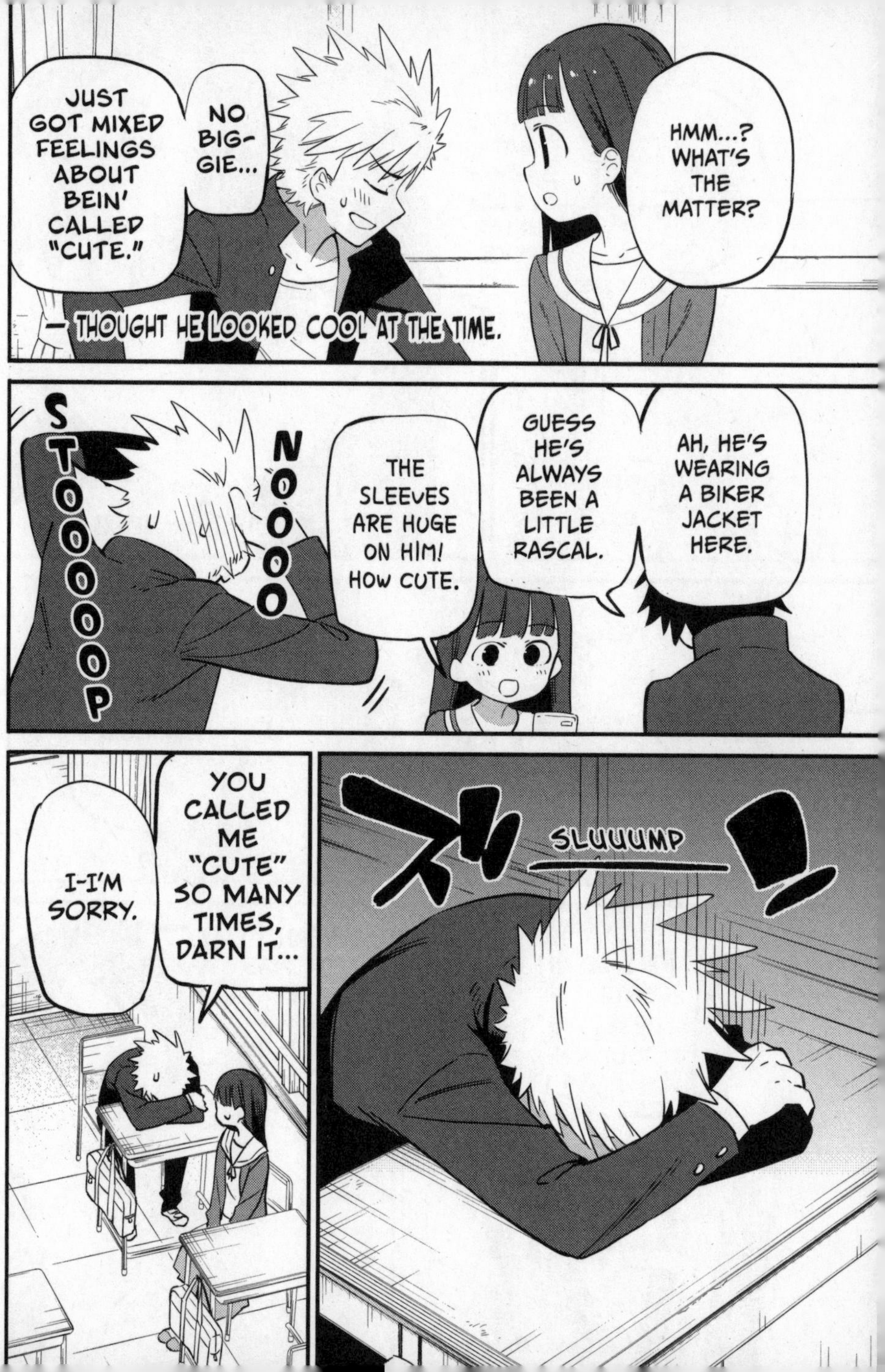
HMM...? WHAT'S THE MATTER?
NO BIG-GIE...
JUST GOT MIXED FEELINGS ABOUT BEIN' CALLED "CUTE."
—THOUGHT HE LOOKED COOL AT THE TIME.
AH, HE'S WEARING A BIKER JACKET HERE.
GUESS HE'S ALWAYS BEEN A LITTLE RASCAL.
THE SLEEVES ARE HUGE ON HIM! HOW CUTE.
NOOOO
STOOOOOOOP
SLUUUMP
YOU CALLED ME "CUTE" SO MANY TIMES, DARN IT...
I-I'M SORRY.

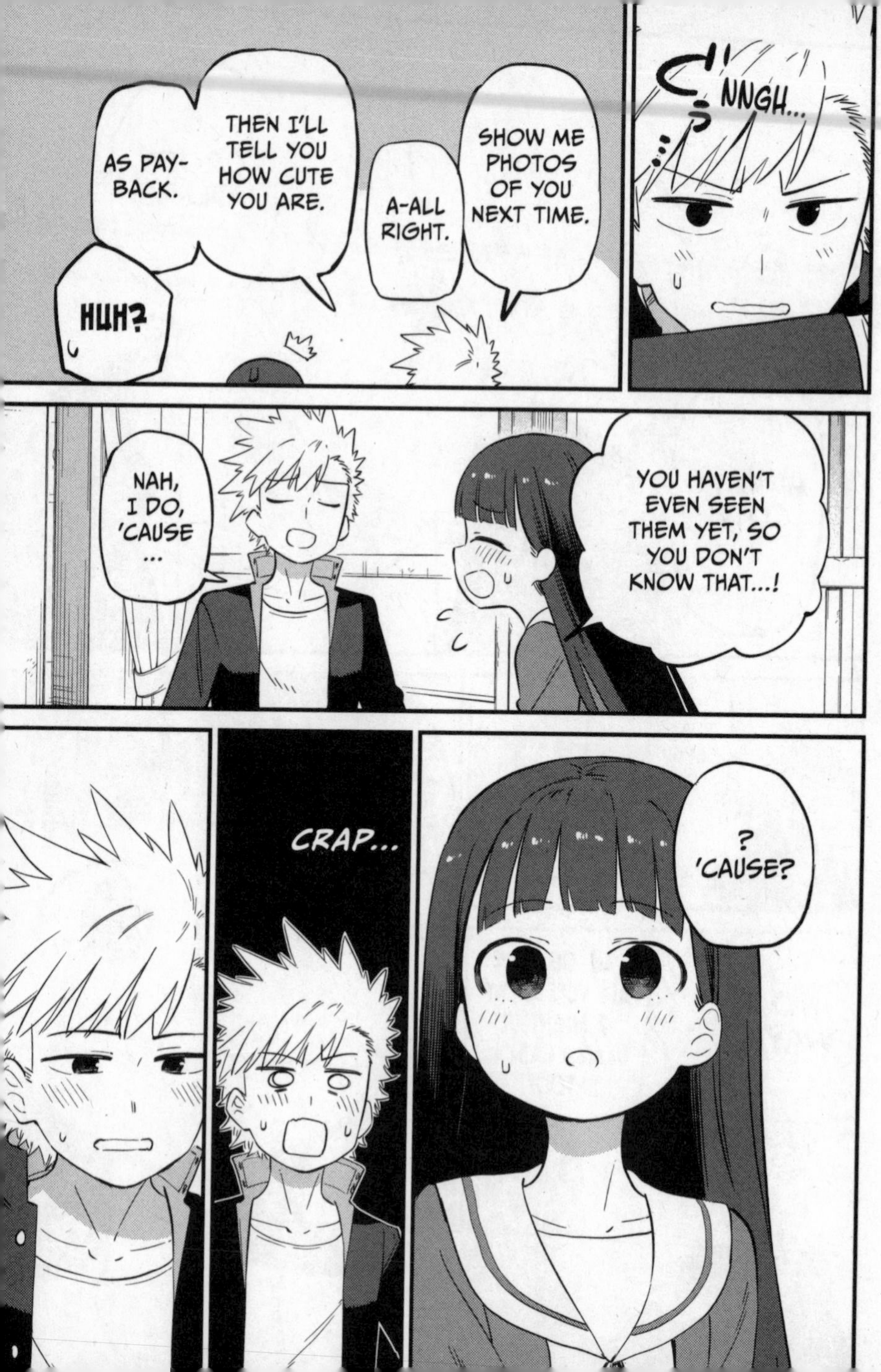
NNGH...
SHOW ME PHOTOS OF YOU NEXT TIME.
A-ALL RIGHT.
THEN I'LL TELL YOU HOW CUTE YOU ARE.
AS PAY-BACK.
HUH?
YOU HAVEN'T EVEN SEEN THEM YET, SO YOU DON'T KNOW THAT...!
NAH, I DO, 'CAUSE ...
? 'CAUSE?
CRAP...

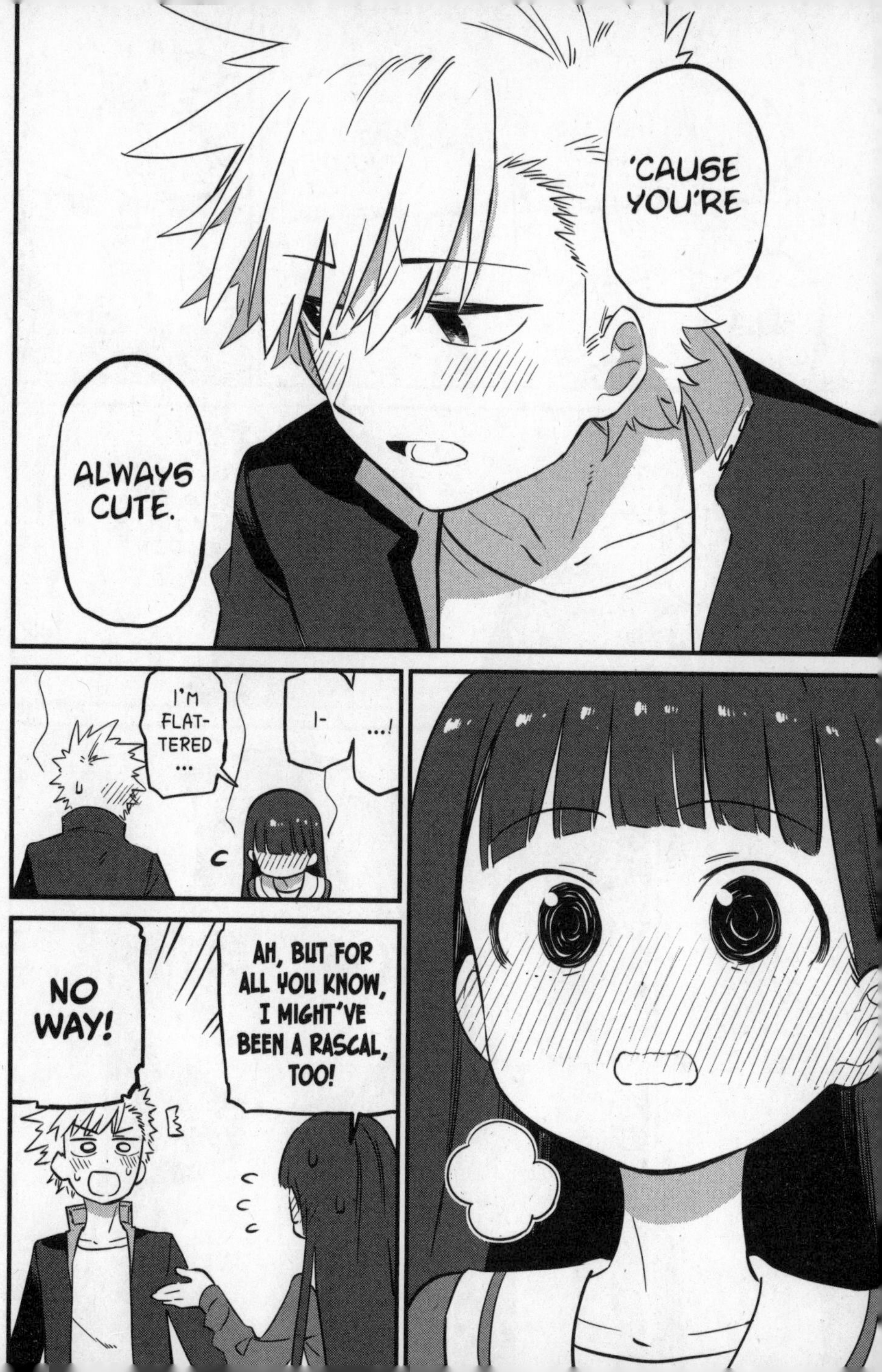
'CAUSE YOU'RE
ALWAYS CUTE.
I- ...!
I'M FLATTERED ...
AH, BUT FOR ALL YOU KNOW, I MIGHT'VE BEEN A RASCAL, TOO!
NO WAY!

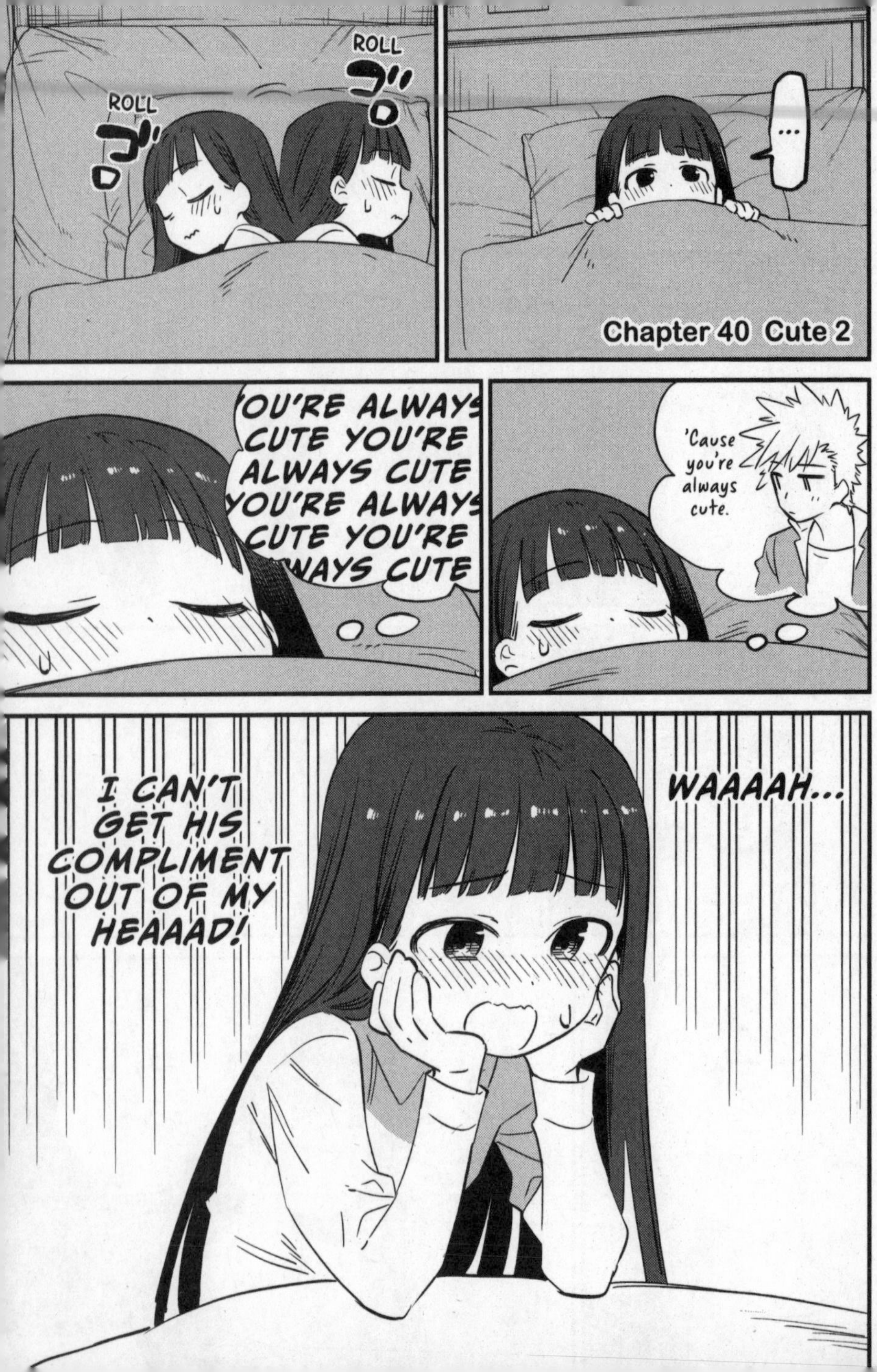
...
Chapter 40 Cute 2
ROLL
ゴロ
ROLL
ゴロ
'Cause you're always cute.
OU'RE ALWAYS CUTE YOU'RE ALWAYS CUTE OU'RE ALWAYS CUTE YOU'RE WAYS CUTE
WAAAAH...
I CAN'T GET HIS COMPLIMENT OUT OF MY HEAAAD!

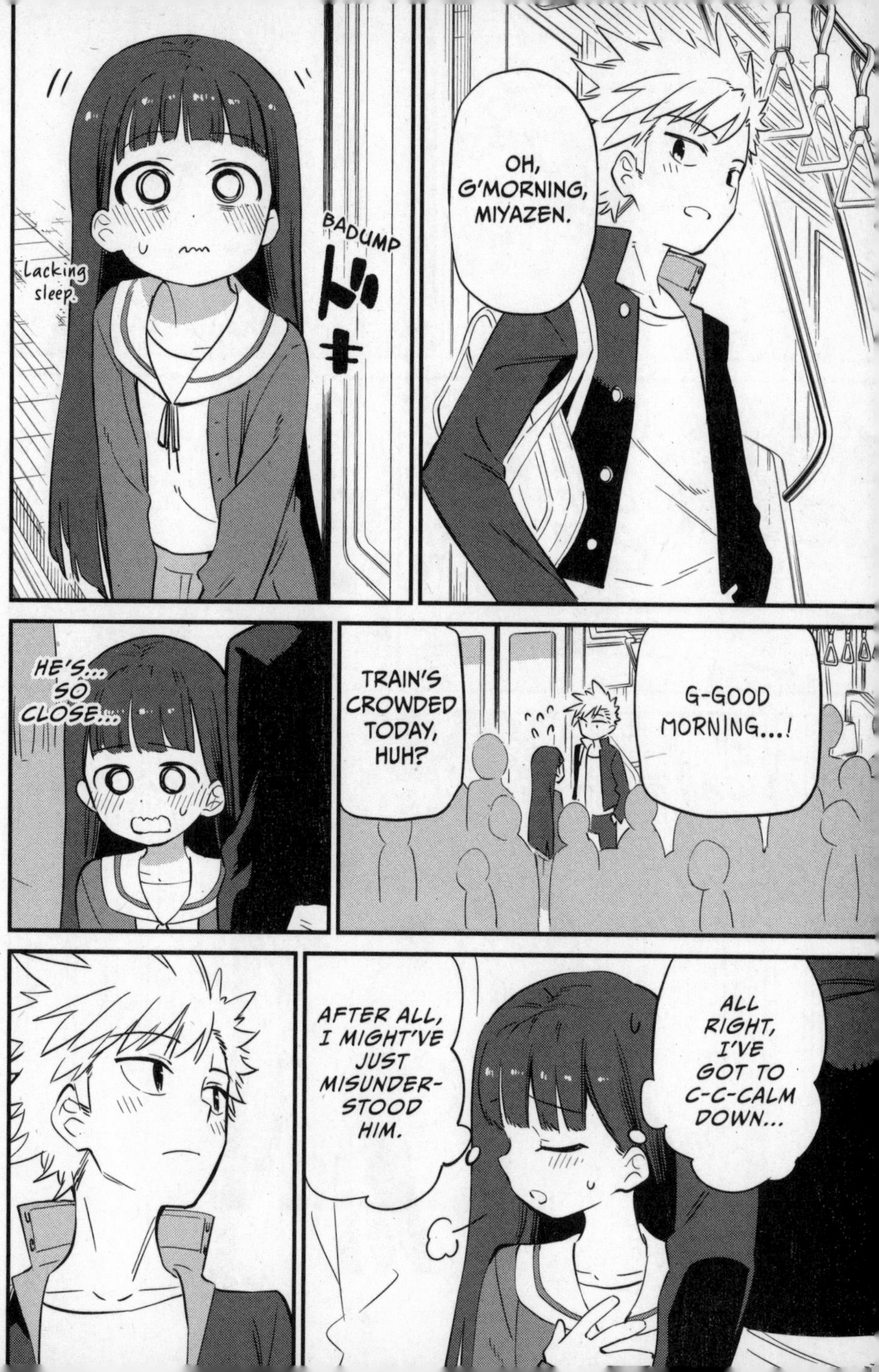

OH, G'MORNING, MIYAZEN.
BADUMP
ドキ
Lacking sleep.
G-GOOD MORNING...!
TRAIN'S CROWDED TODAY, HUH?
HE'S... SO CLOSE...
ALL RIGHT, I'VE GOT TO C-C-CALM DOWN...
AFTER ALL, I MIGHT'VE JUST MISUNDERSTOOD HIM.

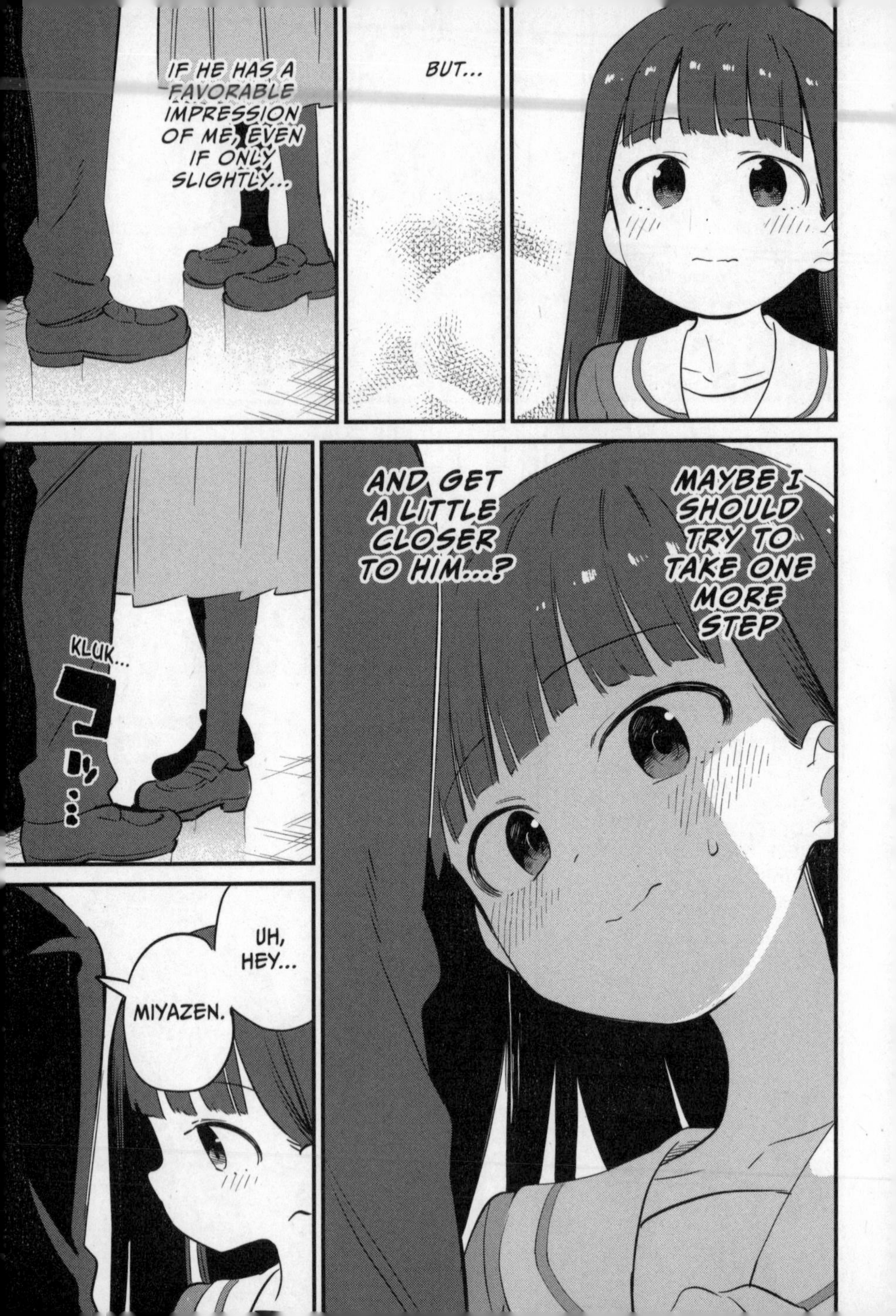
BUT...
IF HE HAS A FAVORABLE IMPRESSION OF ME, EVEN IF ONLY SLIGHTLY...
MAYBE I SHOULD TRY TO TAKE ONE MORE STEP
AND GET A LITTLE CLOSER TO HIM...?
KLUK...
コッ..
UH, HEY...
MIYAZEN.

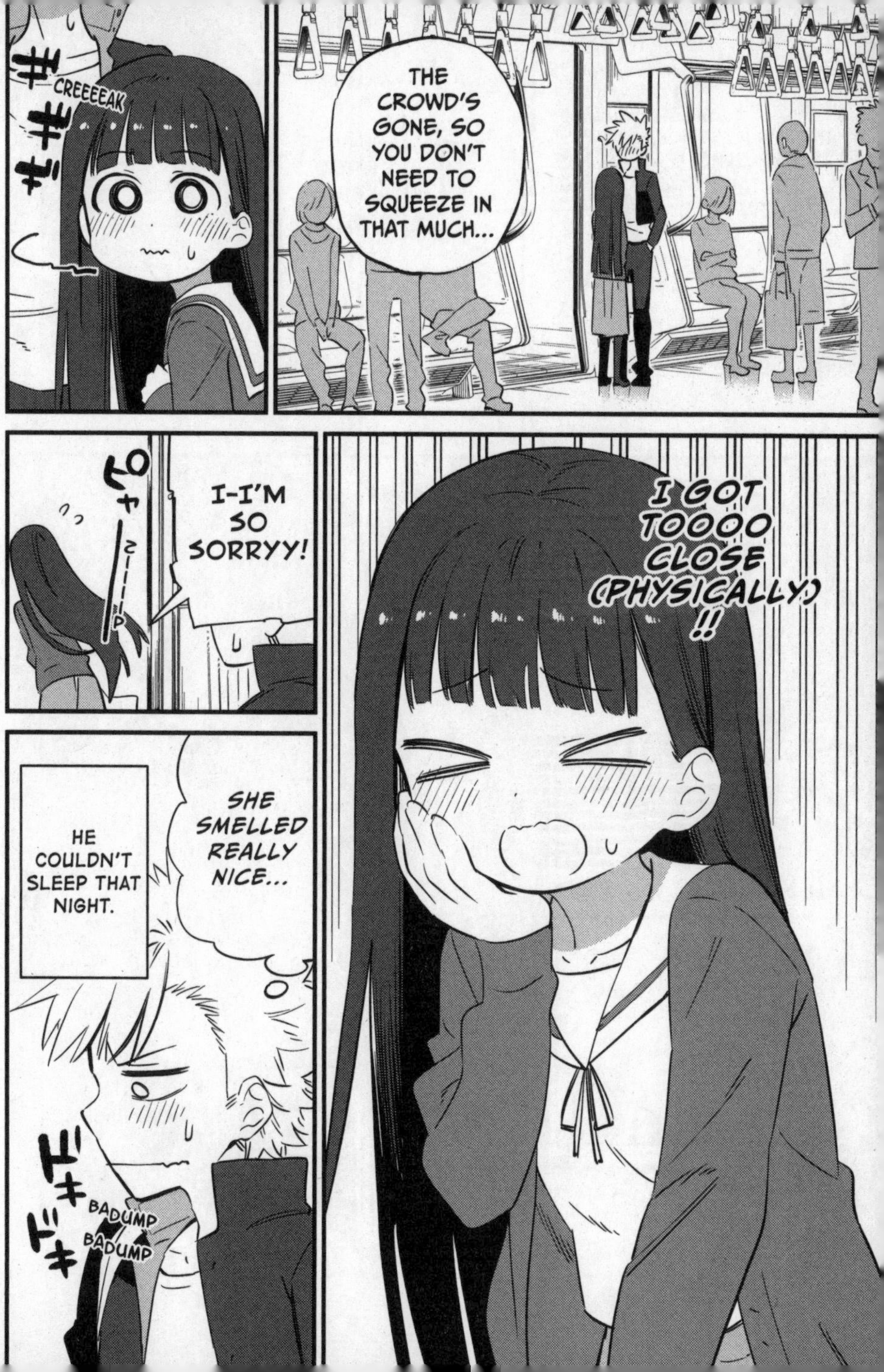
THE CROWD'S GONE, SO YOU DON'T NEED TO SQUEEZE IN THAT MUCH...
CREEEEAK
I GOT TOOOO CLOSE (PHYSICALLY) !!
I-I'M SO SORRYY!
P
SHE SMELLED REALLY NICE...
HE COULDN'T SLEEP THAT NIGHT.
BADUMP
BADUMP

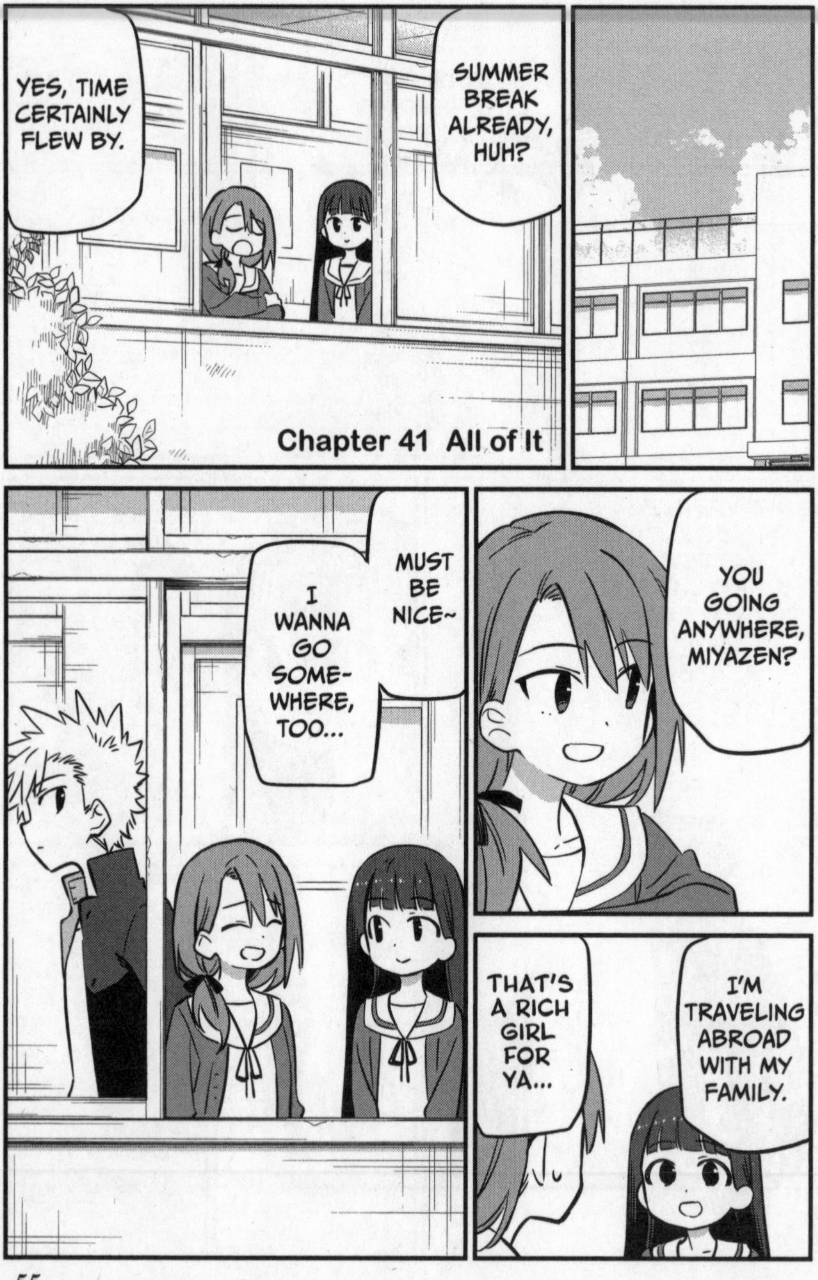
SUMMER BREAK ALREADY, HUH?
YES, TIME CERTAINLY FLEW BY.
Chapter 41 All of It
YOU GOING ANYWHERE, MIYAZEN?
I'M TRAVELING ABROAD WITH MY FAMILY.
THAT'S A RICH GIRL FOR YA...
MUST BE NICE~
I WANNA GO SOMEWHERE, TOO...

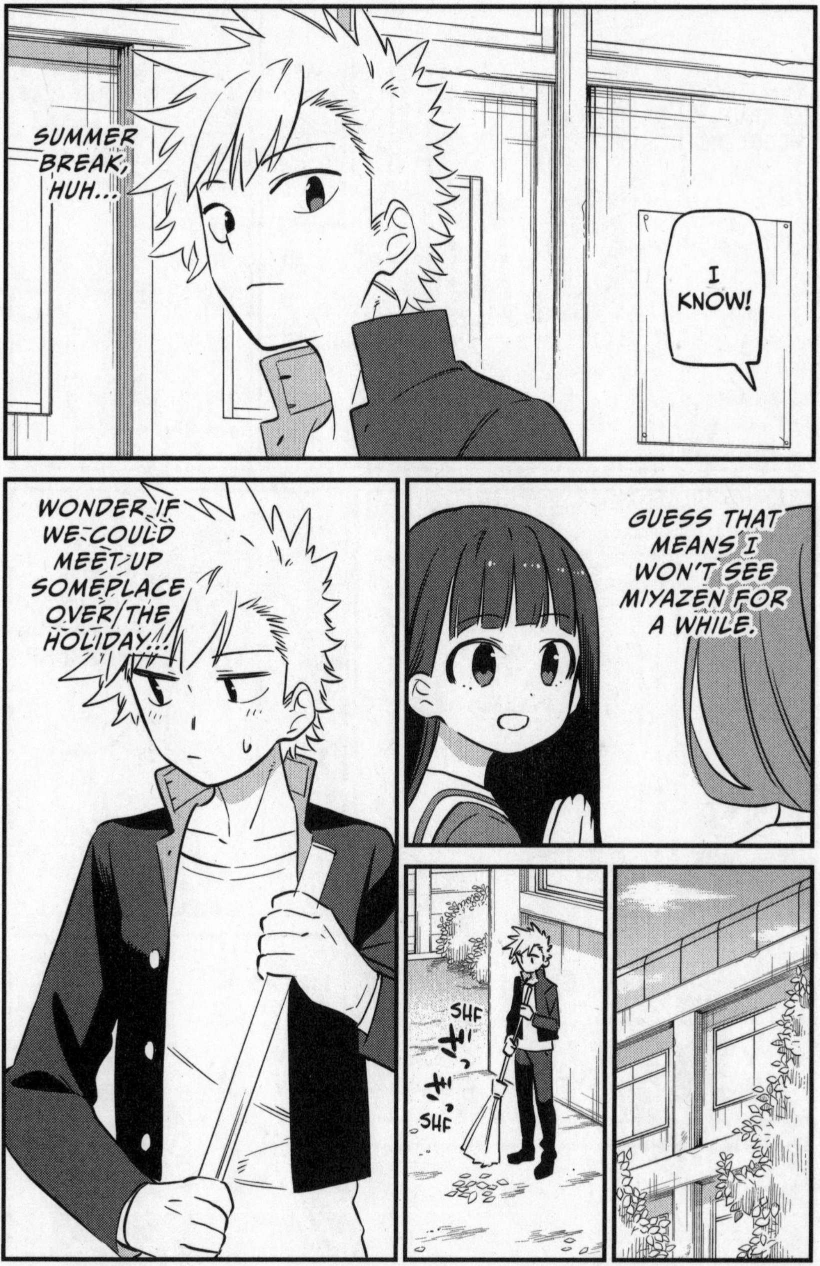
I KNOW!
SUMMER BREAK, HUH...
GUESS THAT MEANS I WON'T SEE MIYAZEN FOR A WHILE.
SHF
SHF
WONDER IF WE COULD MEET UP SOMEPLACE OVER THE HOLIDAY...

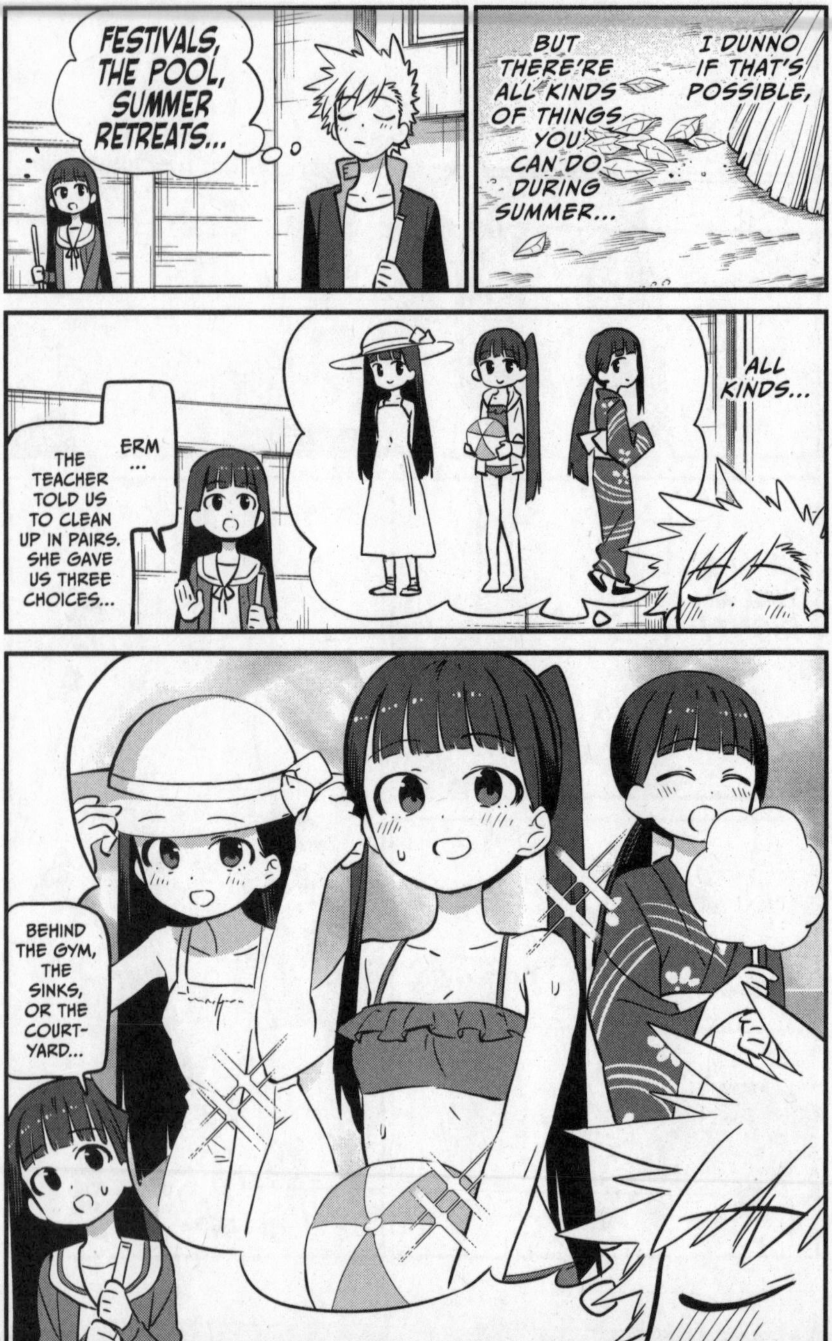
I DUNNO IF THAT'S POSSIBLE,
BUT THERE'RE ALL KINDS OF THINGS YOU CAN DO DURING SUMMER...
FESTIVALS, THE POOL, SUMMER RETREATS...
ALL KINDS...
ERM ...
THE TEACHER TOLD US TO CLEAN UP IN PAIRS. SHE GAVE US THREE CHOICES...
BEHIND THE GYM, THE SINKS, OR THE COURT-YARD...

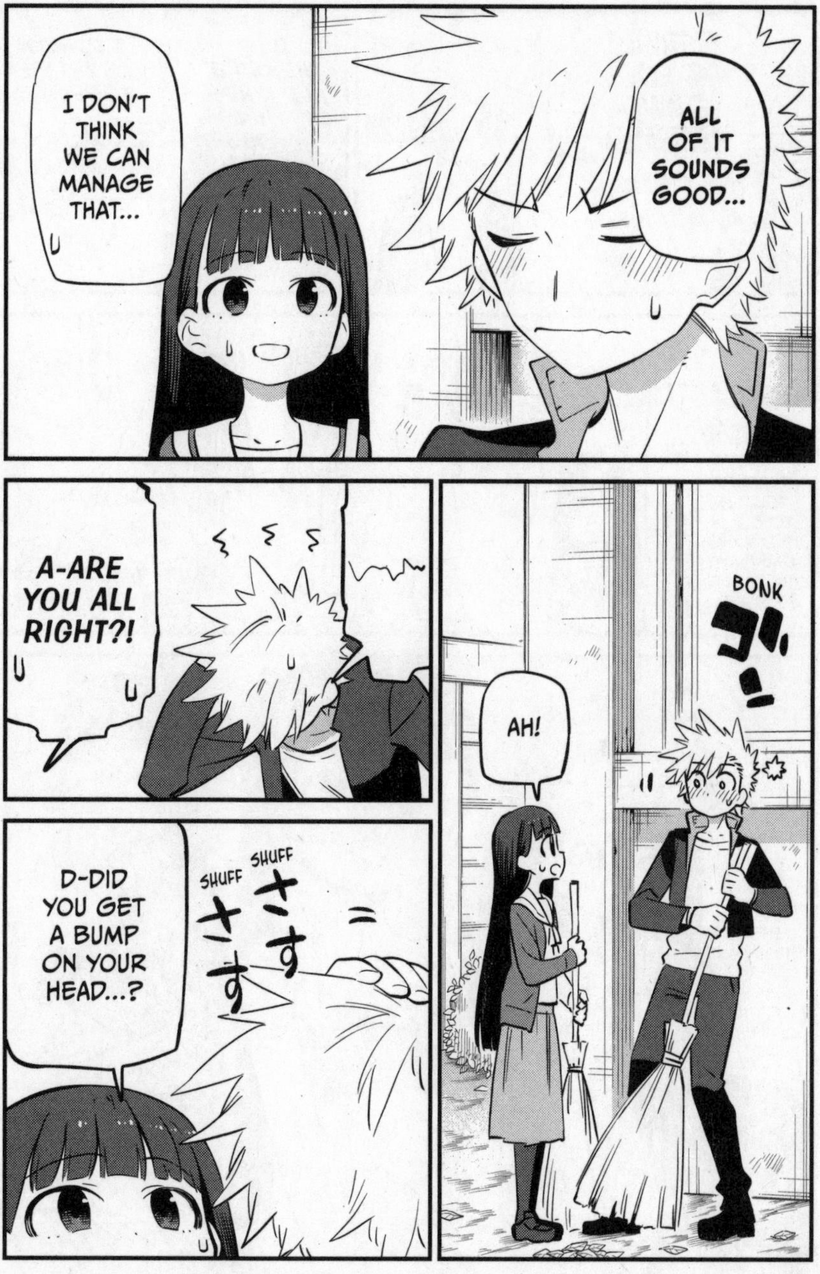
ALL OF IT SOUNDS GOOD...
I DON'T THINK WE CAN MANAGE THAT...
BONK
ゴッ
AH!
A-ARE YOU ALL RIGHT?!
SHUFF
さす
SHUFF
さす
D-DID YOU GET A BUMP ON YOUR HEAD...?

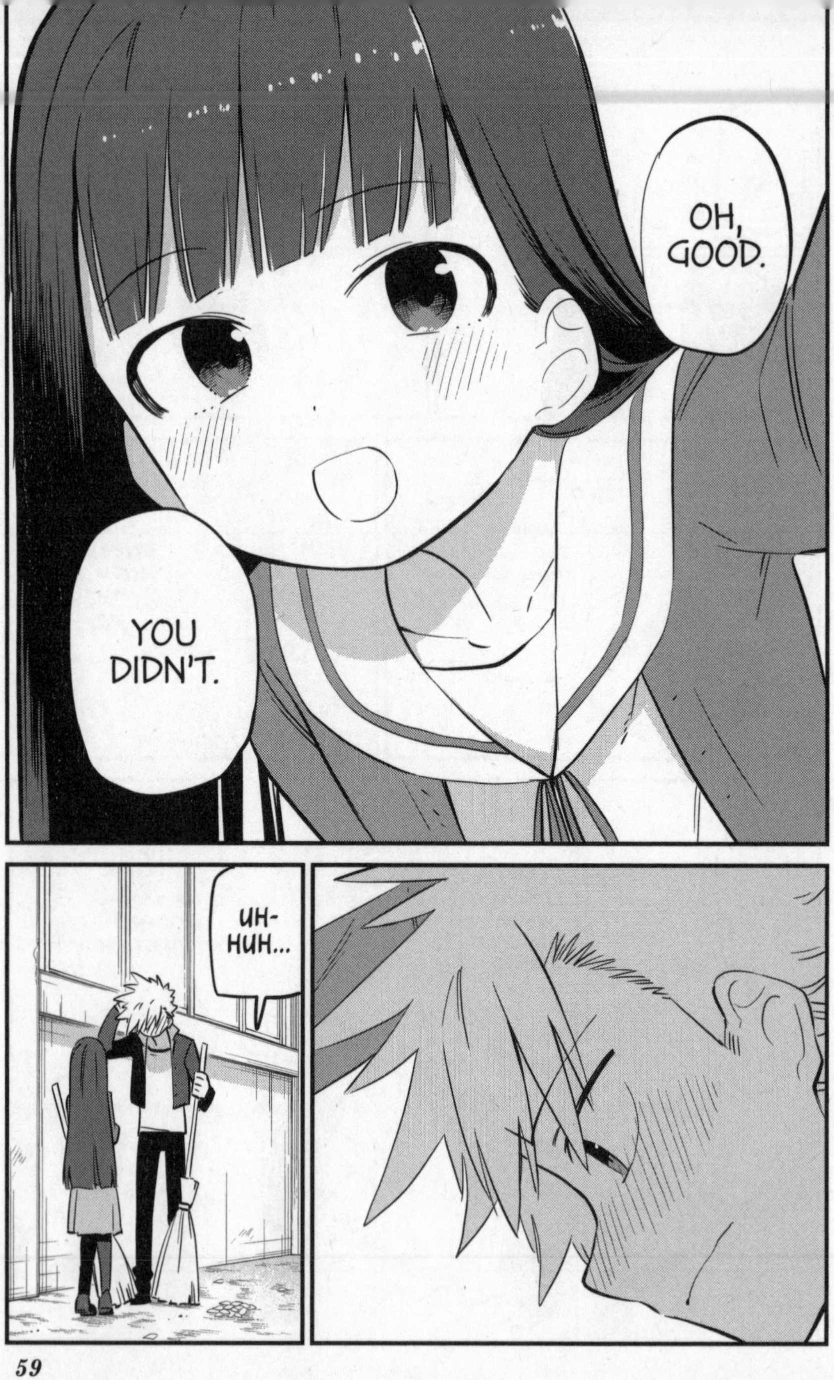
OH, GOOD.
YOU DIDN'T.
UH-HUH...

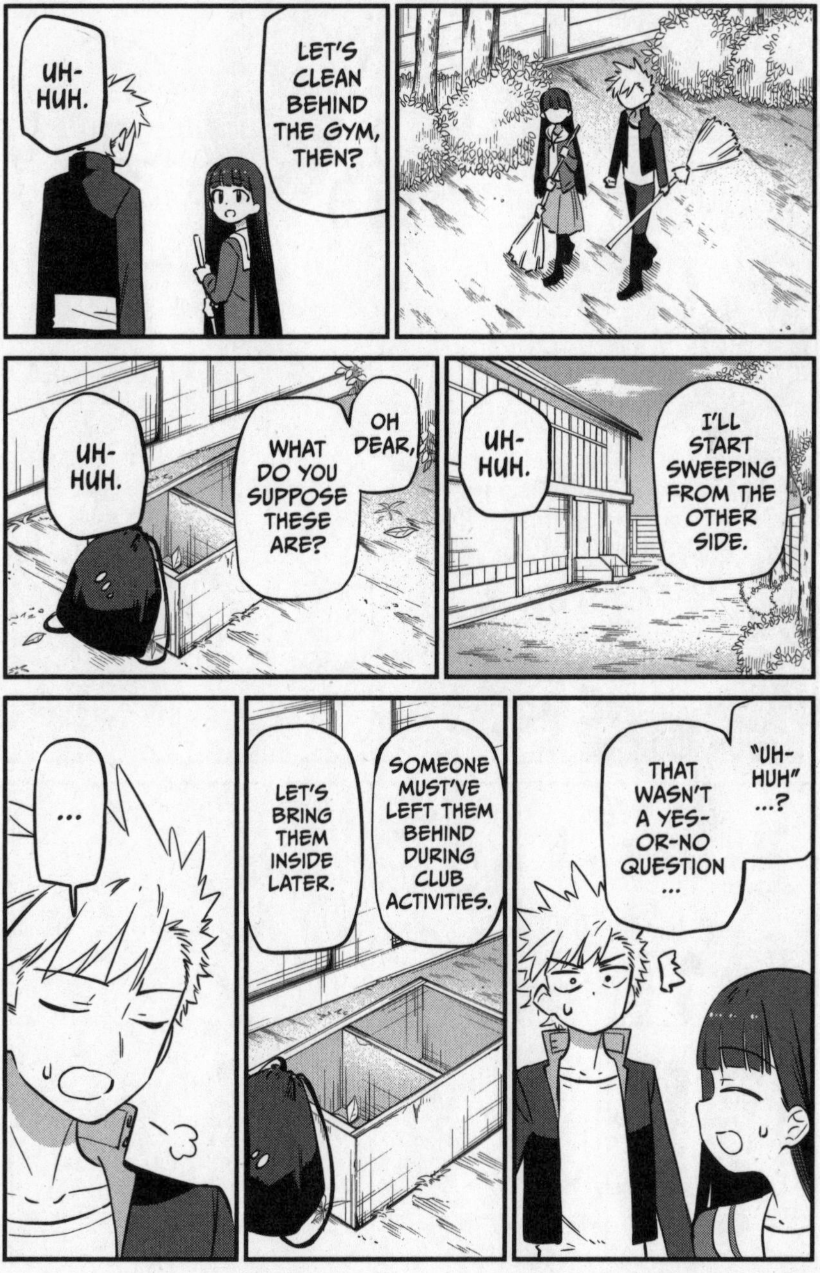
LET'S CLEAN BEHIND THE GYM, THEN?
UH-HUH.
I'LL START SWEEPING FROM THE OTHER SIDE.
UH-HUH.
OH DEAR, WHAT DO YOU SUPPOSE THESE ARE?
UH-HUH.
"UH-HUH" ...?
THAT WASN'T A YES-OR-NO QUESTION ...
SOMEONE MUST'VE LEFT THEM BEHIND DURING CLUB ACTIVITIES.
LET'S BRING THEM INSIDE LATER.
...

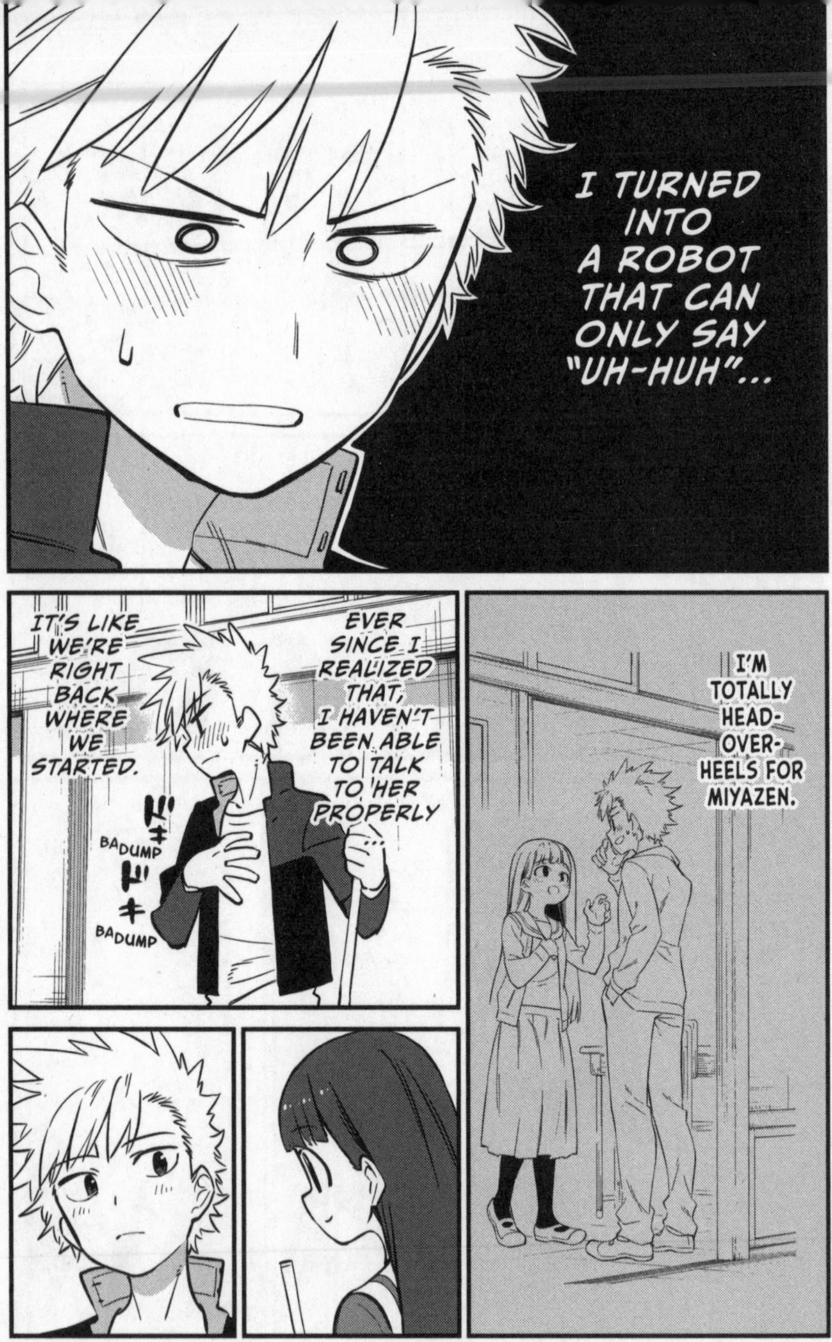
I TURNED INTO A ROBOT THAT CAN ONLY SAY "UH-HUH"...
I'M TOTALLY HEAD-OVER-HEELS FOR MIYAZEN.
EVER SINCE I REALIZED THAT, I HAVEN'T BEEN ABLE TO TALK TO HER PROPERLY...
IT'S LIKE WE'RE RIGHT BACK WHERE WE STARTED.
ドキ
BADUMP
ドキ
BADUMP

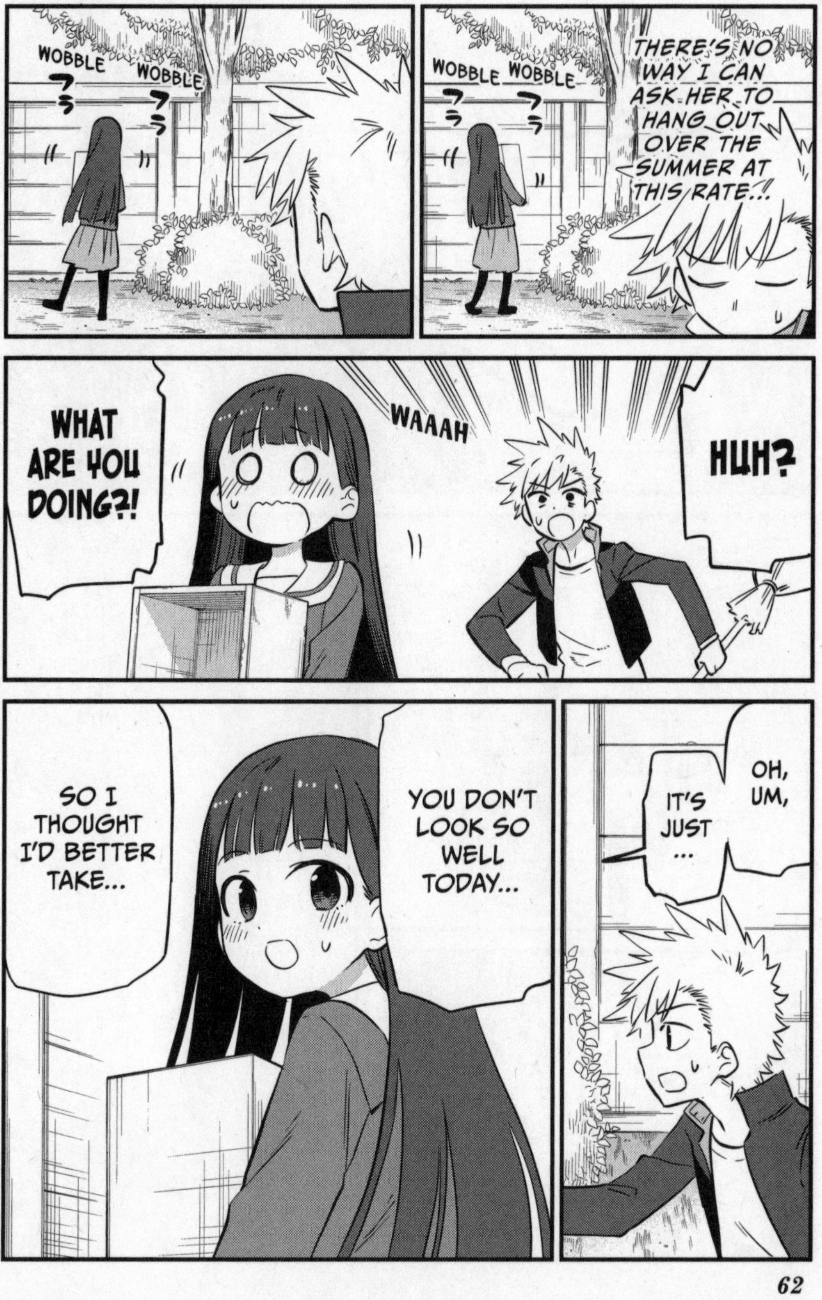
THERE'S NO WAY I CAN ASK HER TO HANG OUT OVER THE SUMMER AT THIS RATE...
WOBBLE
WOBBLE
WOBBLE
WOBBLE
HUH?
WAAAH
WHAT ARE YOU DOING?!
OH, UM,
IT'S JUST ...
YOU DON'T LOOK SO WELL TODAY...
SO I THOUGHT I'D BETTER TAKE...

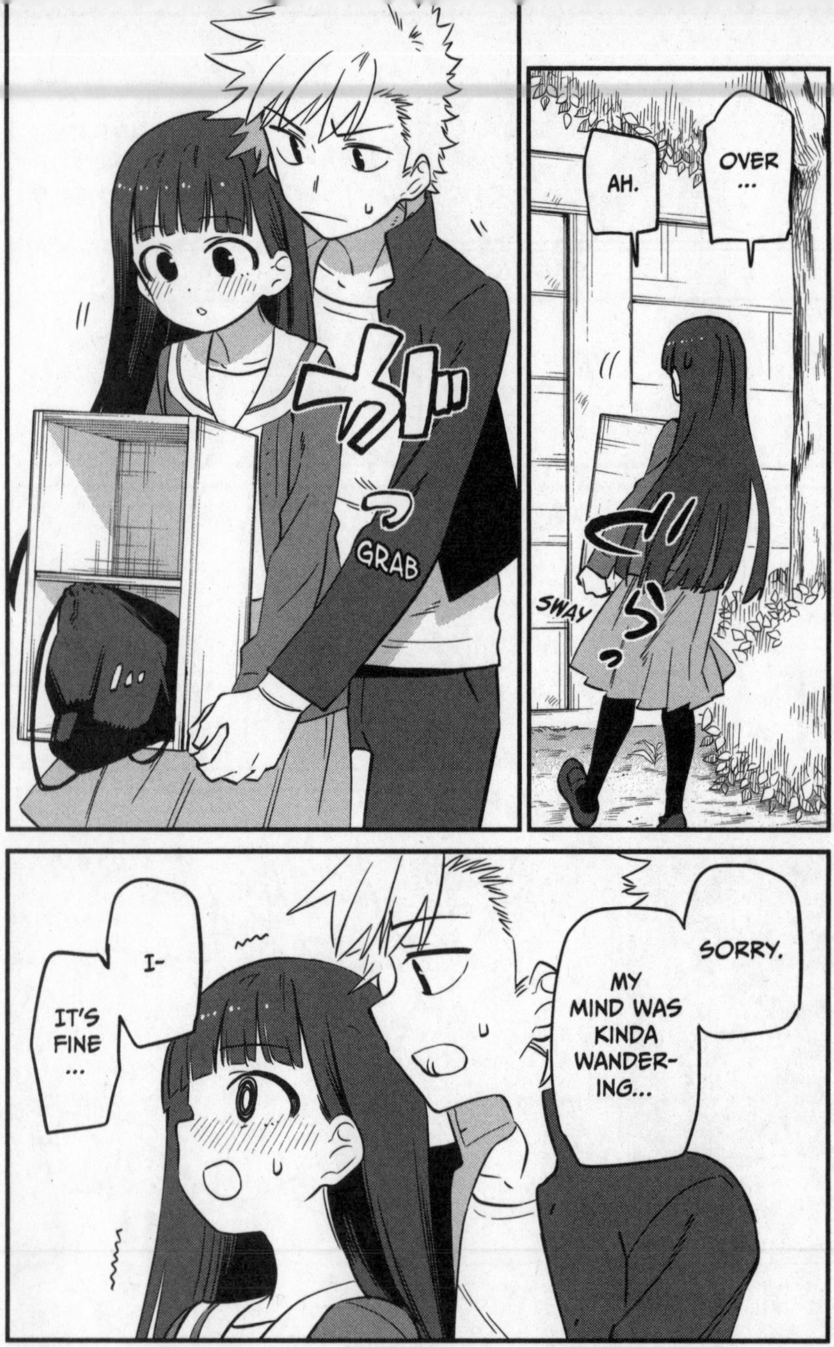
OVER ...
AH.
SWAY
GRAB
SORRY.
MY MIND WAS KINDA WANDER-ING...
I-
IT'S FINE ...

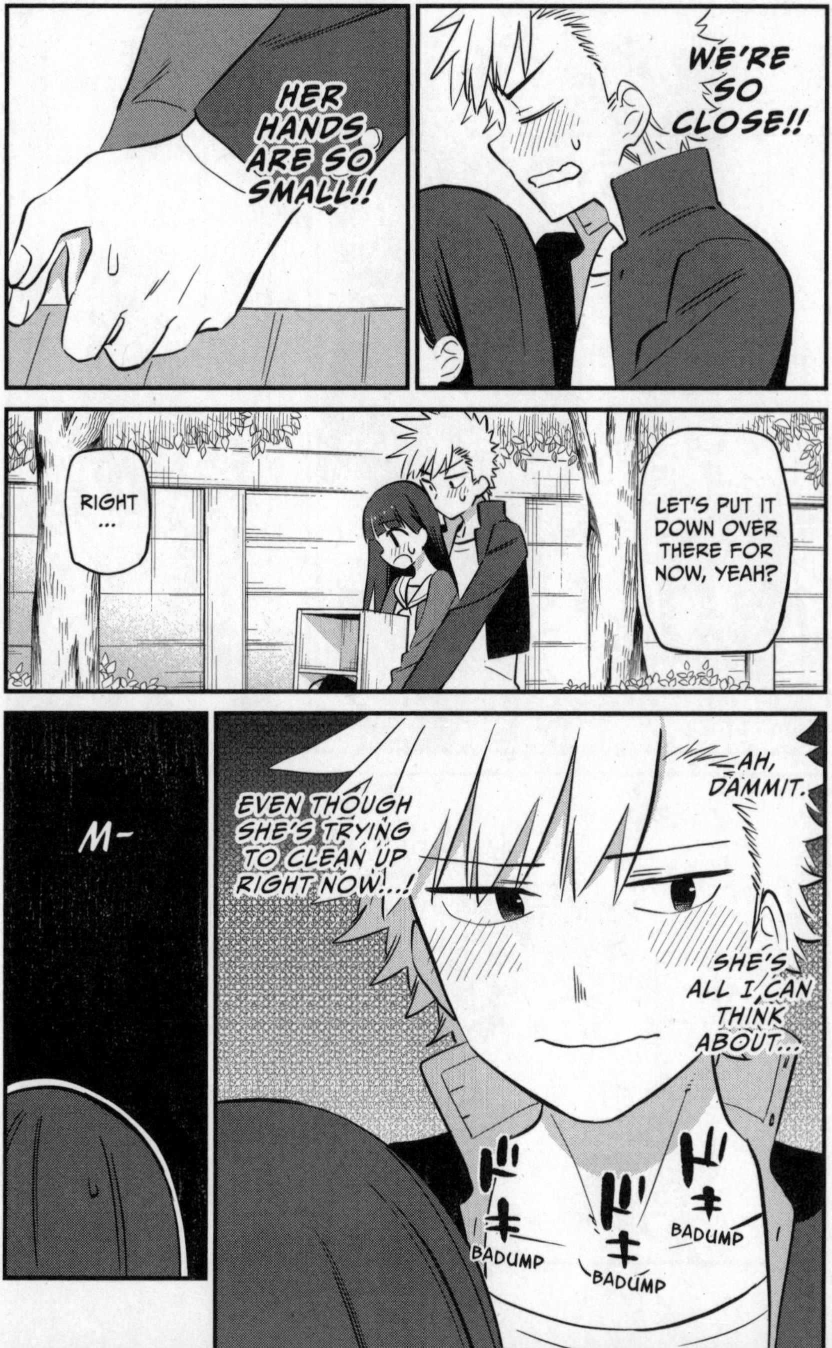
WE'RE SO CLOSE!!
HER HANDS ARE SO SMALL!!
LET'S PUT IT DOWN OVER THERE FOR NOW, YEAH?
RIGHT ...
AH, DAMMIT.
EVEN THOUGH SHE'S TRYING TO CLEAN UP RIGHT NOW...!
SHE'S ALL I CAN THINK ABOUT...
ドキ
BADUMP
ドキ
BADUMP
ドキ
BADUMP
M-

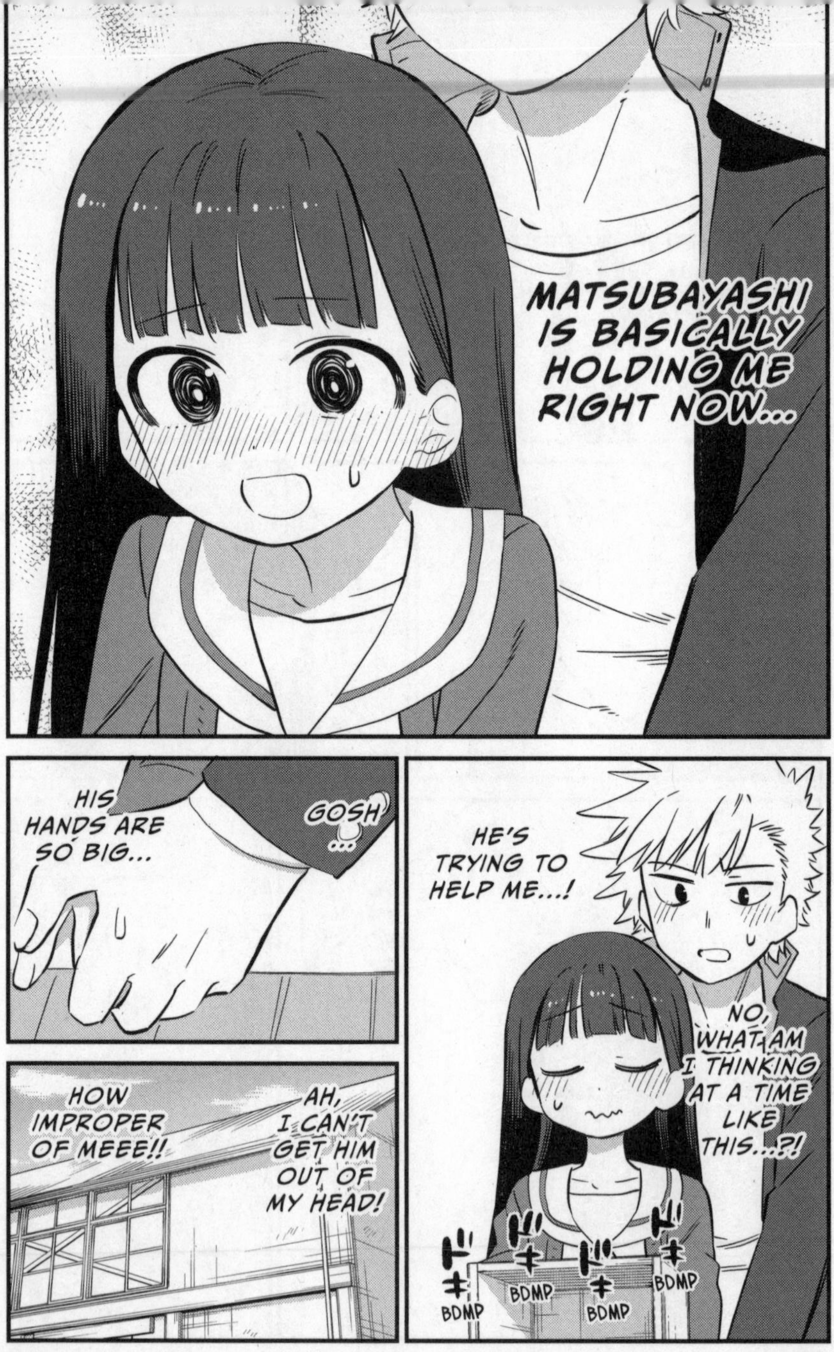
MATSUBAYASHI IS BASICALLY HOLDING ME RIGHT NOW...
HE'S TRYING TO HELP ME...!
NO, WHAT AM I THINKING AT A TIME LIKE THIS...?!
ドキ ドキ ドキ ドキ
BDMP BDMP BDMP BDMP
GOSH...
HIS HANDS ARE SO BIG...
AH, I CAN'T GET HIM OUT OF MY HEAD!
HOW IMPROPER OF MEEE!!

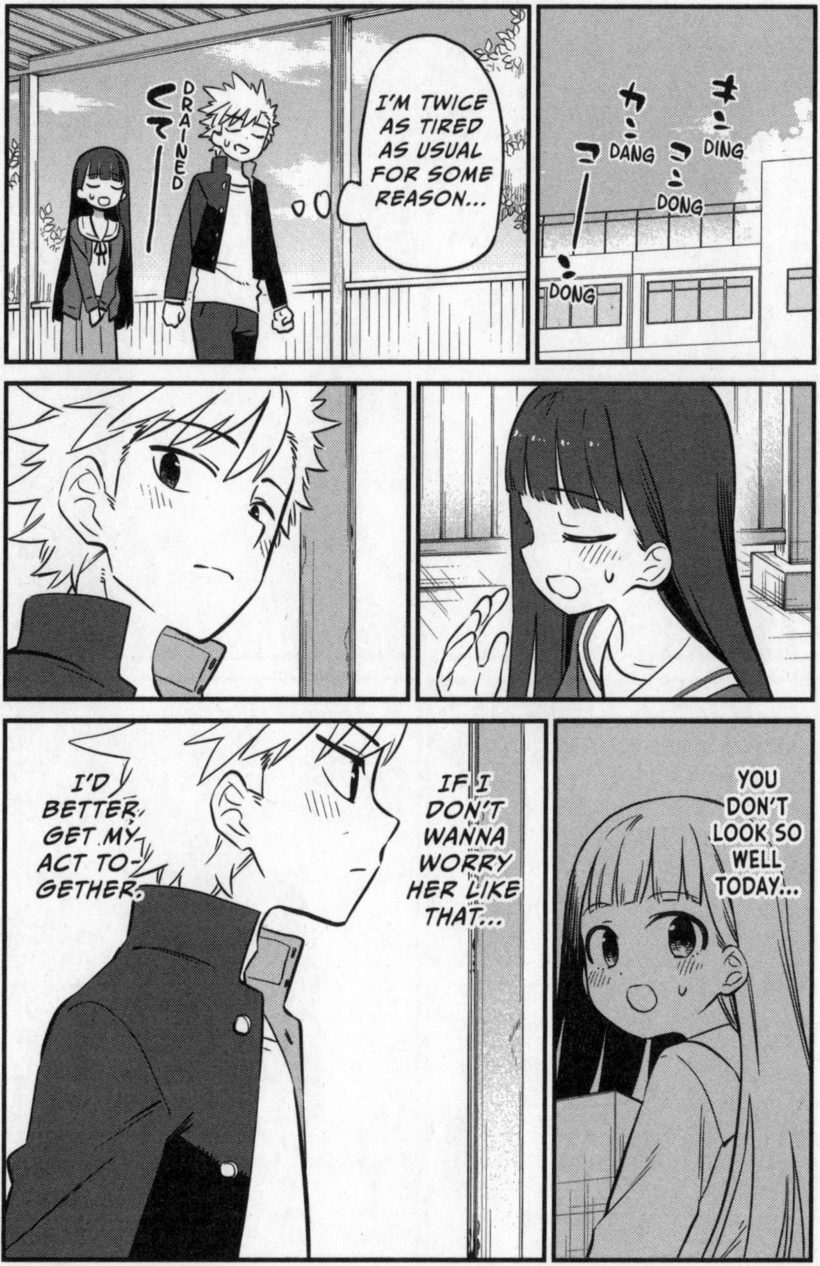
DING
DONG
DANG
DONG
I'M TWICE AS TIRED AS USUAL FOR SOME REASON...
DRAINED
YOU DON'T LOOK SO WELL TODAY...
IF I DON'T WANNA WORRY HER LIKE THAT...
I'D BETTER GET MY ACT TOGETHER.

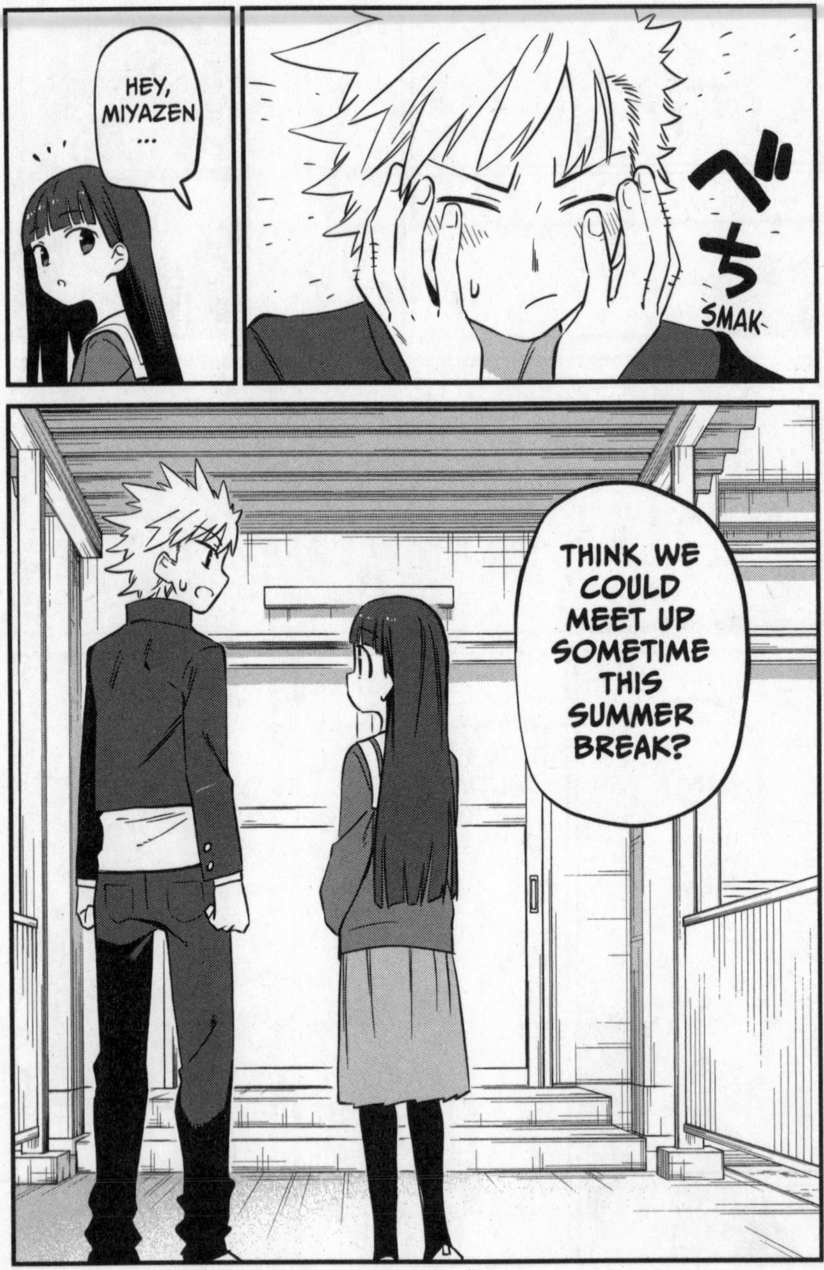
べち
SMAK
HEY, MIYAZEN ...
THINK WE COULD MEET UP SOMETIME THIS SUMMER BREAK?

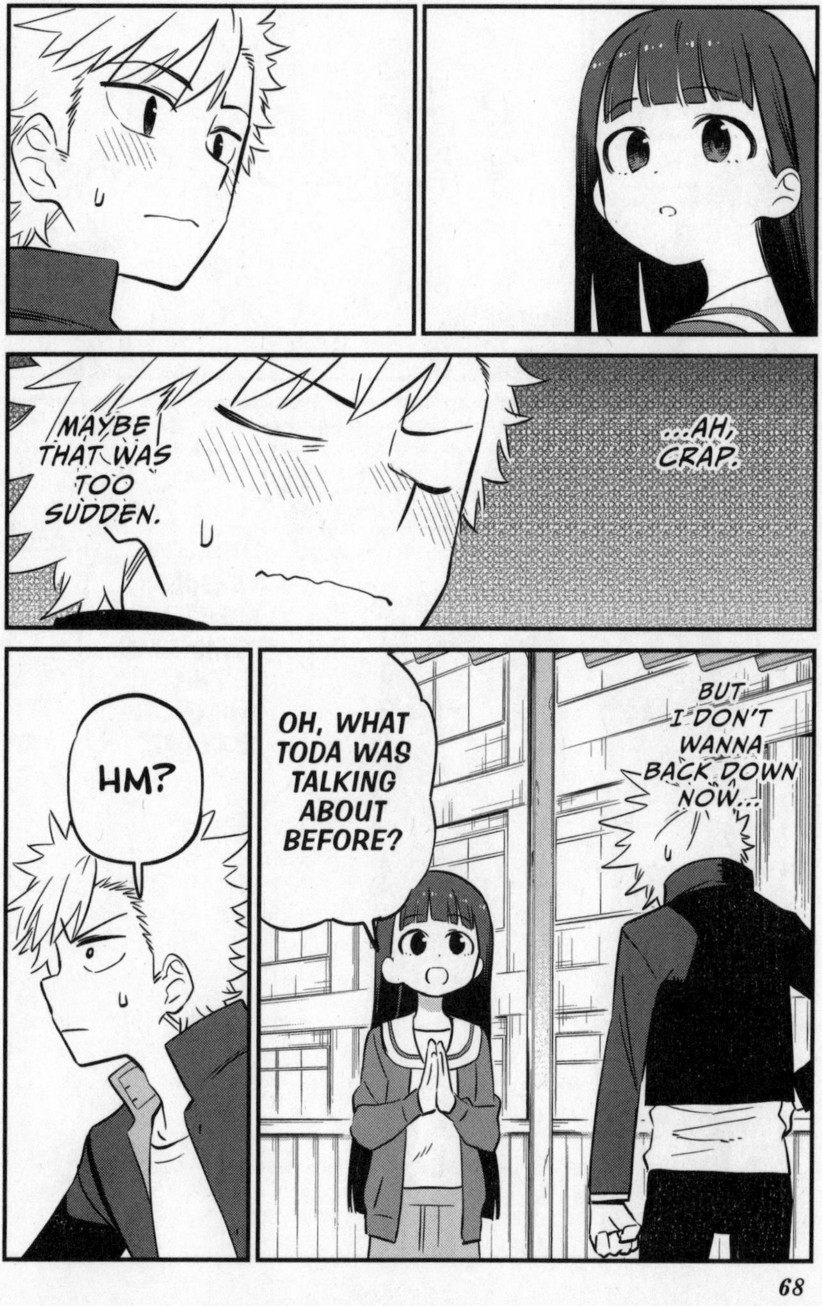
...AH, CRAP.
MAYBE THAT WAS TOO SUDDEN.
BUT I DON'T WANNA BACK DOWN NOW...
OH, WHAT TODA WAS TALKING ABOUT BEFORE?
HM?

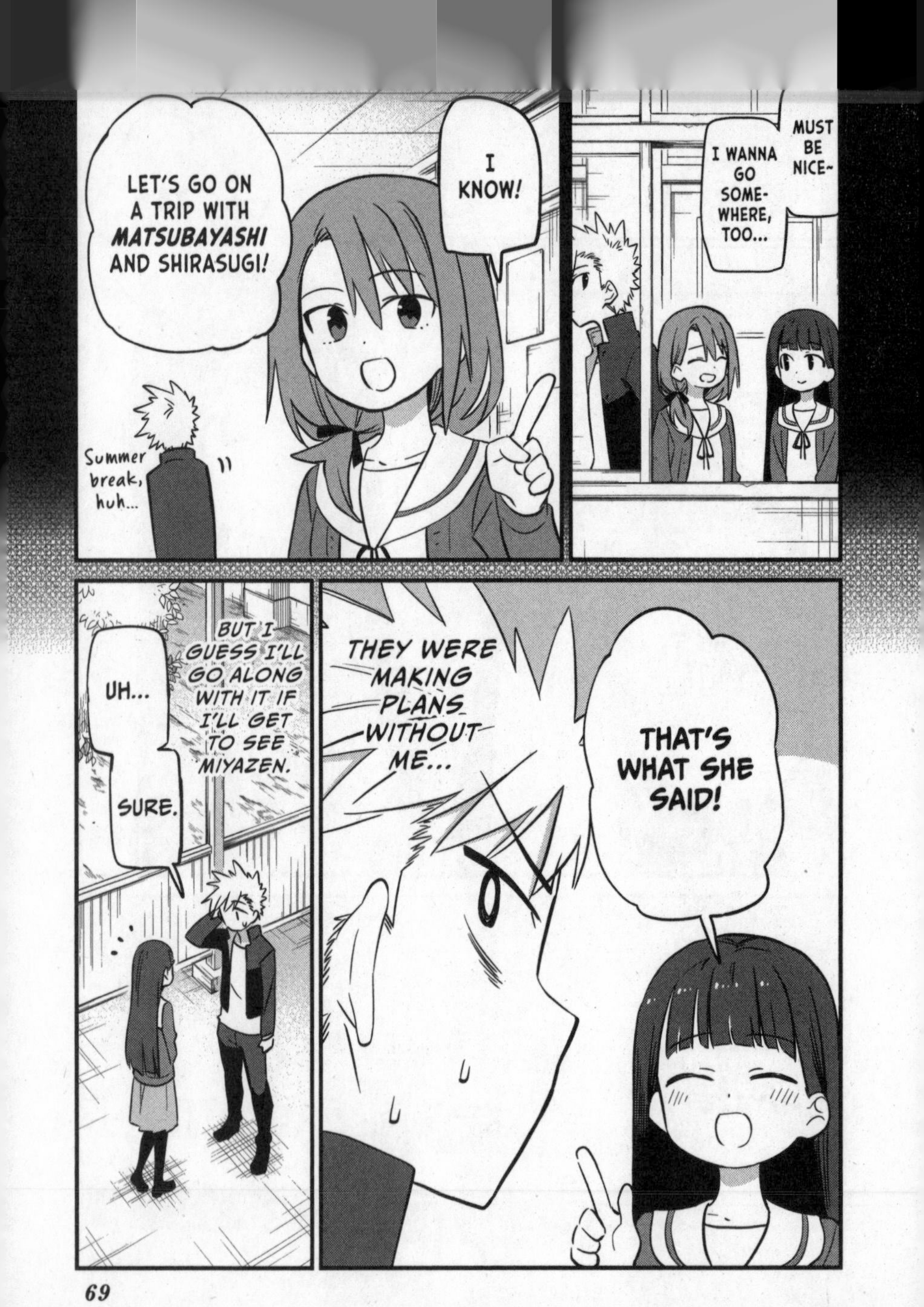
MUST BE NICE~
I WANNA GO SOME-WHERE, TOO...
I KNOW!
LET'S GO ON A TRIP WITH MATSUBAYASHI AND SHIRASUGI!
Summer break, huh...
THAT'S WHAT SHE SAID!
THEY WERE MAKING PLANS WITHOUT ME...
BUT I GUESS I'LL GO ALONG WITH IT IF I'LL GET TO SEE MIYAZEN.
UH...
SURE.

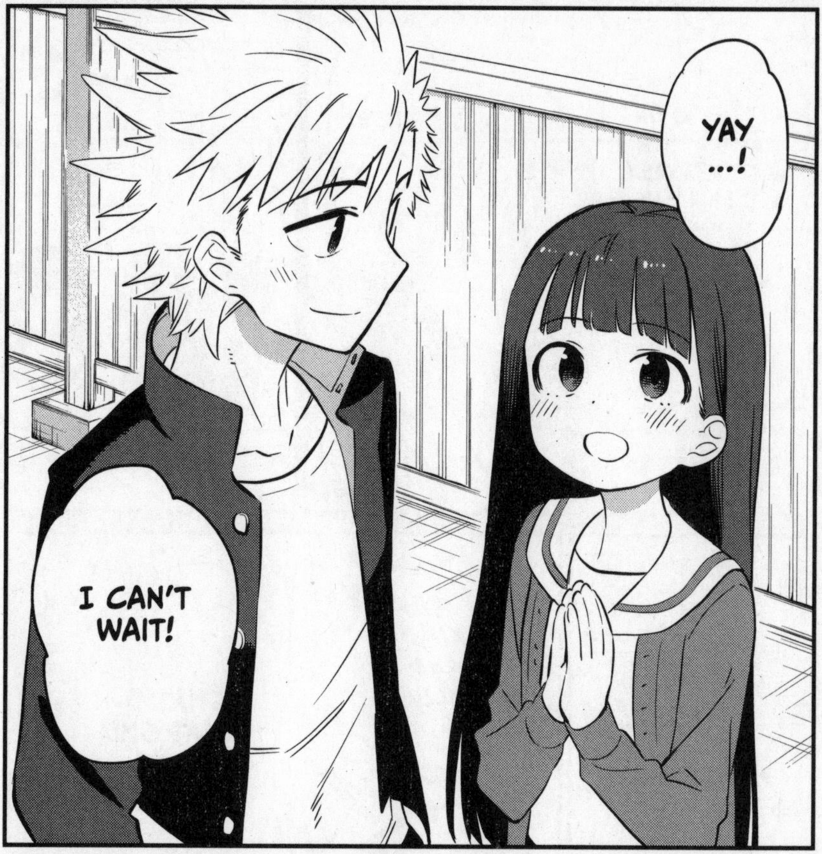
YAY ...!
I CAN'T WAIT!

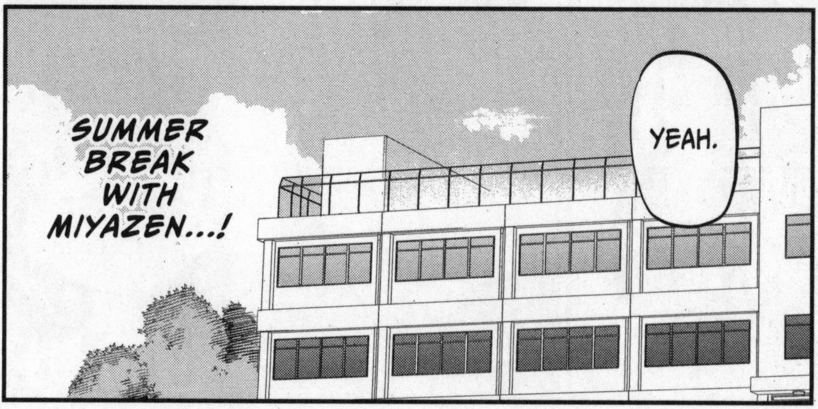
YEAH.
SUMMER BREAK WITH MIYAZEN...!

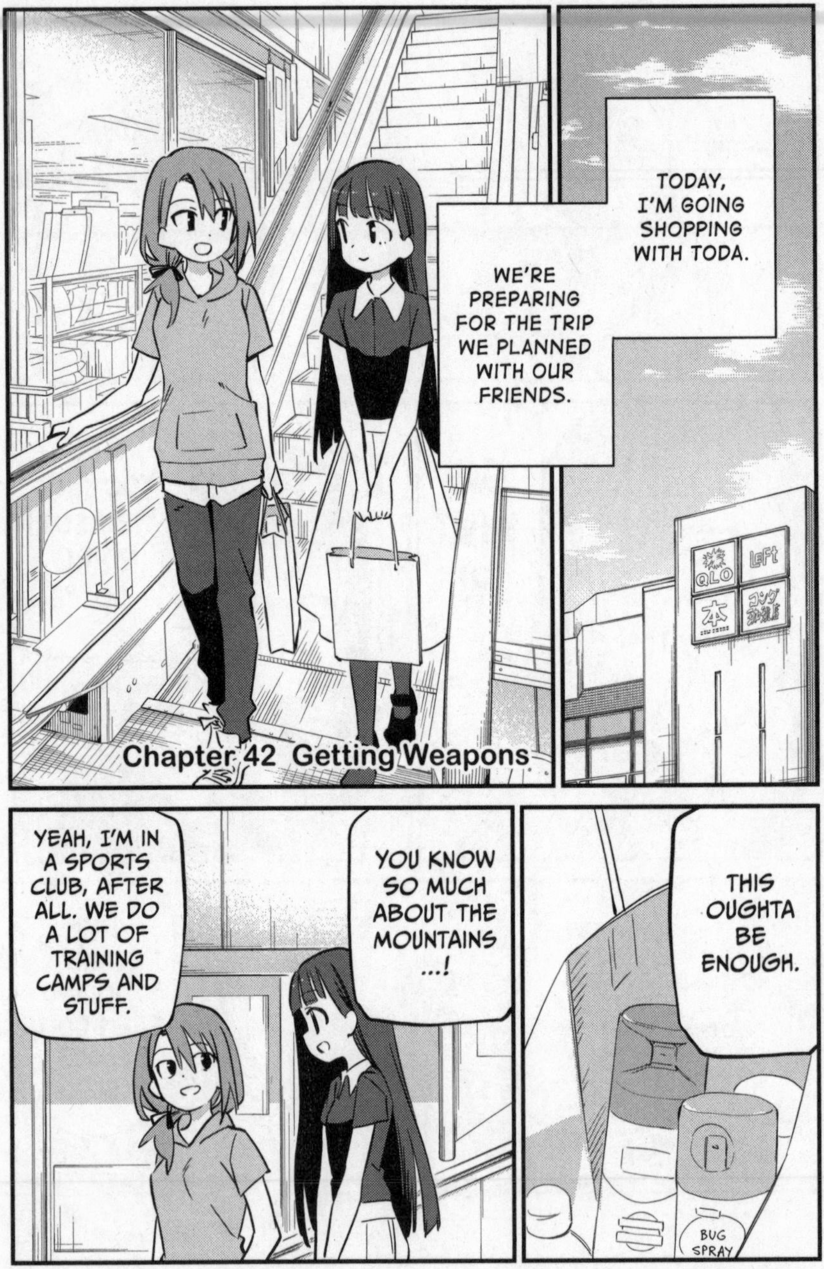
TODAY, I'M GOING SHOPPING WITH TODA.
WE'RE PREPARING FOR THE TRIP WE PLANNED WITH OUR FRIENDS.
QLO
LeFt
本
Chapter 42 Getting Weapons
THIS OUGHTA BE ENOUGH.
BUG SPRAY
YOU KNOW SO MUCH ABOUT THE MOUNTAINS ...!
YEAH, I'M IN A SPORTS CLUB, AFTER ALL. WE DO A LOT OF TRAINING CAMPS AND STUFF.

Sign: Konda's Coffee

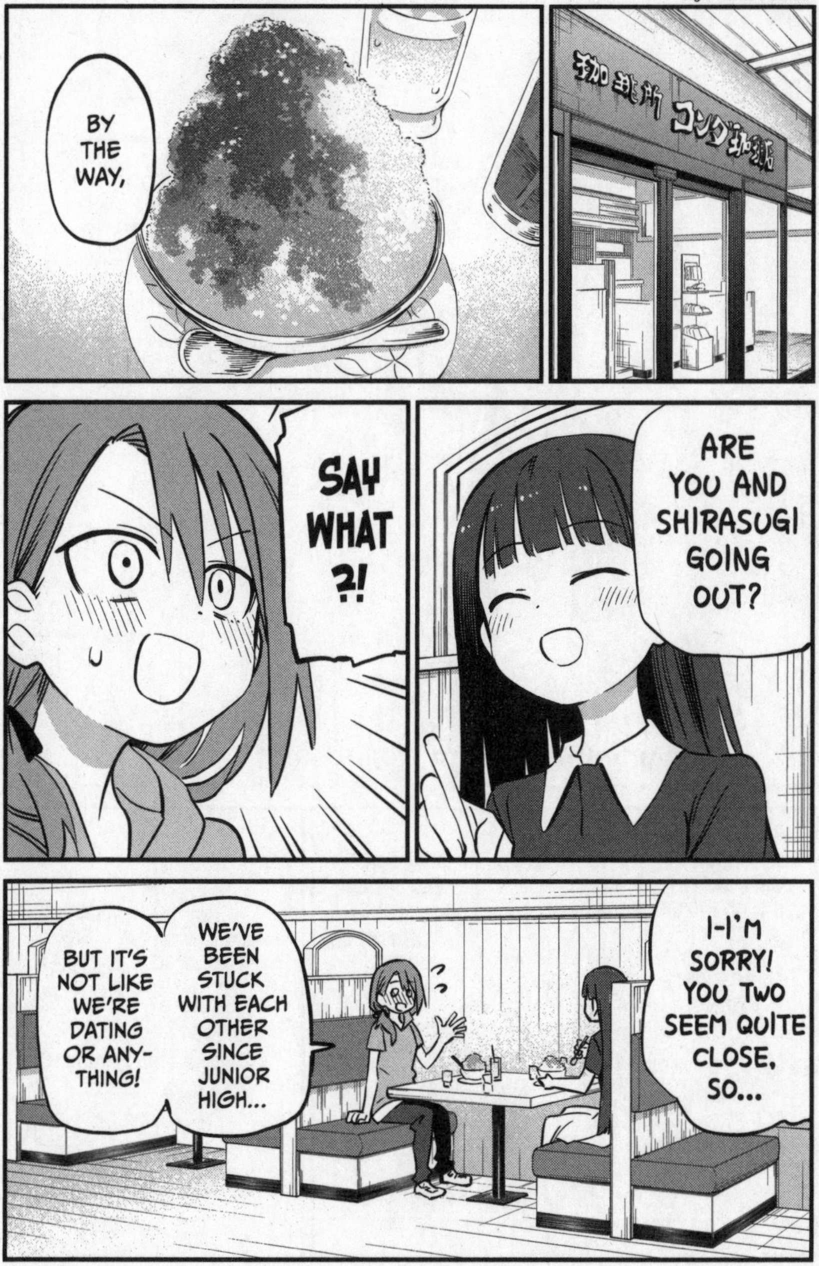
BY THE WAY,
ARE YOU AND SHIRASUGI GOING OUT?
SAY WHAT ?!
I-I'M SORRY! YOU TWO SEEM QUITE CLOSE, SO...
WE'VE BEEN STUCK WITH EACH OTHER SINCE JUNIOR HIGH...
BUT IT'S NOT LIKE WE'RE DATING OR ANY-THING!

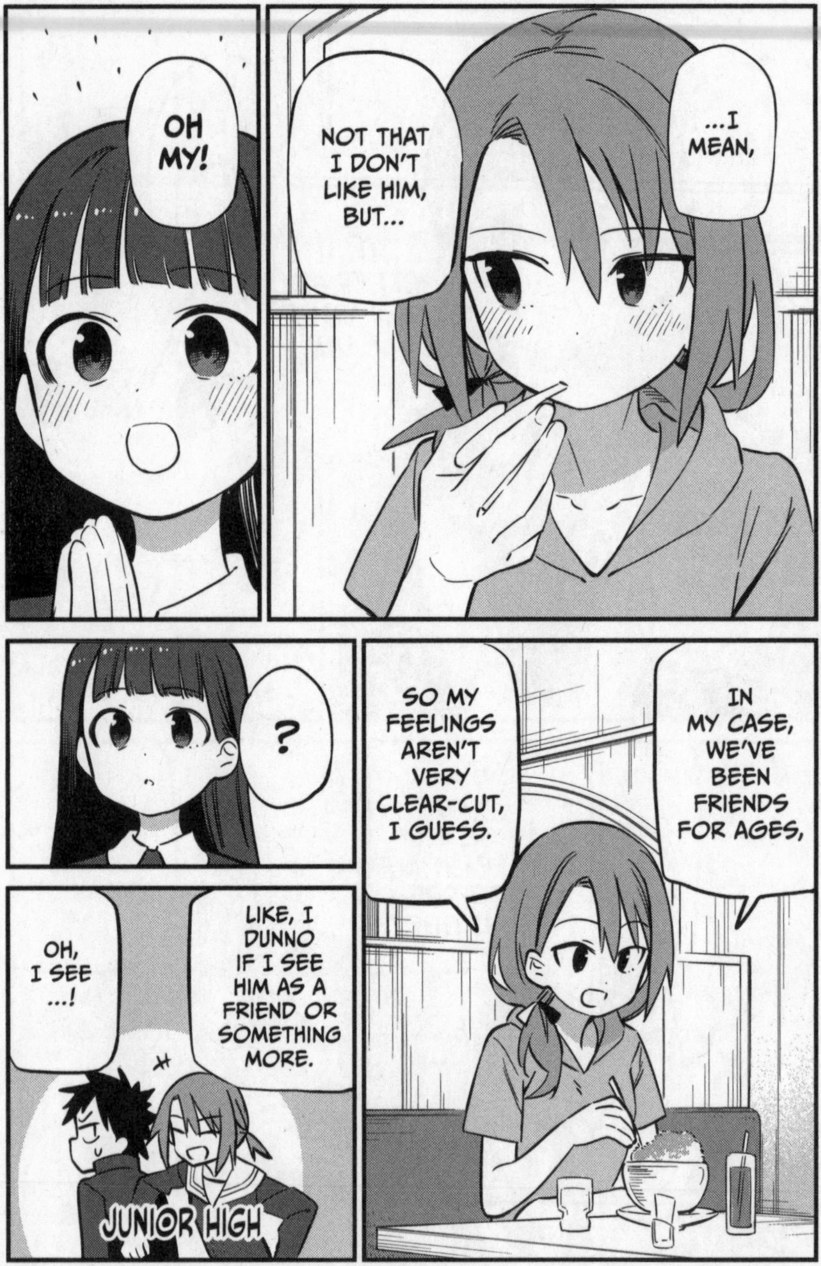
...I MEAN,
NOT THAT I DON'T LIKE HIM, BUT...
OH MY!
IN MY CASE, WE'VE BEEN FRIENDS FOR AGES,
SO MY FEELINGS AREN'T VERY CLEAR-CUT, I GUESS.
?
LIKE, I DUNNO IF I SEE HIM AS A FRIEND OR SOMETHING MORE.
OH, I SEE ...!
JUNIOR HIGH

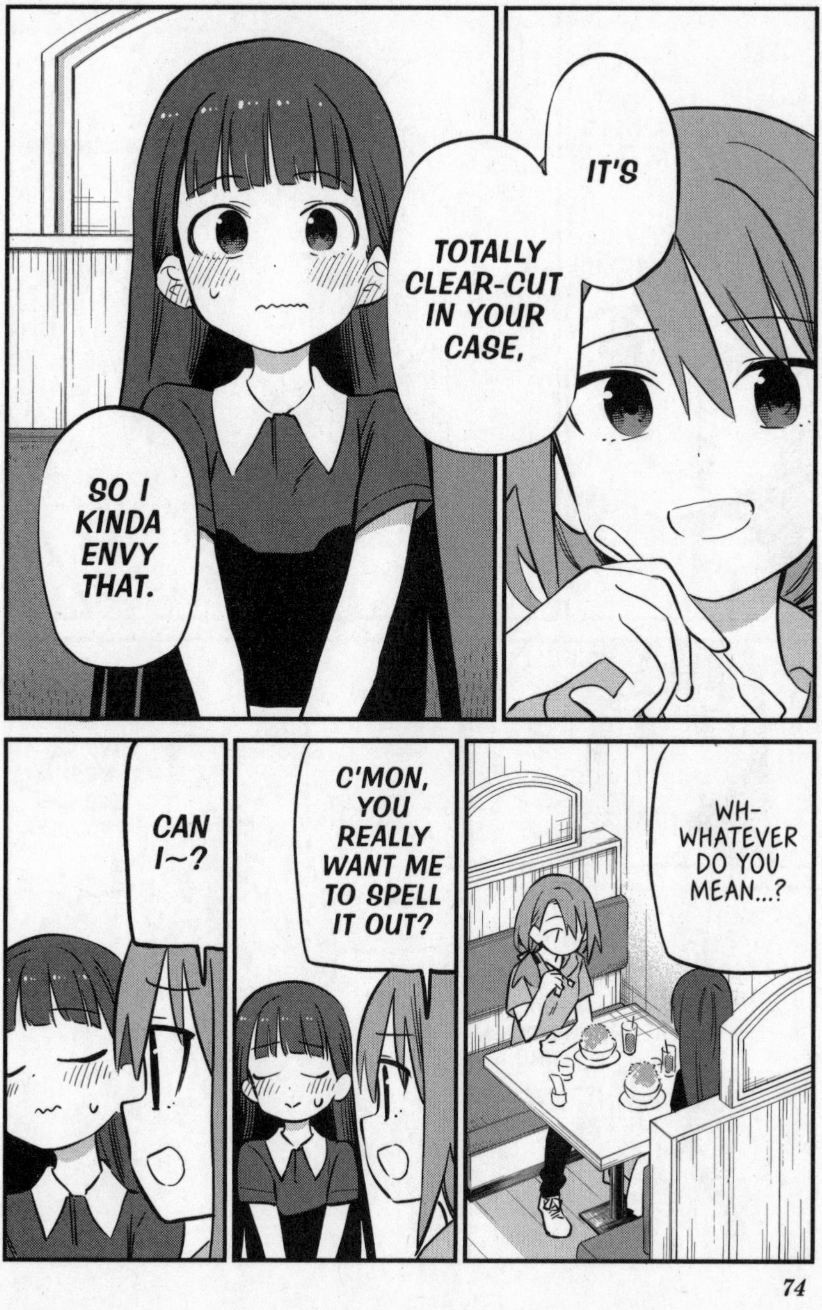
IT'S
TOTALLY CLEAR-CUT IN YOUR CASE,
SO I KINDA ENVY THAT.
WH-WHATEVER DO YOU MEAN...?
C'MON, YOU REALLY WANT ME TO SPELL IT OUT?
CAN I~?

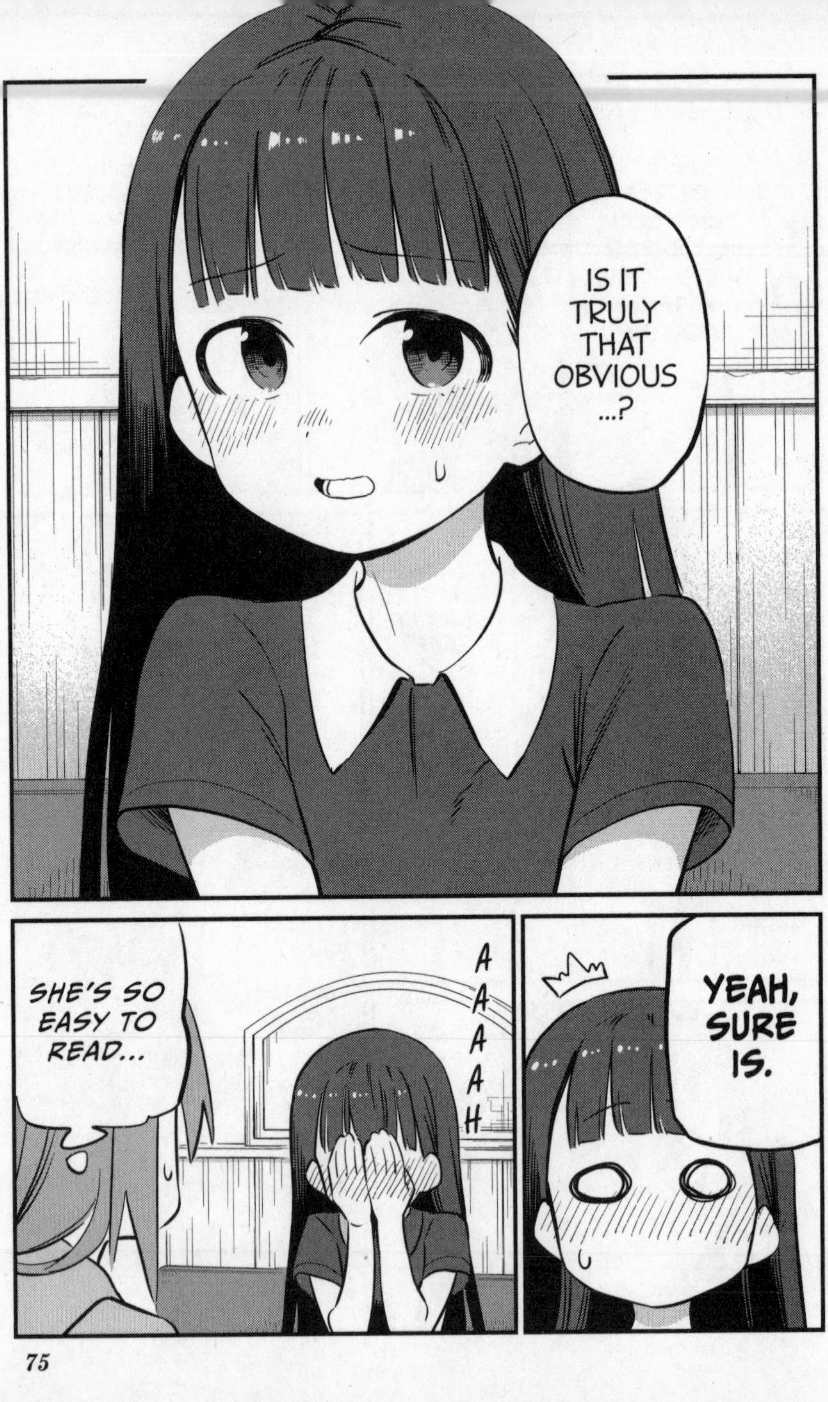
IS IT TRULY THAT OBVIOUS ...?
YEAH, SURE IS.
AAAAAH
SHE'S SO EASY TO READ...

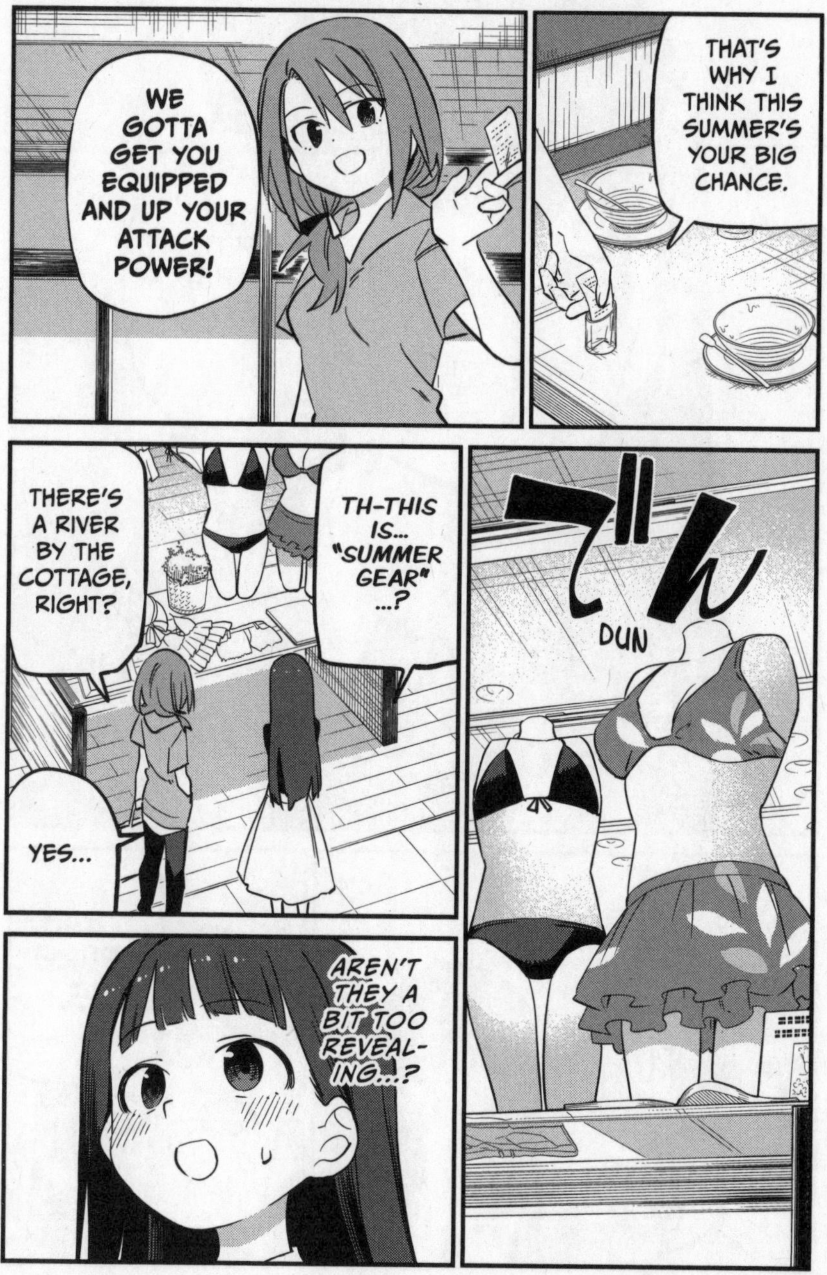
THAT'S WHY I THINK THIS SUMMER'S YOUR BIG CHANCE.
WE GOTTA GET YOU EQUIPPED AND UP YOUR ATTACK POWER!
でん
DUN
TH-THIS IS... "SUMMER GEAR" ...?
THERE'S A RIVER BY THE COTTAGE, RIGHT?
YES...
AREN'T THEY A BIT TOO REVEAL-ING...?

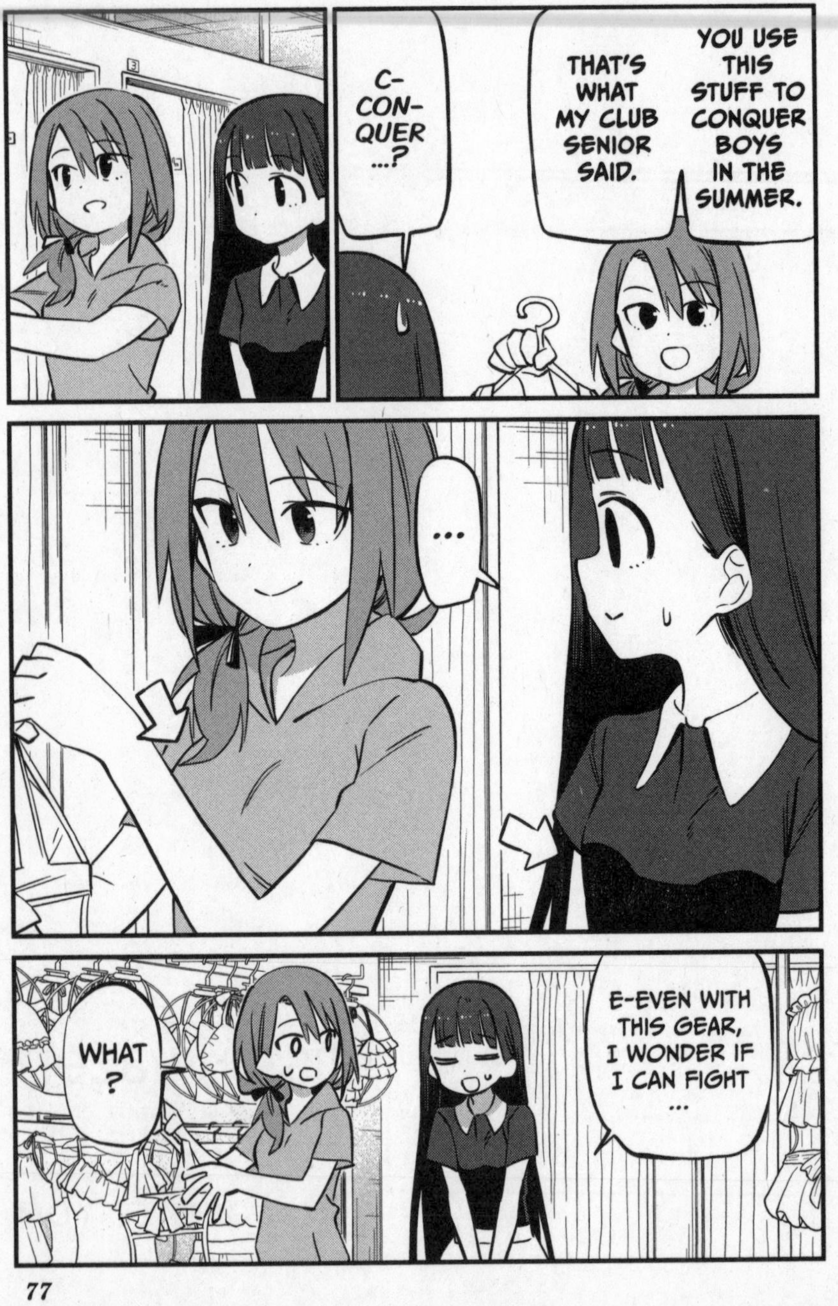
YOU USE THIS STUFF TO CONQUER BOYS IN THE SUMMER.
THAT'S WHAT MY CLUB SENIOR SAID.
C-CONQUER ...?
...
E-EVEN WITH THIS GEAR, I WONDER IF I CAN FIGHT ...
WHAT?

Miss Miyazen
Would Love to
Get Closer to You

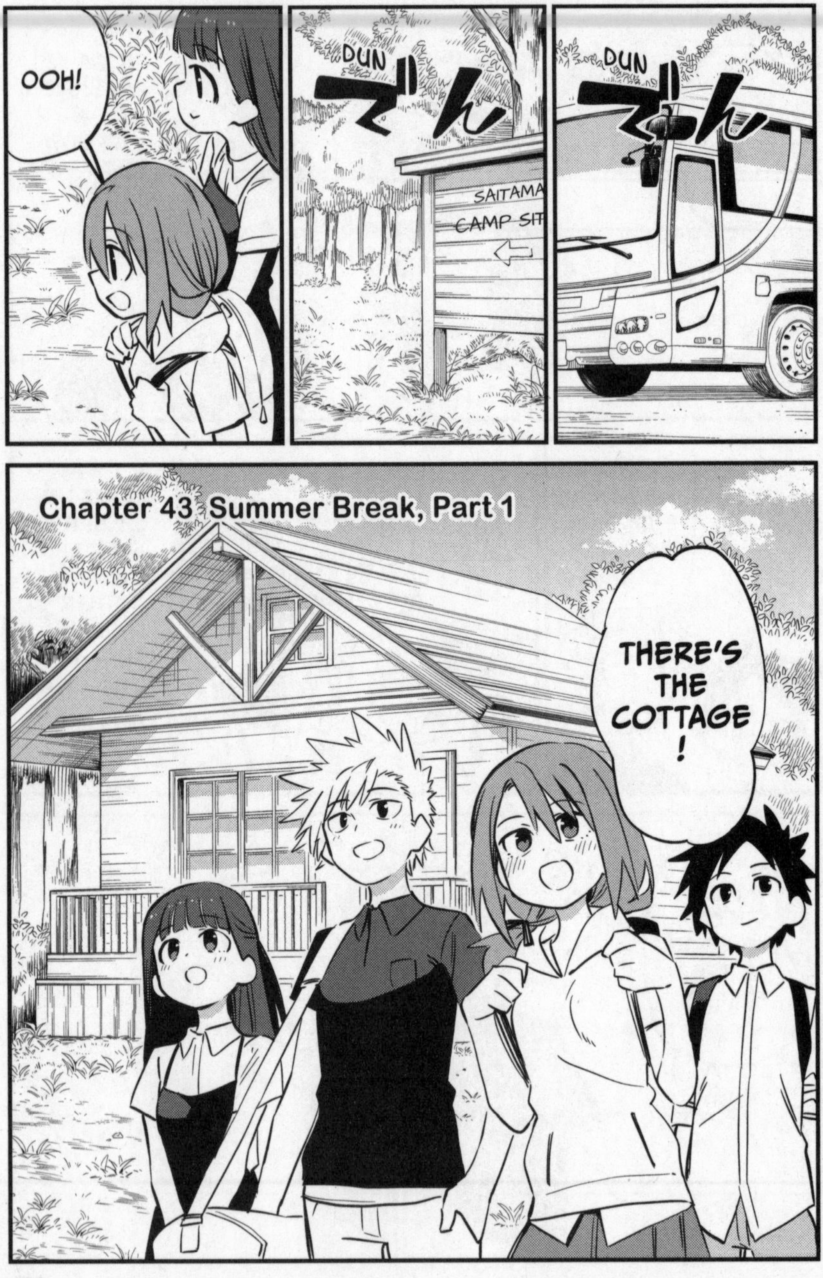
DUN
でん
DUN
でん
SAITAMA
CAMP SIT
OOH!
Chapter 43 Summer Break, Part 1
THERE'S THE COTTAGE!

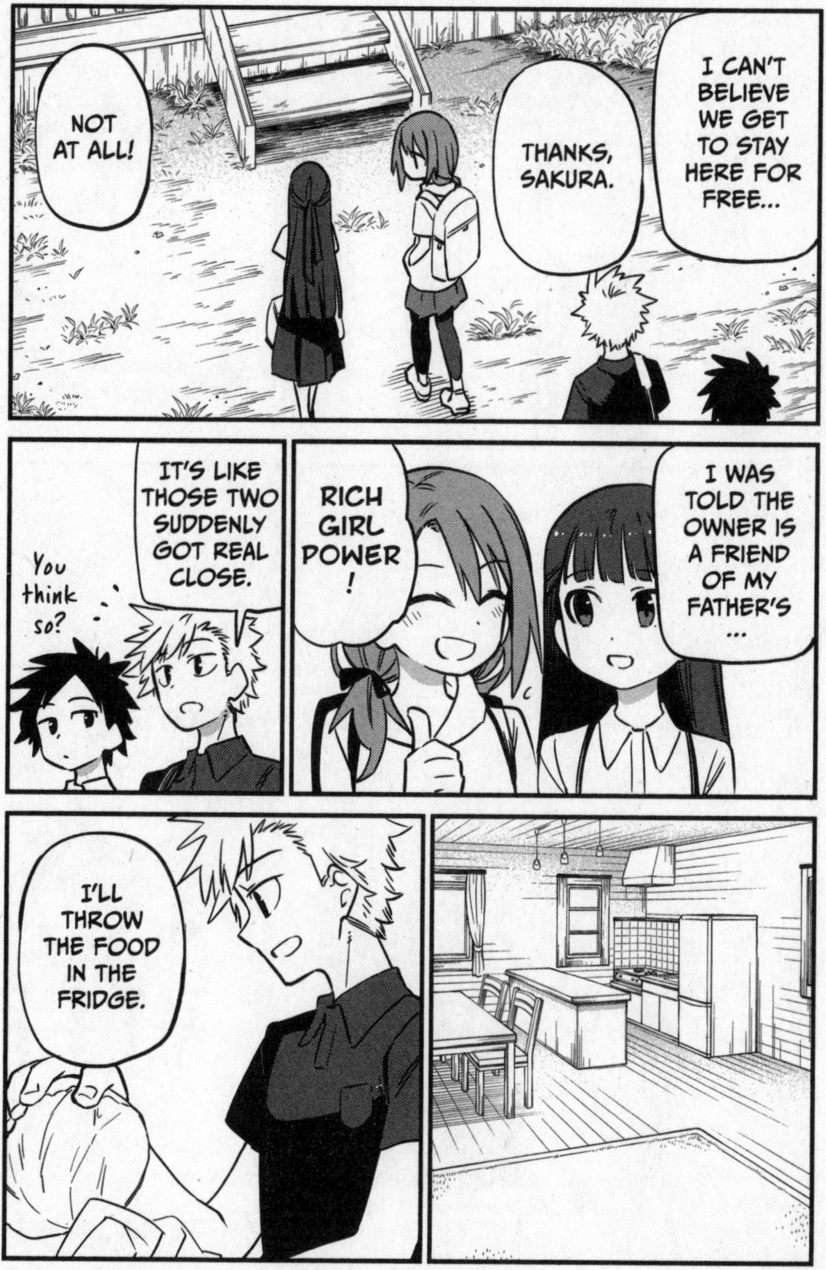
I CAN'T BELIEVE WE GET TO STAY HERE FOR FREE...
THANKS, SAKURA.
NOT AT ALL!
I WAS TOLD THE OWNER IS A FRIEND OF MY FATHER'S ...
RICH GIRL POWER!
IT'S LIKE THOSE TWO SUDDENLY GOT REAL CLOSE.
You think so?
I'LL THROW THE FOOD IN THE FRIDGE.

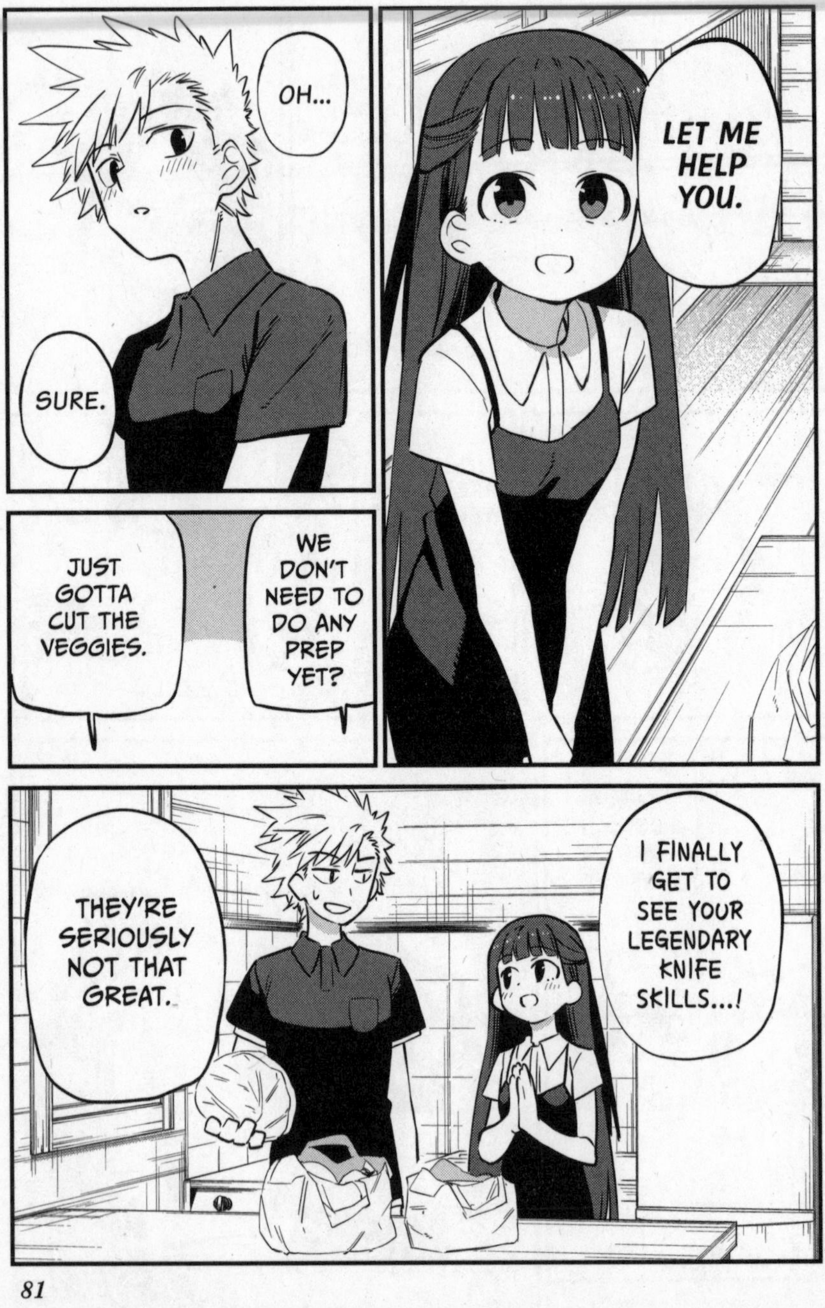
LET ME HELP YOU.
OH...
SURE.
WE DON'T NEED TO DO ANY PREP YET?
JUST GOTTA CUT THE VEGGIES.
I FINALLY GET TO SEE YOUR LEGENDARY KNIFE SKILLS...!
THEY'RE SERIOUSLY NOT THAT GREAT.

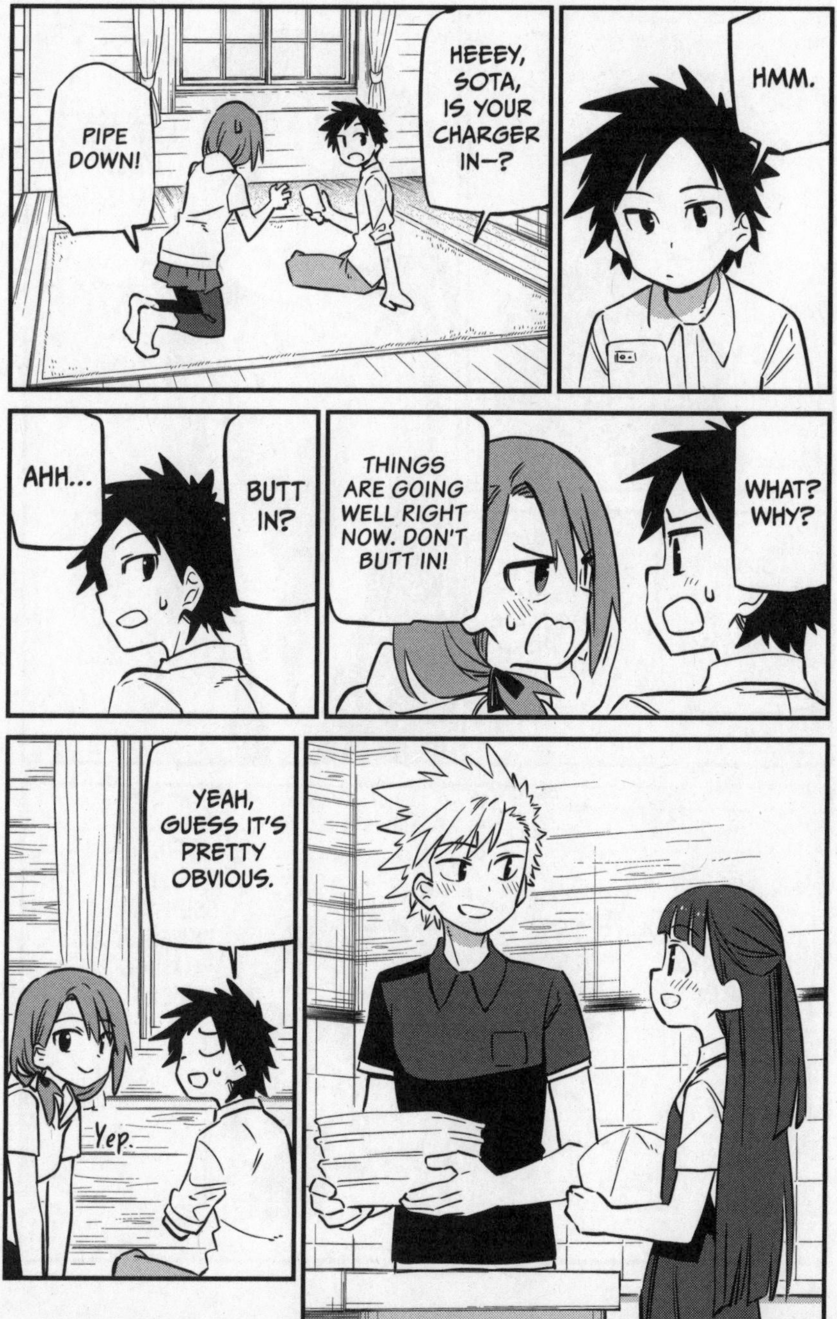
HMM.
HEEEY, SOTA, IS YOUR CHARGER IN–?
PIPE DOWN!
WHAT? WHY?
THINGS ARE GOING WELL RIGHT NOW. DON'T BUTT IN!
BUTT IN?
AHH...
YEAH, GUESS IT'S PRETTY OBVIOUS.
Yep.

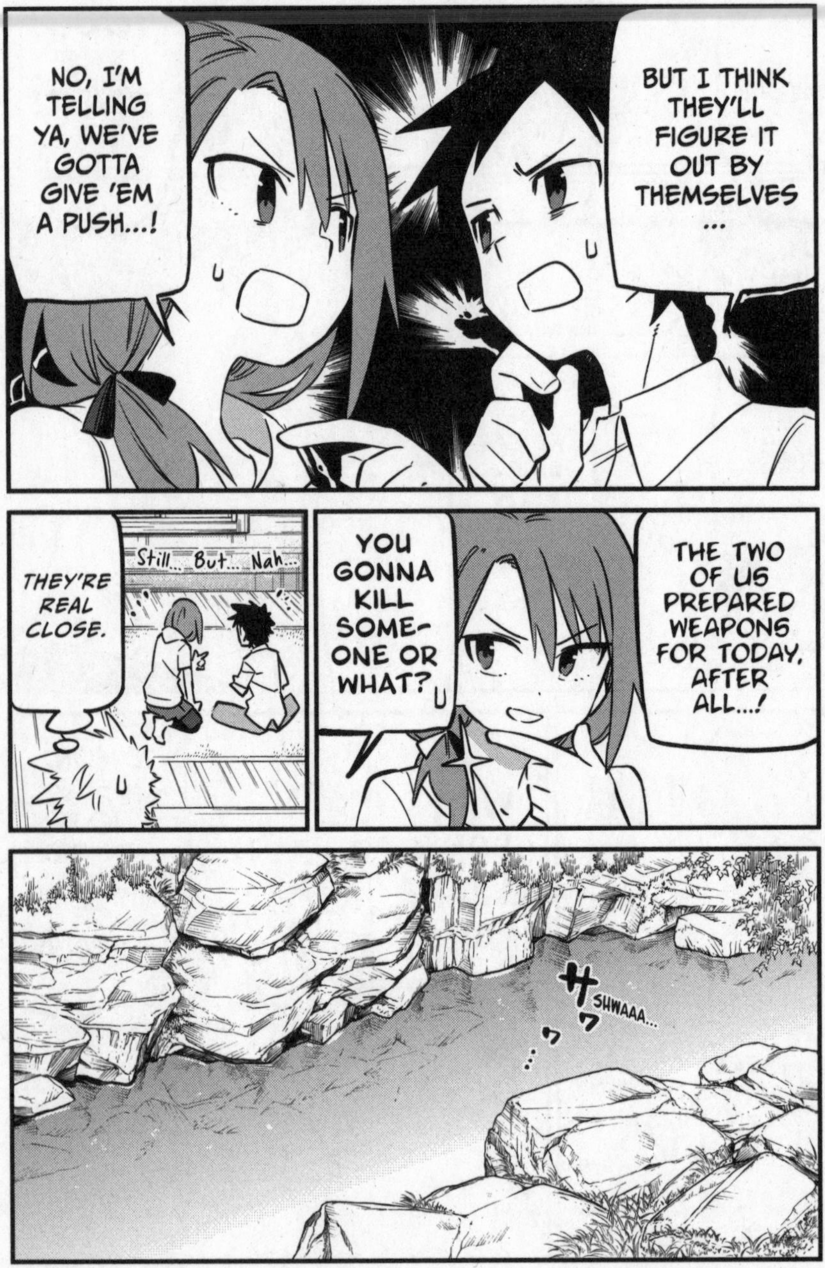
BUT I THINK THEY'LL FIGURE IT OUT BY THEMSELVES ...
NO, I'M TELLING YA, WE'VE GOTTA GIVE 'EM A PUSH...!
THE TWO OF US PREPARED WEAPONS FOR TODAY, AFTER ALL...!
YOU GONNA KILL SOME-ONE OR WHAT?
Still... But... Nah...
THEY'RE REAL CLOSE.
SHWAAA...

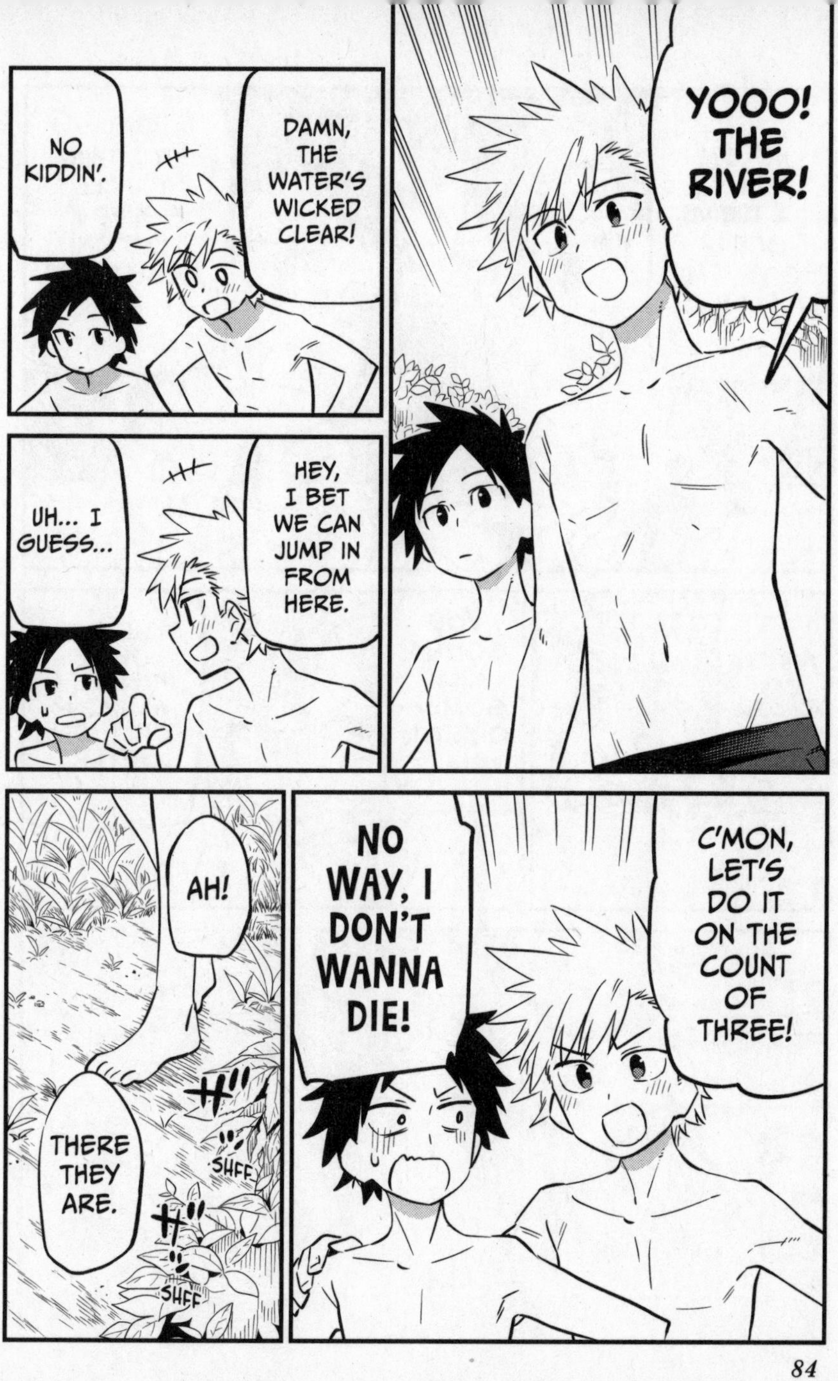
YOOO! THE RIVER!
DAMN, THE WATER'S WICKED CLEAR!
NO KIDDIN'.
HEY, I BET WE CAN JUMP IN FROM HERE.
UH... I GUESS...
C'MON, LET'S DO IT ON THE COUNT OF THREE!
NO WAY, I DON'T WANNA DIE!
AH!
THERE THEY ARE.
SHFF
SHFF

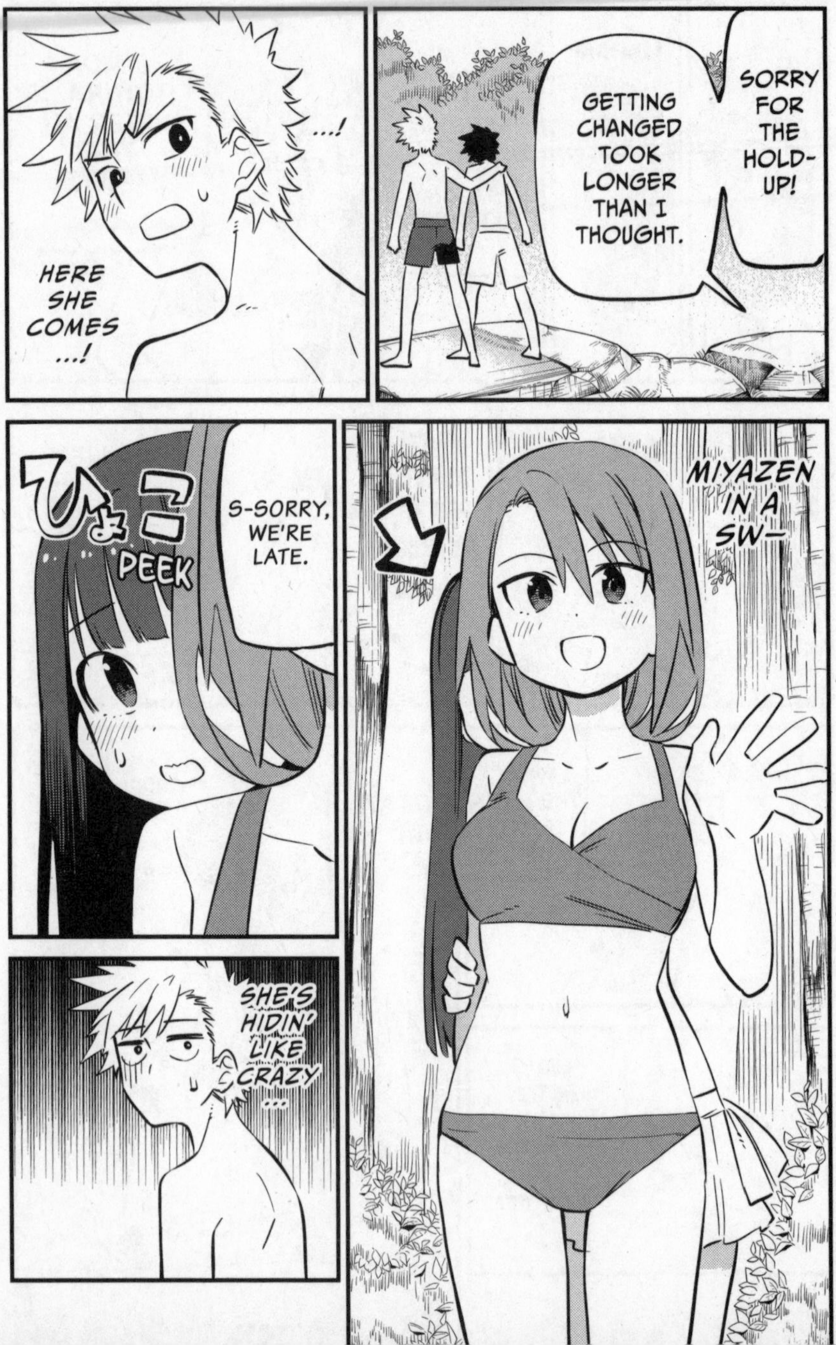
SORRY FOR THE HOLD-UP!
GETTING CHANGED TOOK LONGER THAN I THOUGHT.
...!
HERE SHE COMES ...!
MIYAZEN IN A SW—
S-SORRY, WE'RE LATE.
ひょこ PEEK
SHE'S HIDIN' LIKE CRAZY ...

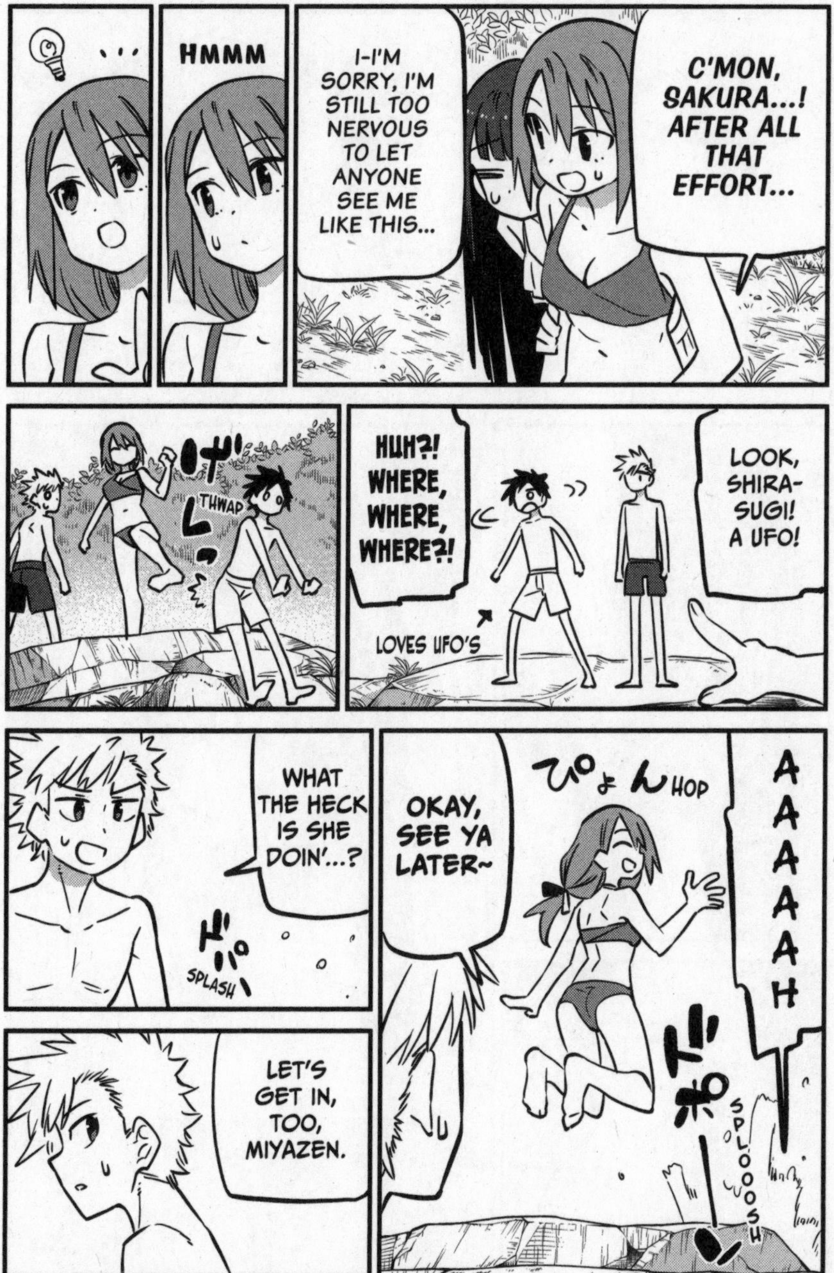
C'MON, SAKURA...! AFTER ALL THAT EFFORT...
I-I'M SORRY, I'M STILL TOO NERVOUS TO LET ANYONE SEE ME LIKE THIS...
HMMM
...
LOOK, SHIRA-SUGI! A UFO!
HUH?! WHERE, WHERE, WHERE?!
LOVES UFO'S
THWAP
AAAAAAH
ぴょん HOP
OKAY, SEE YA LATER~
SPLOOOOSH
WHAT THE HECK IS SHE DOIN'...?
SPLASH
LET'S GET IN, TOO, MIYAZEN.

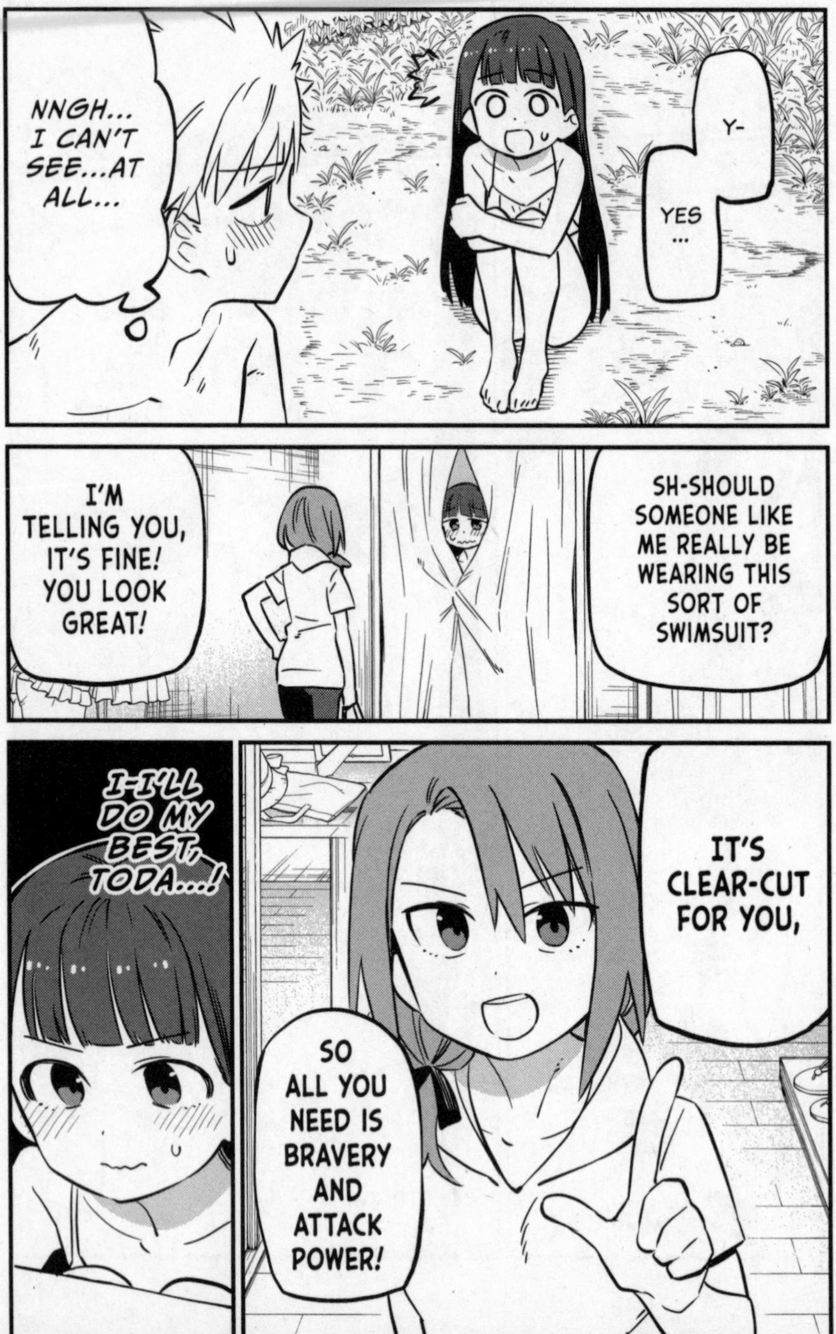
Y- YES...
NNGH... I CAN'T SEE...AT ALL...
SH-SHOULD SOMEONE LIKE ME REALLY BE WEARING THIS SORT OF SWIMSUIT?
I'M TELLING YOU, IT'S FINE! YOU LOOK GREAT!
IT'S CLEAR-CUT FOR YOU,
SO ALL YOU NEED IS BRAVERY AND ATTACK POWER!
I-I'LL DO MY BEST, TODA...!

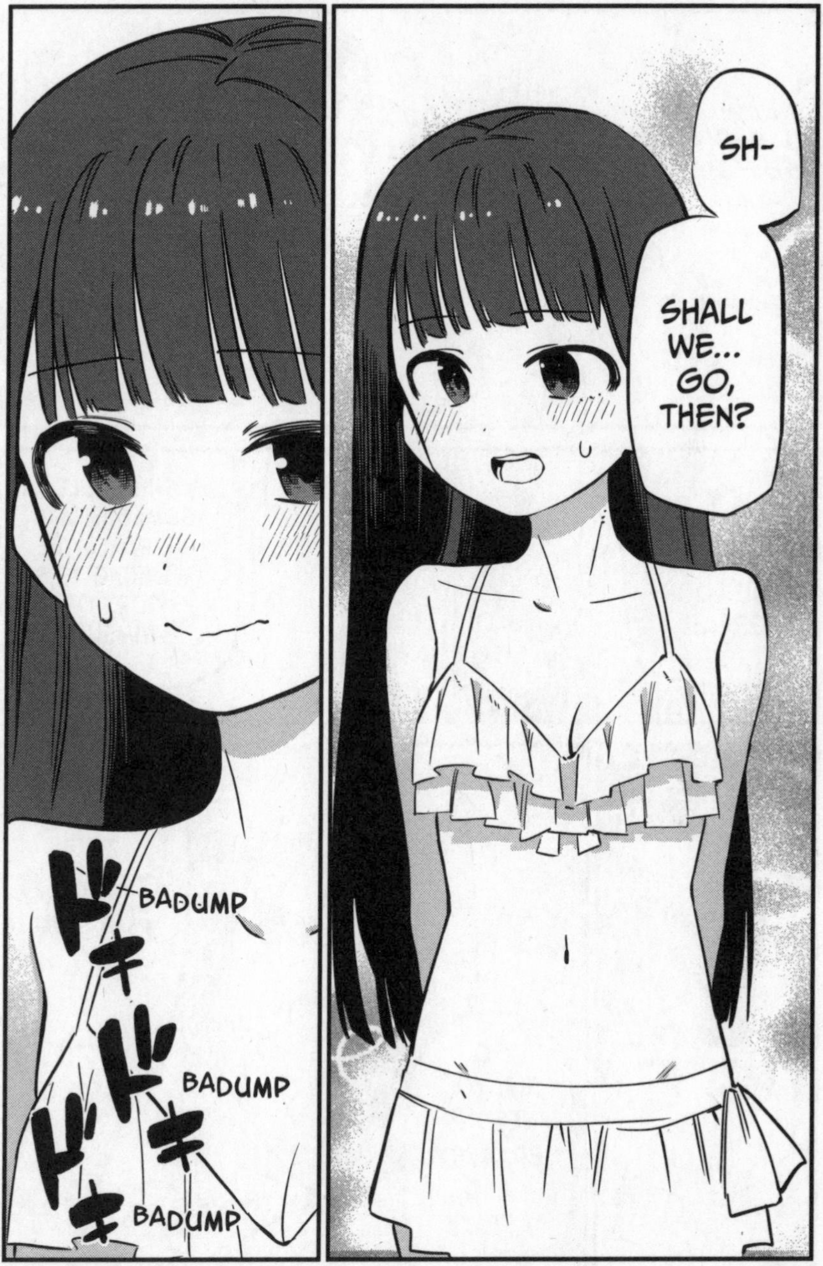
SH-
SHALL WE... GO, THEN?
ドキ
BADUMP
ドキ
BADUMP
ドキ
BADUMP

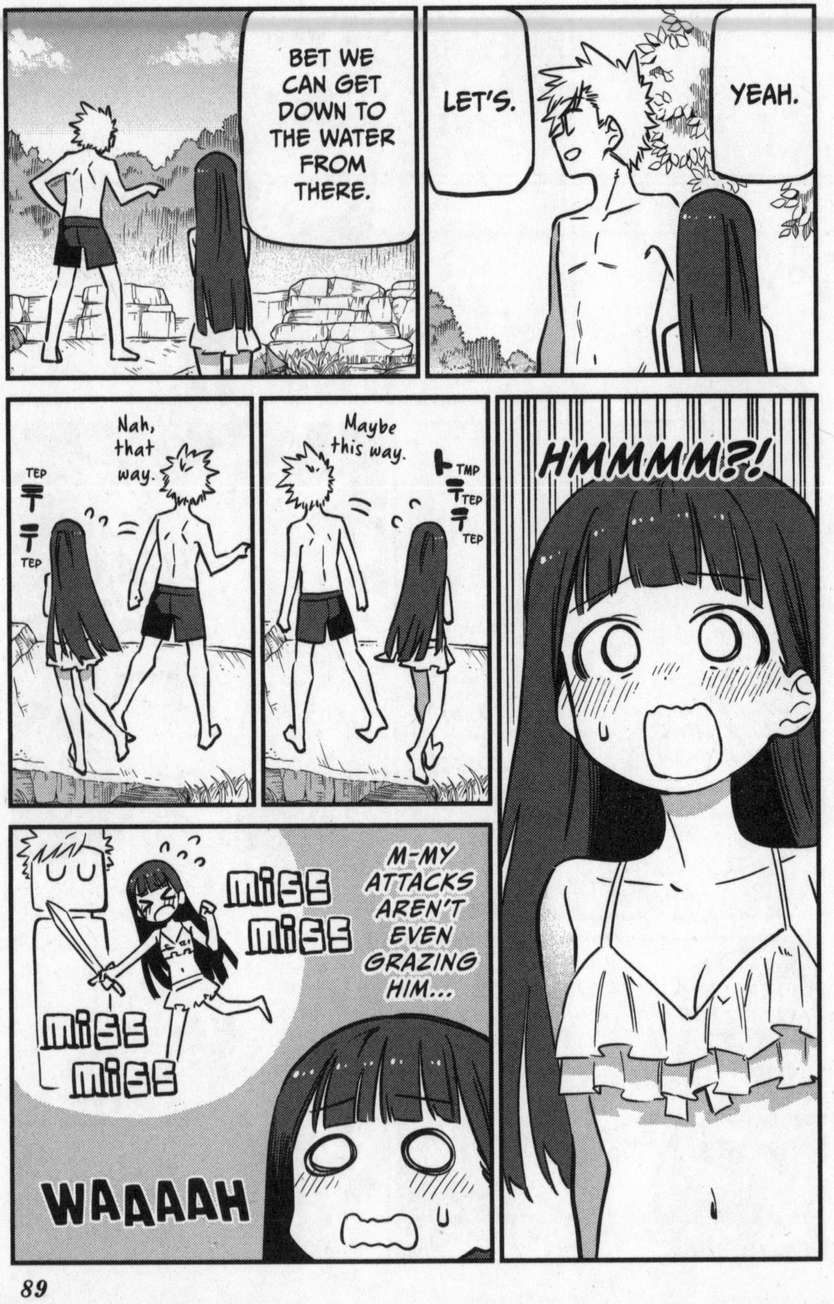
BET WE CAN GET DOWN TO THE WATER FROM THERE.
LET'S.
YEAH.
Nah, that way.
TEP TEP
Maybe this way.
TMP TEP TEP
HMMMM?!
MISS MISS
M-MY ATTACKS AREN'T EVEN GRAZING HIM...
MISS MISS
WAAAAH

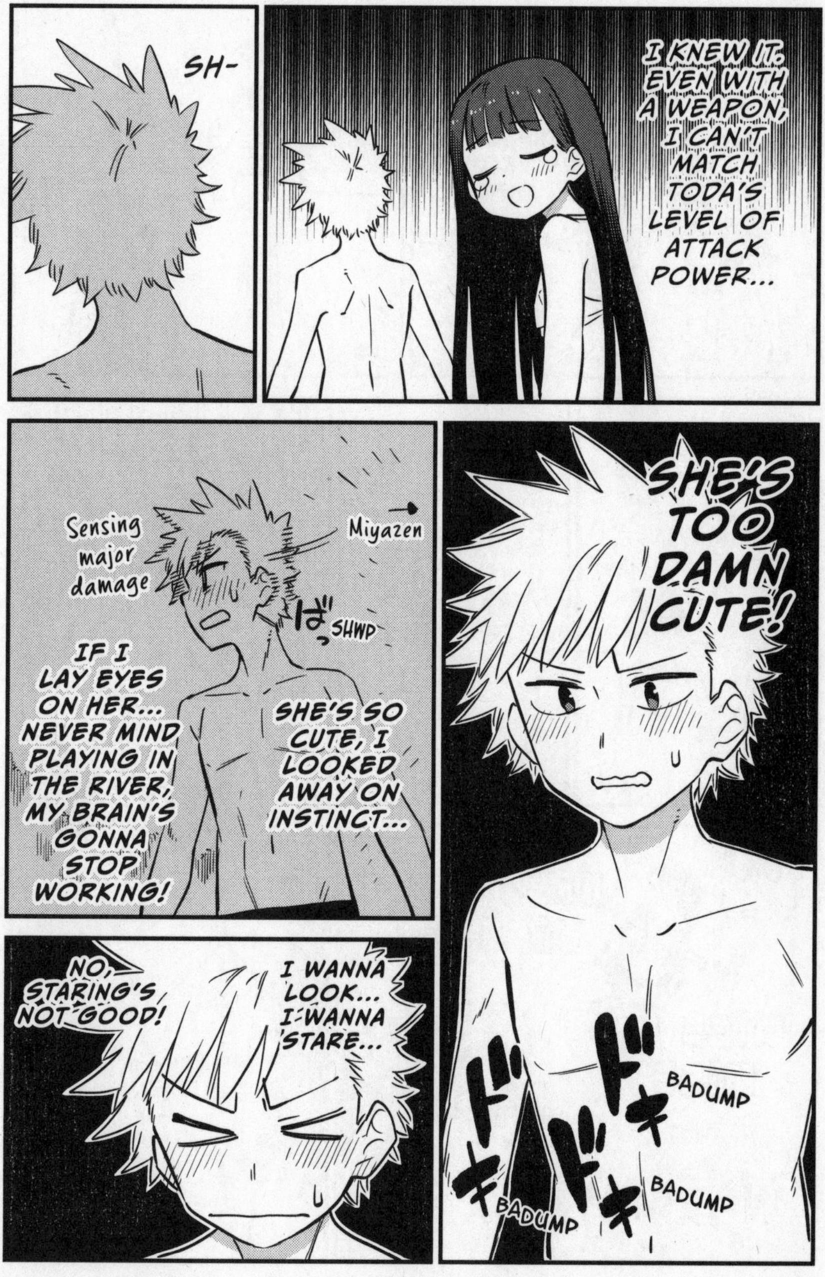
I KNEW IT. EVEN WITH A WEAPON, I CAN'T MATCH TODA'S LEVEL OF ATTACK POWER...
SH-
SHE'S TOO DAMN CUTE!
BADUMP
BADUMP
BADUMP
Miyazen
Sensing major damage
SHWP
SHE'S SO CUTE, I LOOKED AWAY ON INSTINCT...
IF I LAY EYES ON HER... NEVER MIND PLAYING IN THE RIVER, MY BRAIN'S GONNA STOP WORKING!
I WANNA LOOK... I WANNA STARE...
NO, STARING'S NOT GOOD!

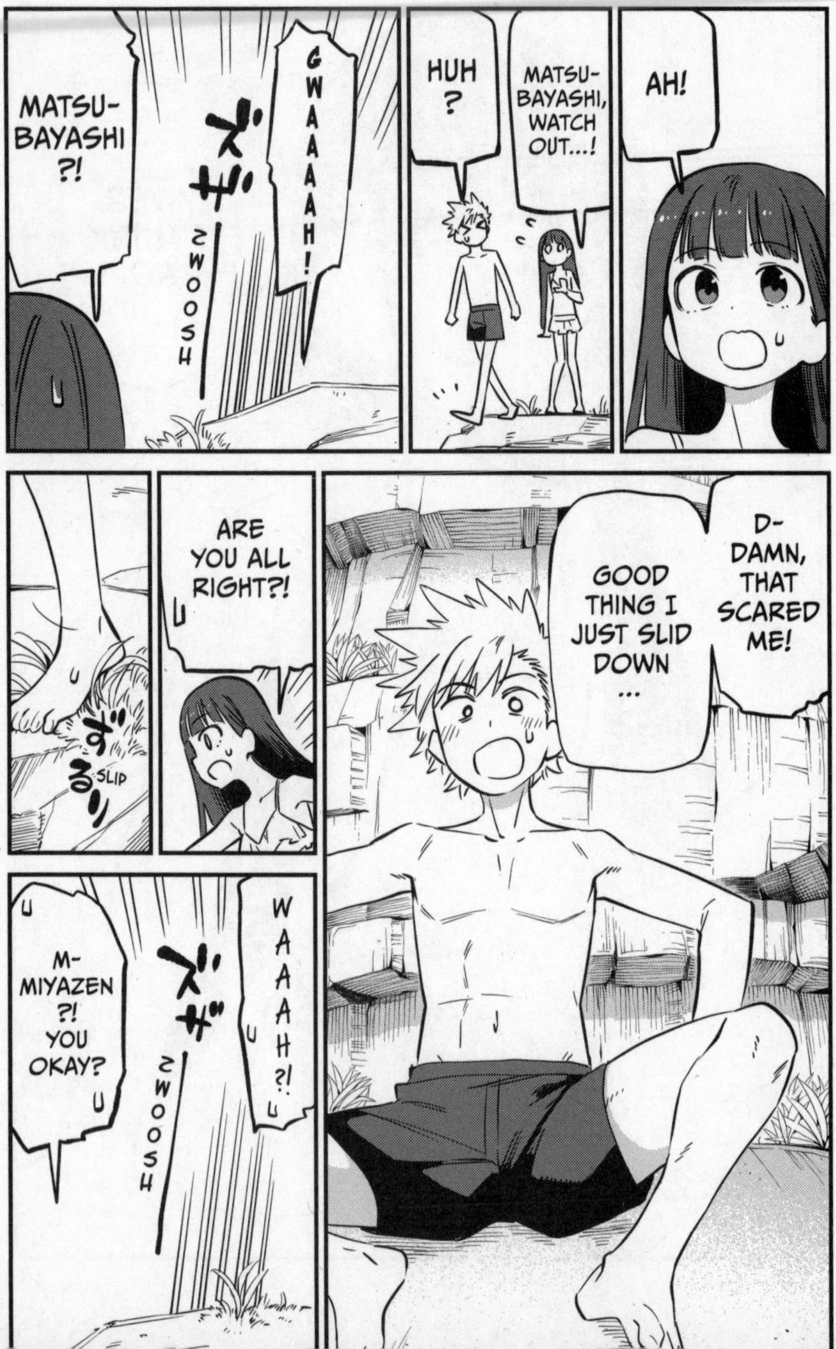
AH!
MATSU-BAYASHI, WATCH OUT...!
HUH?
GWAAAAAH!
ZWOOSH
MATSU-BAYASHI?!
D-DAMN, THAT SCARED ME!
GOOD THING I JUST SLID DOWN ...
ARE YOU ALL RIGHT?!
SLIP
WAAAAH?!
ZWOOSH
M-MIYAZEN?! YOU OKAY?

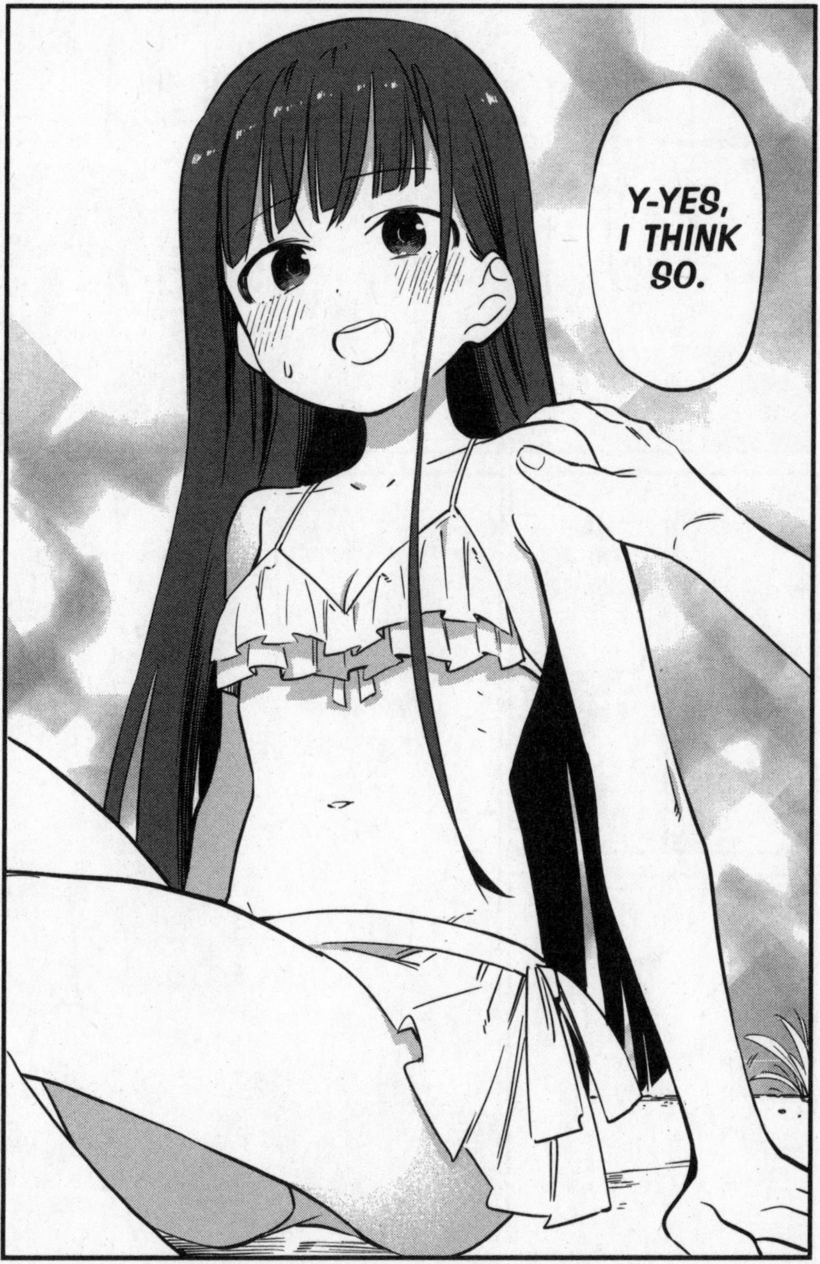
Y-YES, I THINK SO.

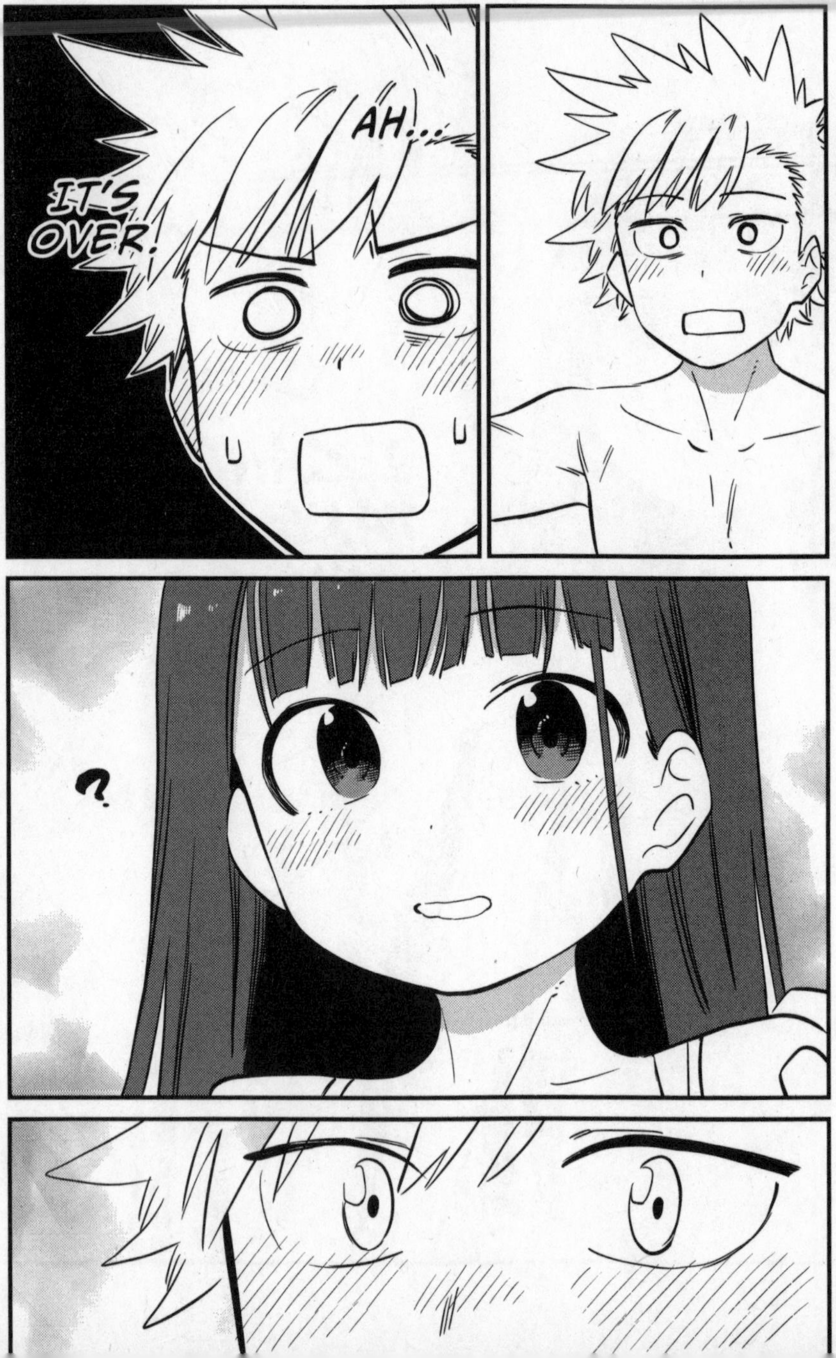
AH...
IT'S OVER!
?

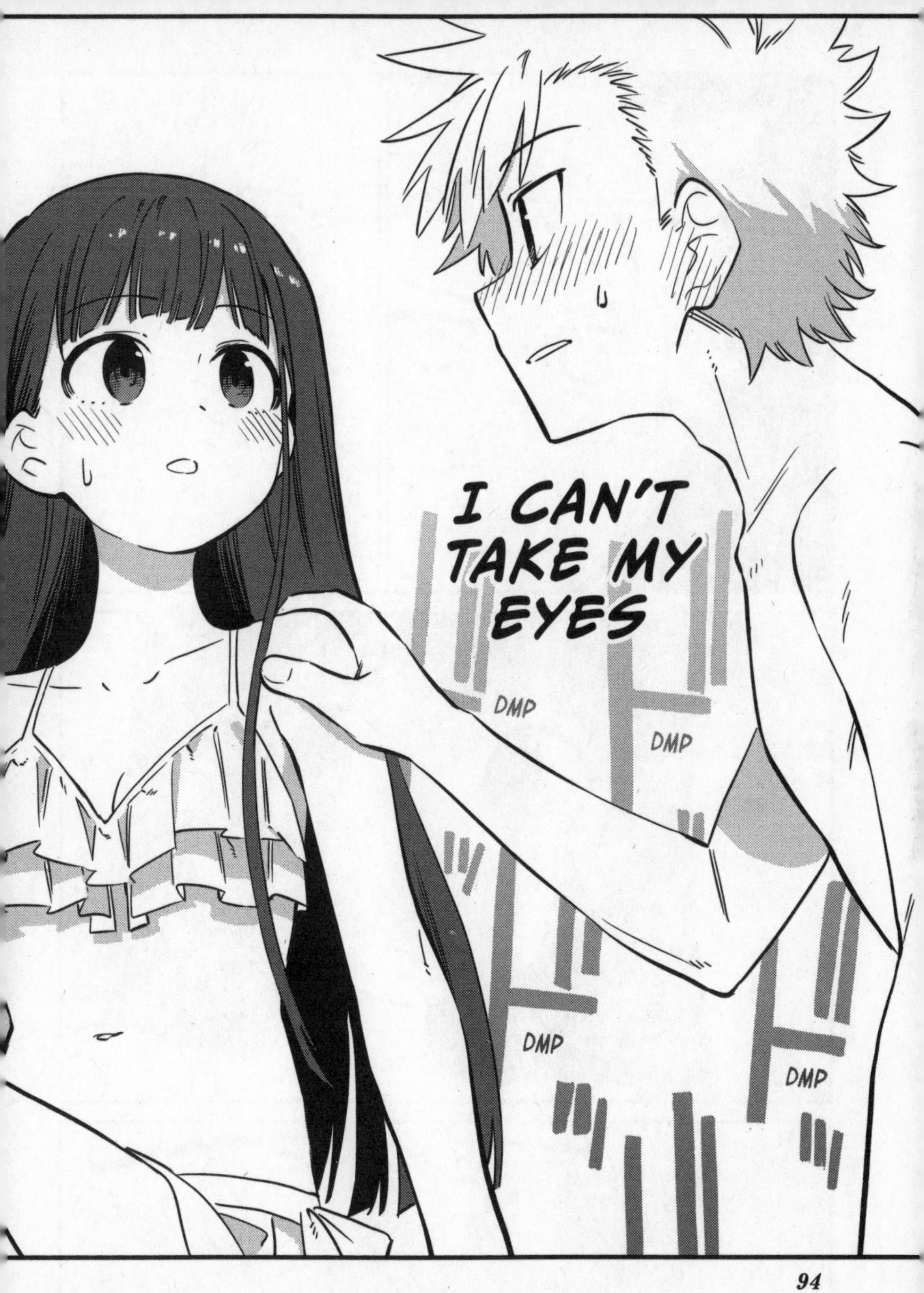
I CAN'T TAKE MY EYES
DMP
DMP
DMP
DMP

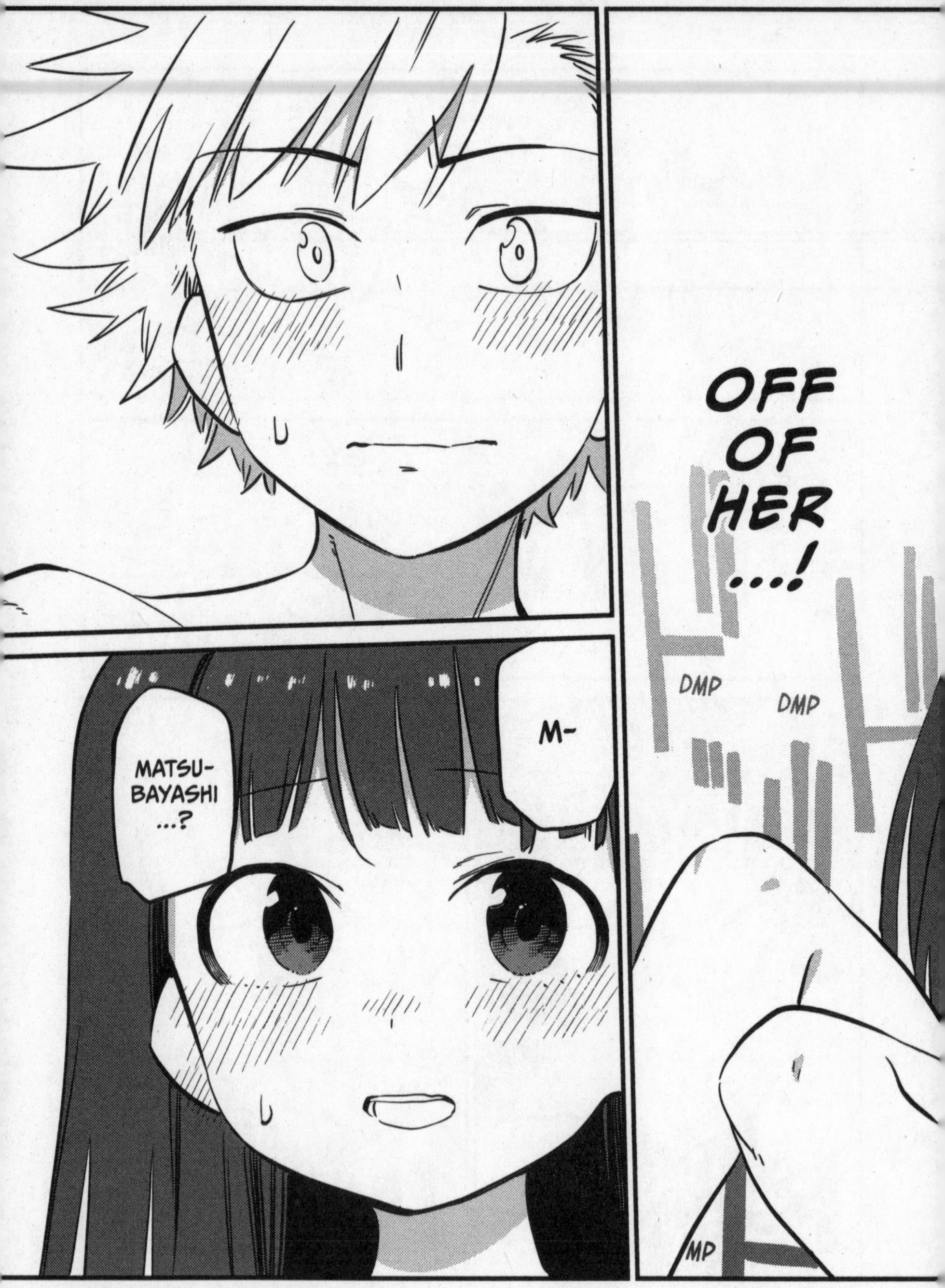
OFF OF HER ...!
DMP
DMP
MP
M-
MATSU-BAYASHI ...?

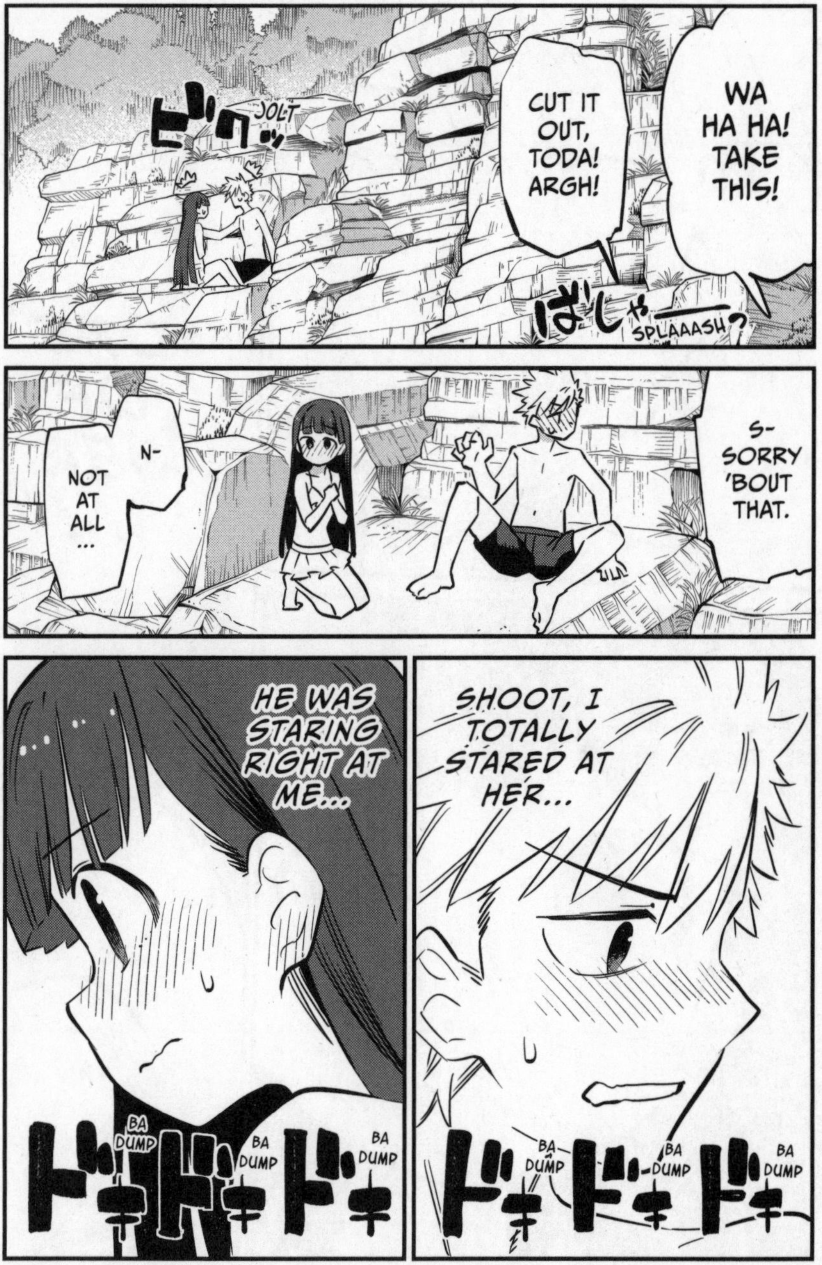
WA HA HA! TAKE THIS!
CUT IT OUT, TODA! ARGH!
ばしゃー
SPLAAASH
ピクッ
JOLT
S-SORRY 'BOUT THAT.
N- NOT AT ALL...
SHOOT, I TOTALLY STARED AT HER...
ドキドキドキ
BA DUMP
BA DUMP
BA DUMP
HE WAS STARING RIGHT AT ME...
ドキドキドキ
BA DUMP
BA DUMP
BA DUMP

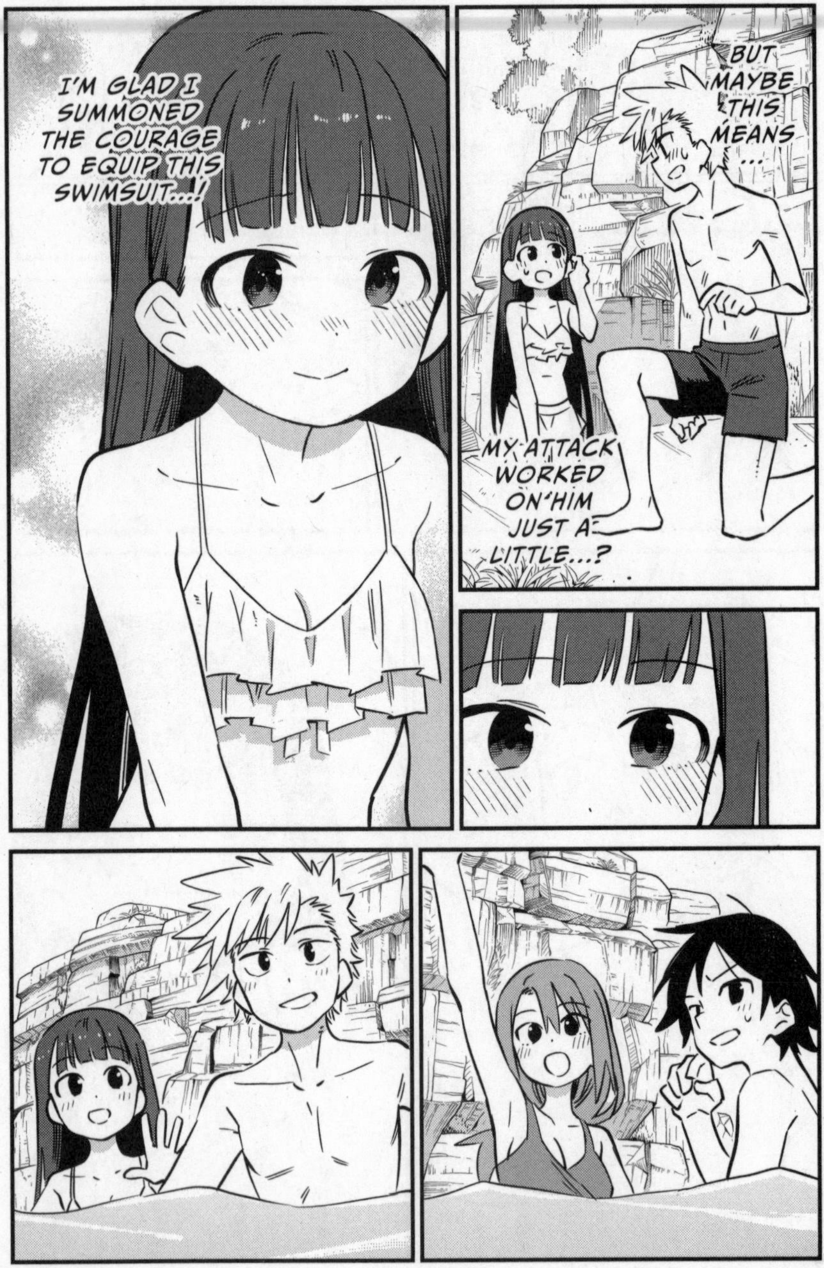
BUT MAYBE THIS MEANS...
MY ATTACK WORKED ON HIM JUST A LITTLE...?
I'M GLAD I SUMMONED THE COURAGE TO EQUIP THIS SWIMSUIT...!

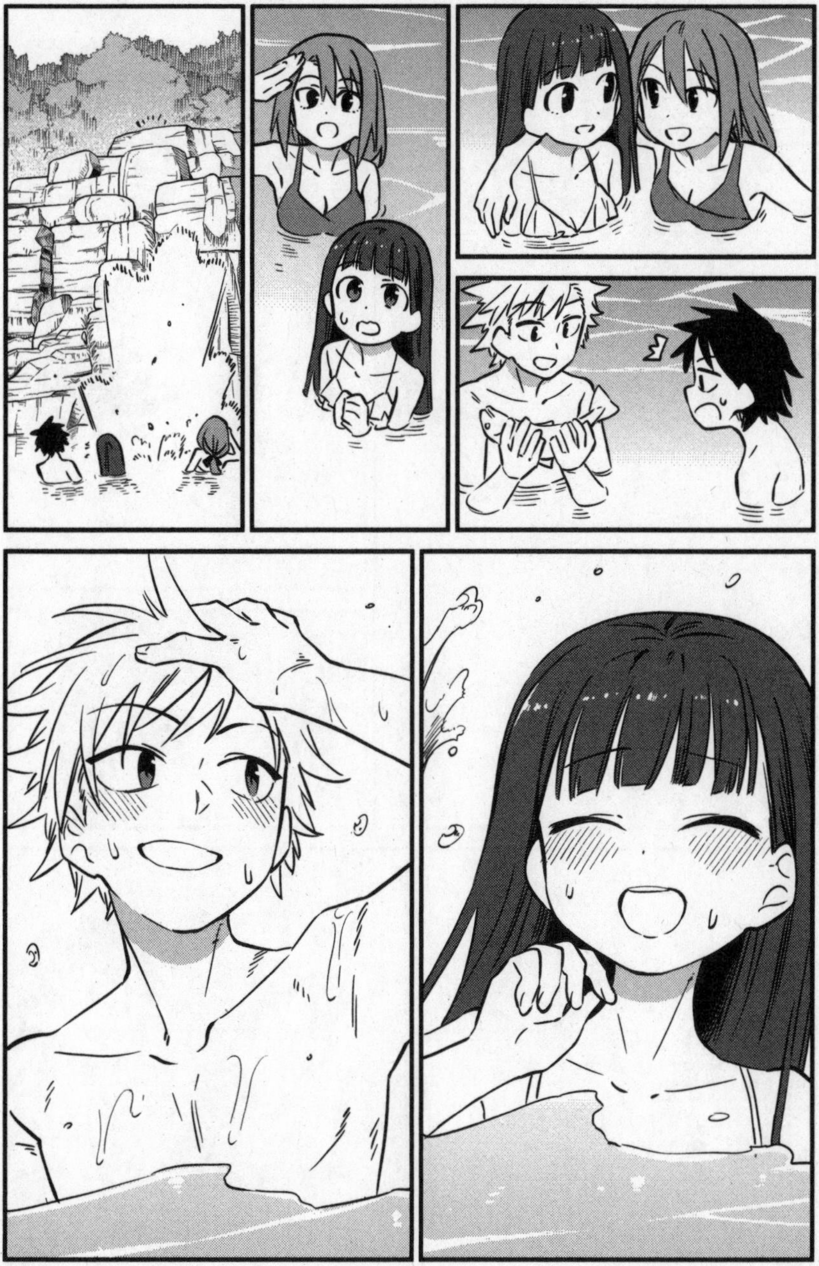

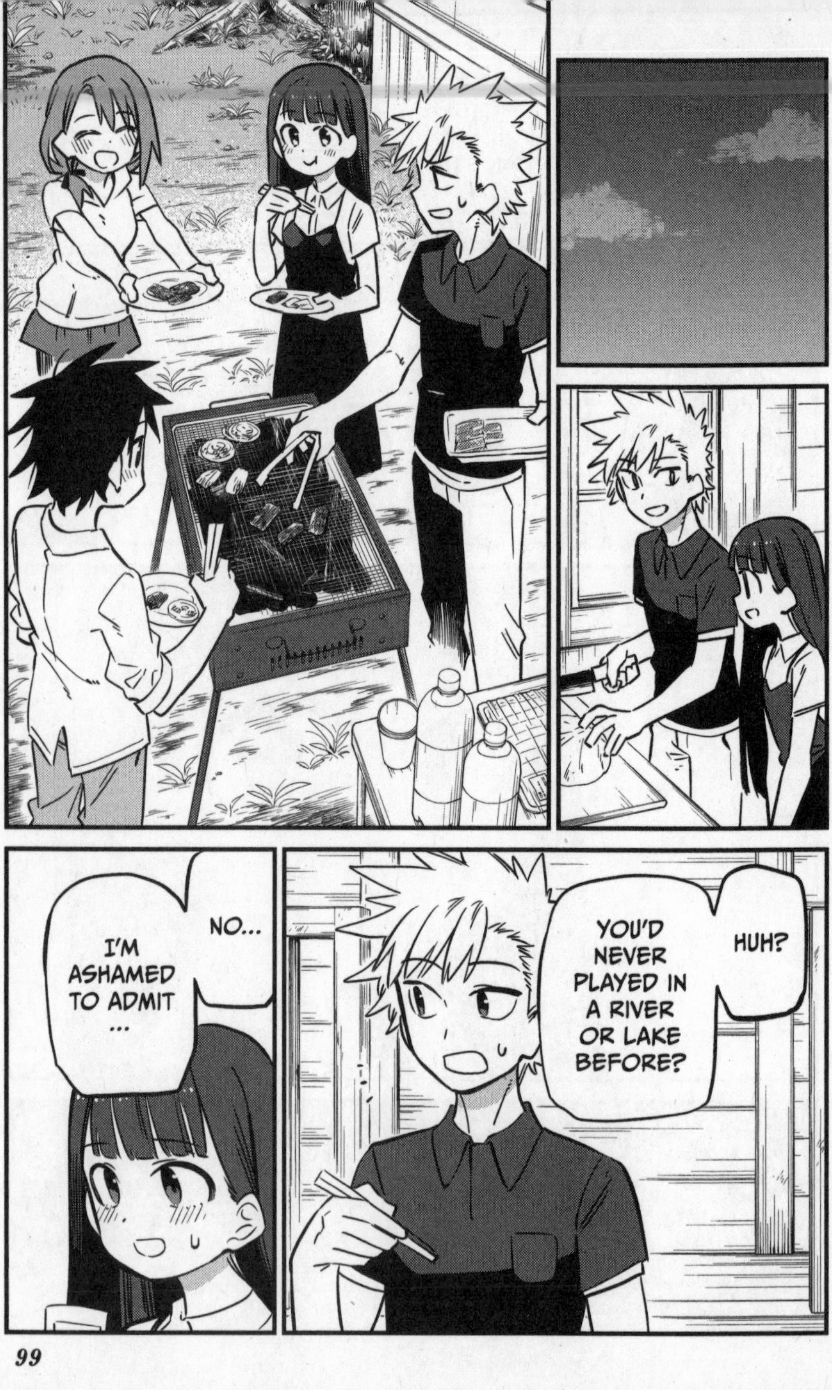
HUH?
YOU'D NEVER PLAYED IN A RIVER OR LAKE BEFORE?
NO...
I'M ASHAMED TO ADMIT ...

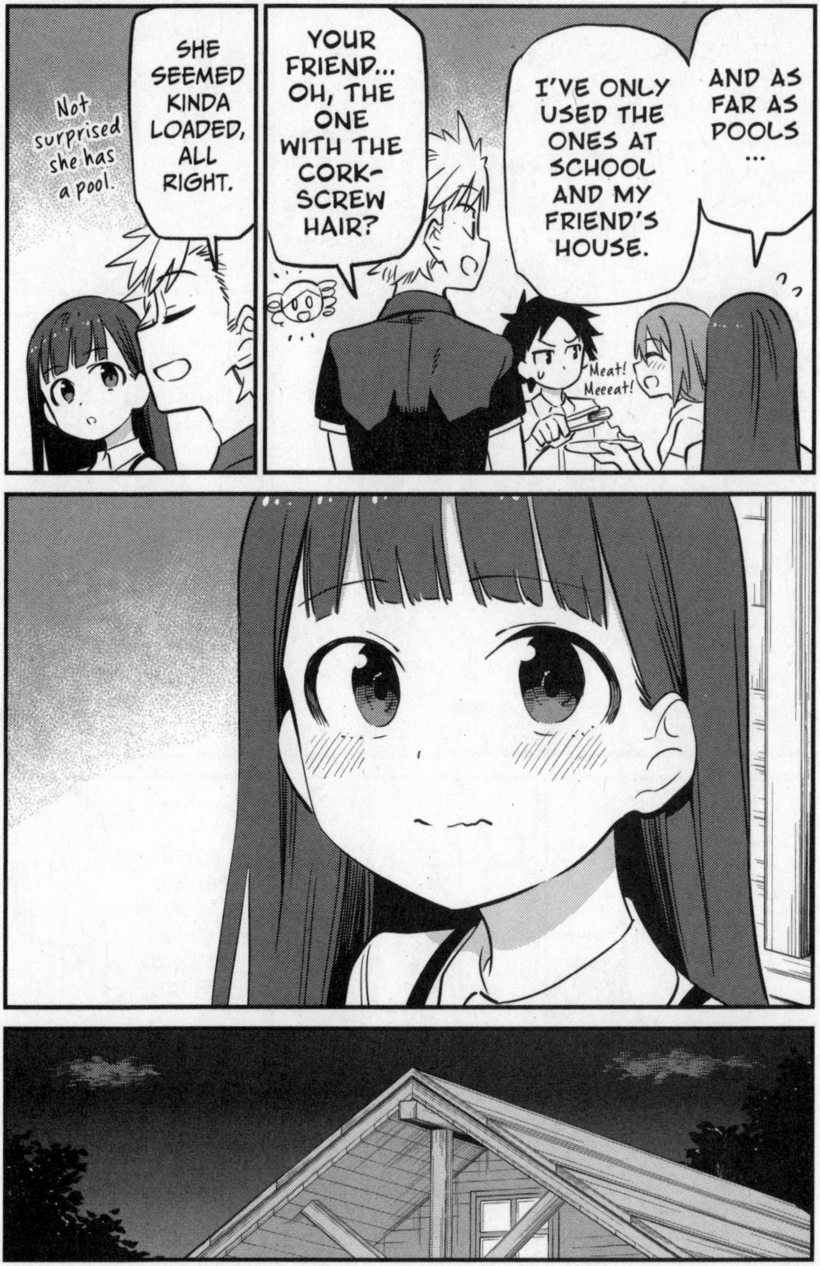
AND AS FAR AS POOLS...
I'VE ONLY USED THE ONES AT SCHOOL AND MY FRIEND'S HOUSE.
YOUR FRIEND... OH, THE ONE WITH THE CORK-SCREW HAIR?
Meat! Meeeat!
SHE SEEMED KINDA LOADED, ALL RIGHT.
Not surprised she has a pool.

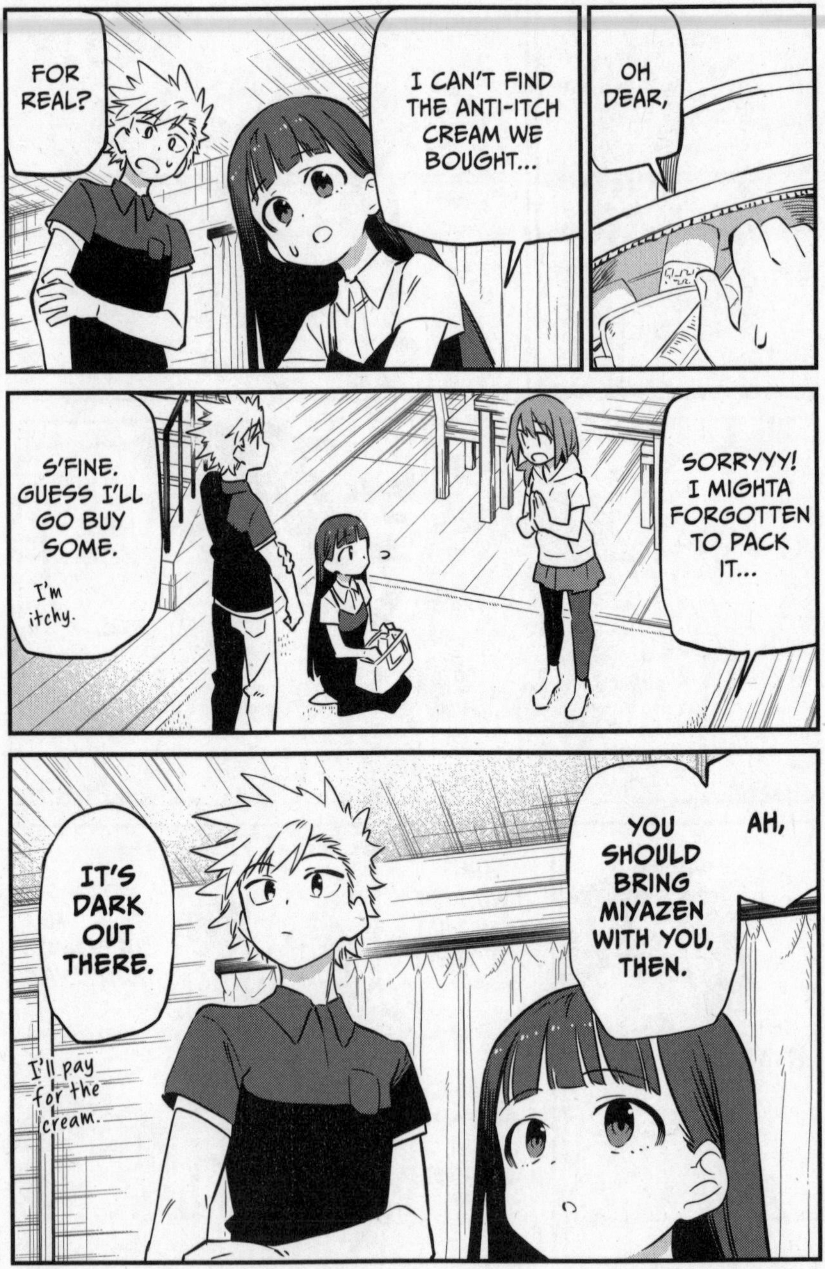
OH DEAR,
I CAN'T FIND THE ANTI-ITCH CREAM WE BOUGHT...
FOR REAL?
SORRYYY! I MIGHTA FORGOTTEN TO PACK IT...
S'FINE. GUESS I'LL GO BUY SOME.
I'm itchy.
AH,
YOU SHOULD BRING MIYAZEN WITH YOU, THEN.
IT'S DARK OUT THERE.
I'll pay for the cream.

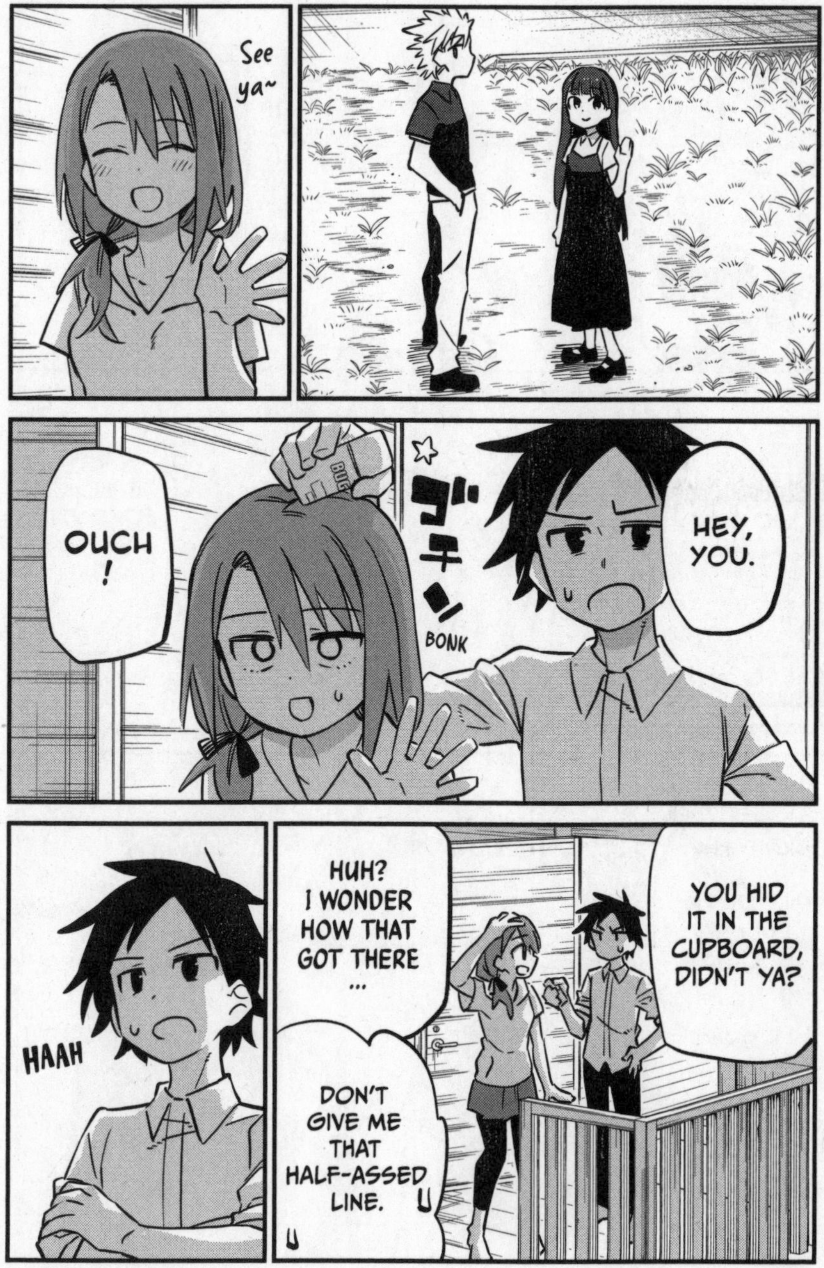
See ya~
HEY, YOU.
ゴチン
BONK
OUCH!
YOU HID IT IN THE CUPBOARD, DIDN'T YA?
HUH? I WONDER HOW THAT GOT THERE ...
DON'T GIVE ME THAT HALF-ASSED LINE.
HAAH

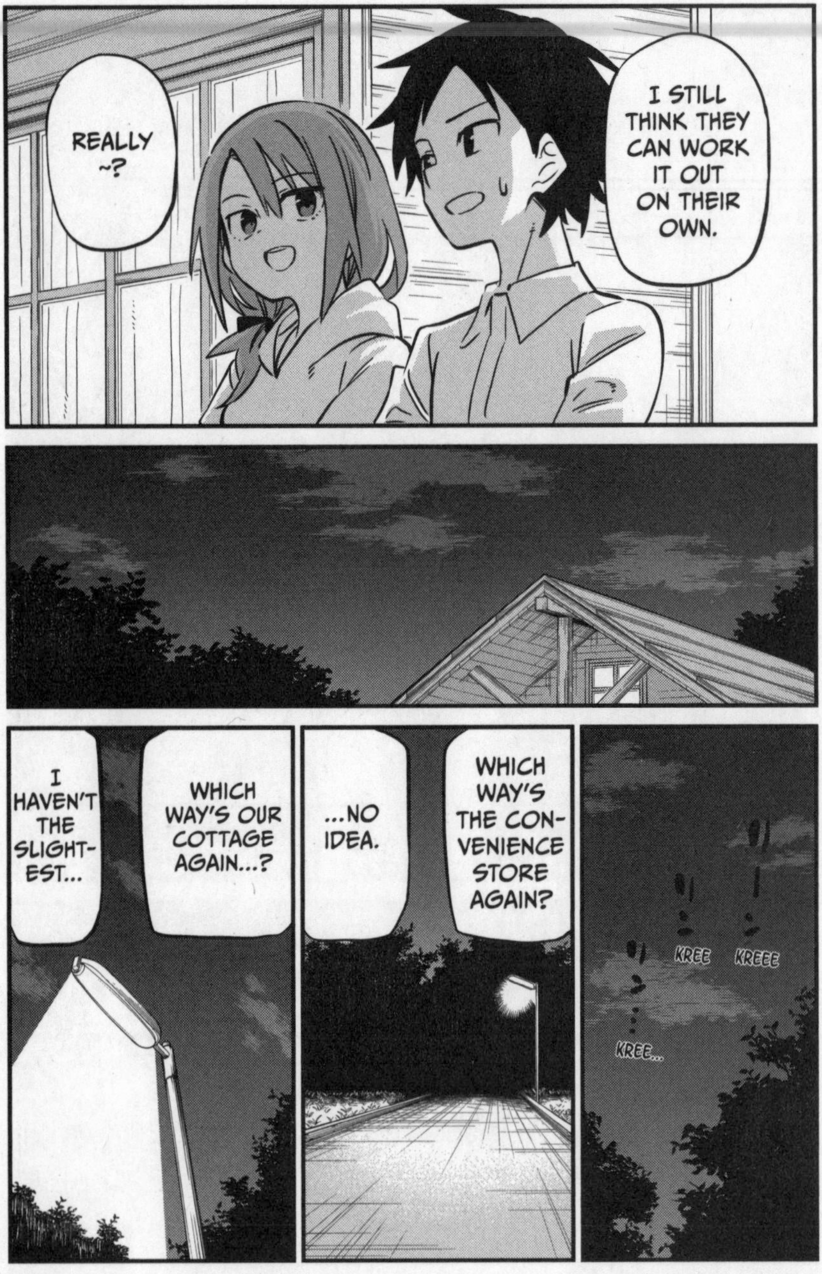
I STILL THINK THEY CAN WORK IT OUT ON THEIR OWN.
REALLY ~?
KREEE
KREE
KREE...
WHICH WAY'S THE CON-VENIENCE STORE AGAIN?
...NO IDEA.
WHICH WAY'S OUR COTTAGE AGAIN...?
I HAVEN'T THE SLIGHT-EST...

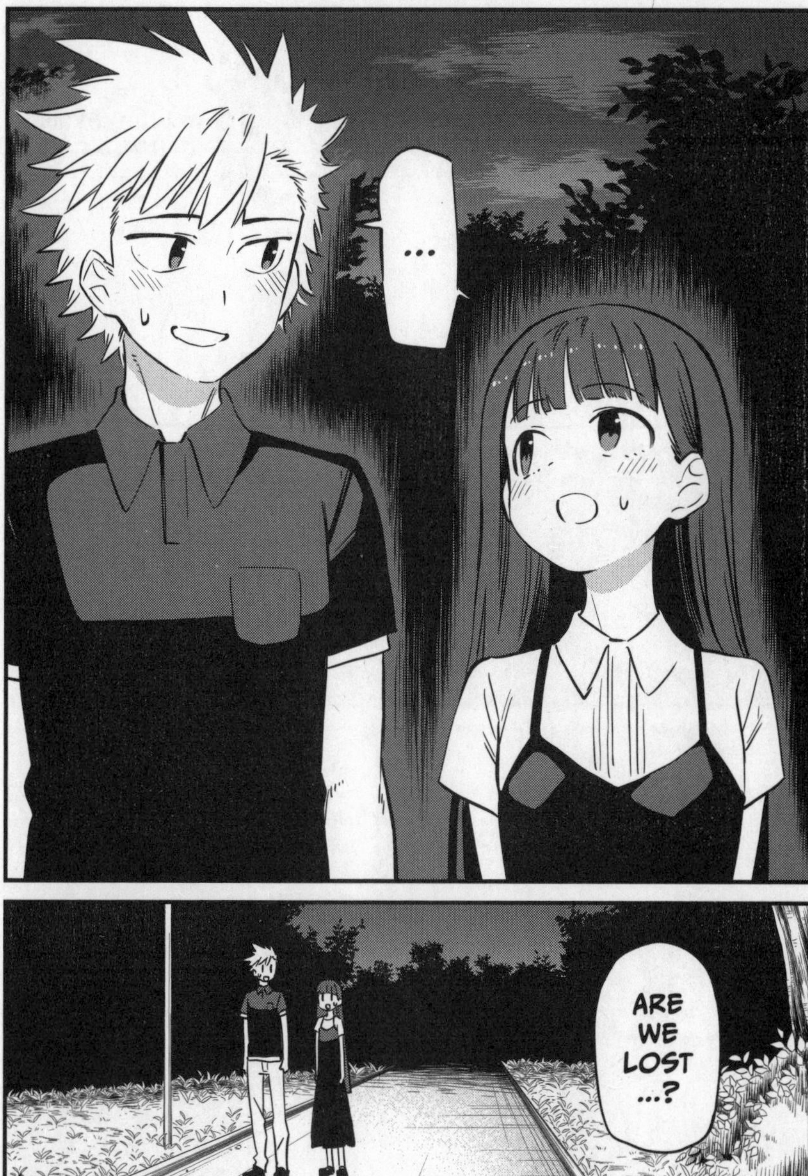
...
ARE WE LOST ...?

Miss Miyazen
Would Love to
Get Closer to You

Miss Miyazen
Would Love to
Get Closer to You

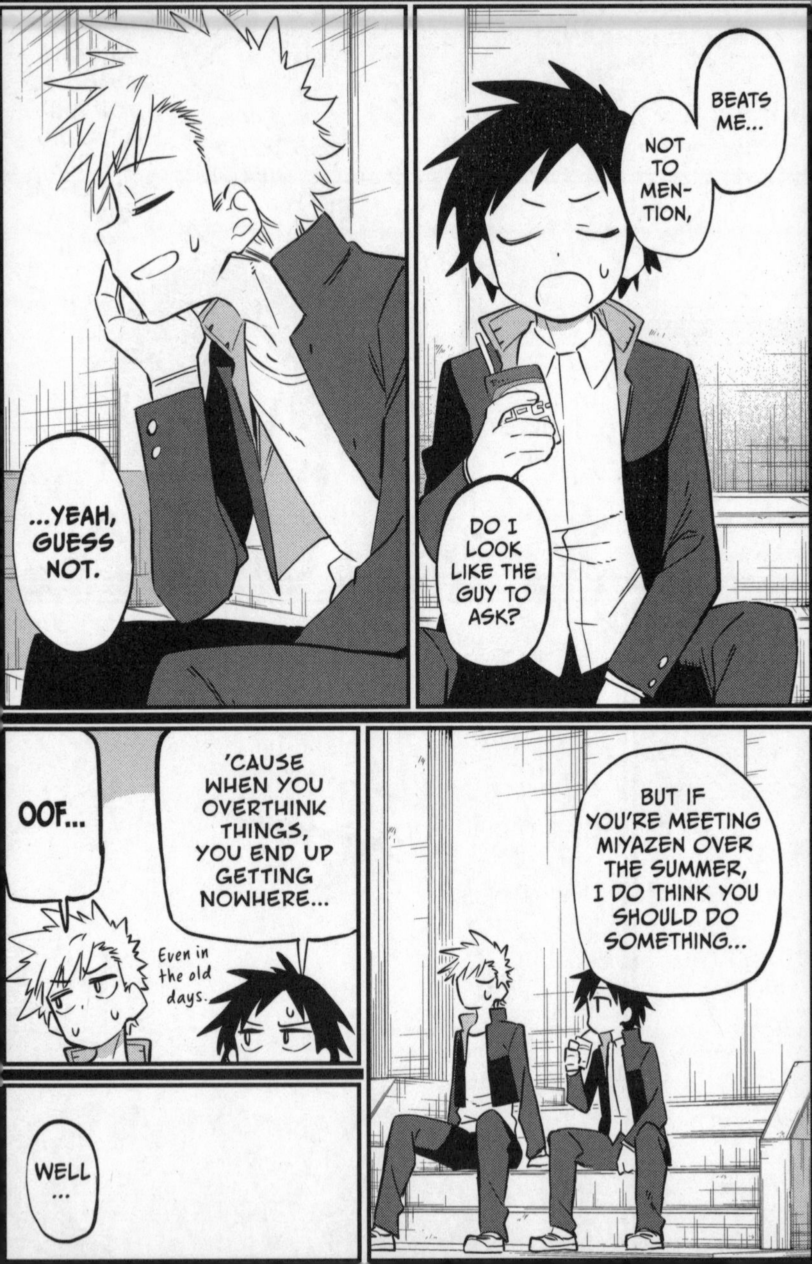
BEATS ME...
NOT TO MENTION,
DO I LOOK LIKE THE GUY TO ASK?
...YEAH, GUESS NOT.
BUT IF YOU'RE MEETING MIYAZEN OVER THE SUMMER, I DO THINK YOU SHOULD DO SOMETHING...
'CAUSE WHEN YOU OVERTHINK THINGS, YOU END UP GETTING NOWHERE...
Even in the old days.
OOF...
WELL ...

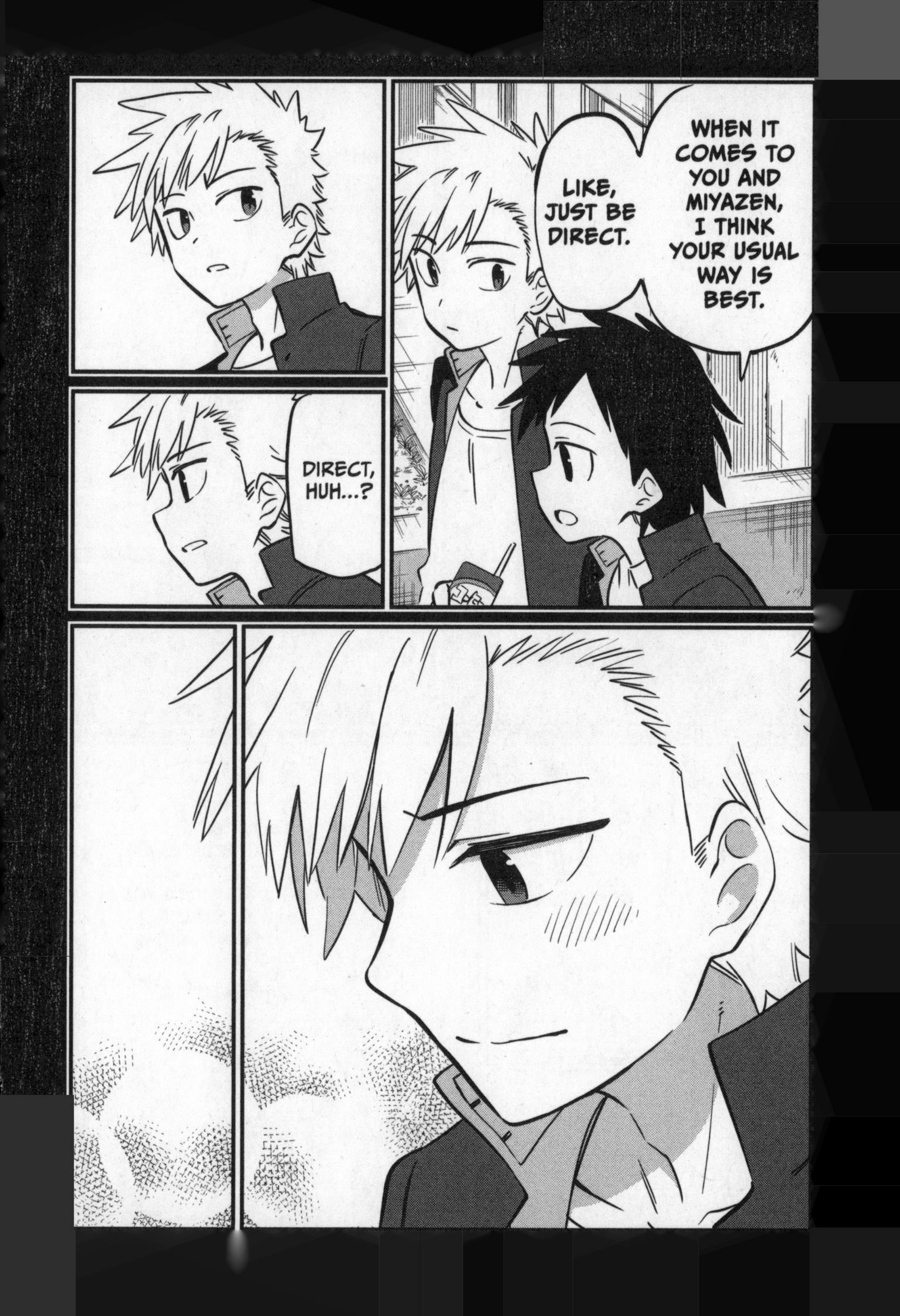
WHEN IT COMES TO YOU AND MIYAZEN, I THINK YOUR USUAL WAY IS BEST.
LIKE, JUST BE DIRECT.
DIRECT, HUH...?

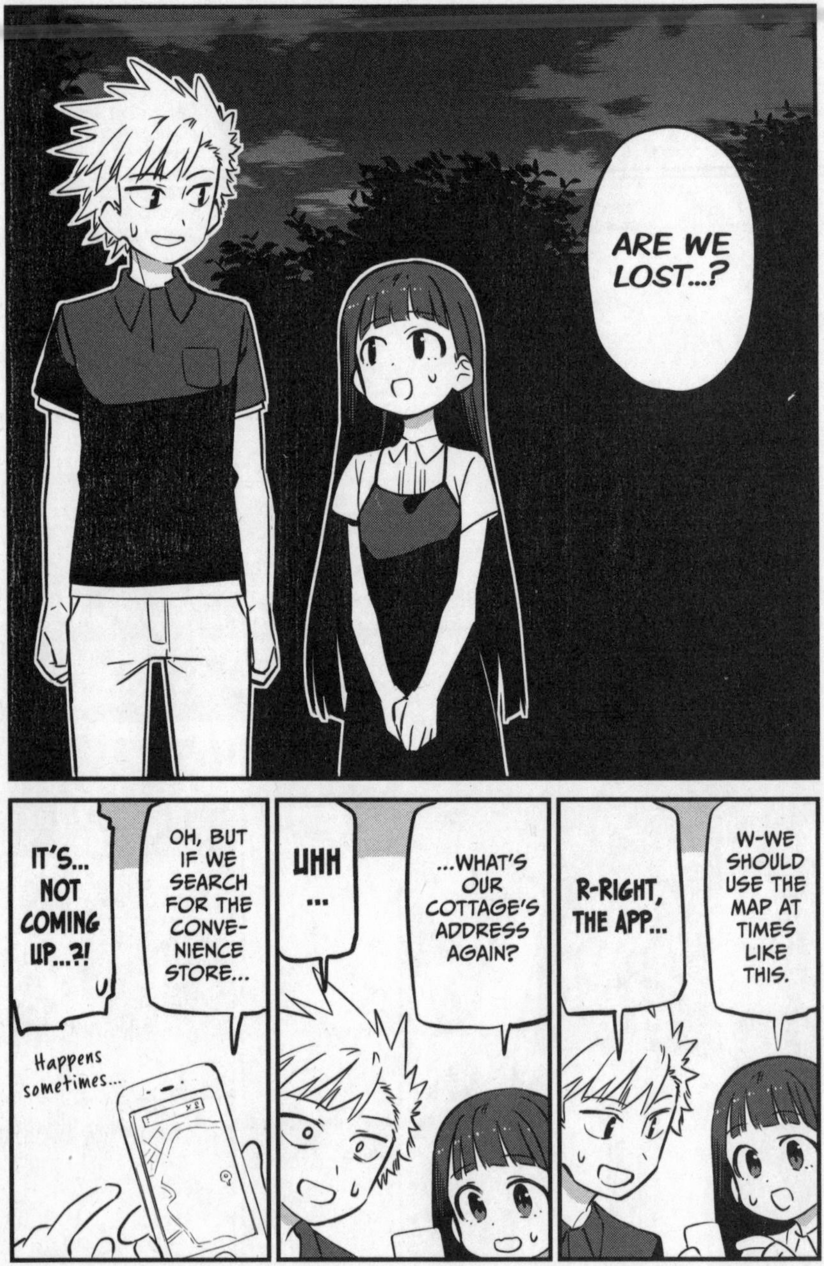
ARE WE LOST...?
W-WE SHOULD USE THE MAP AT TIMES LIKE THIS.
R-RIGHT, THE APP...
...WHAT'S OUR COTTAGE'S ADDRESS AGAIN?
UHH ...
OH, BUT IF WE SEARCH FOR THE CONVENIENCE STORE...
IT'S... NOT COMING UP...?!
Happens sometimes...

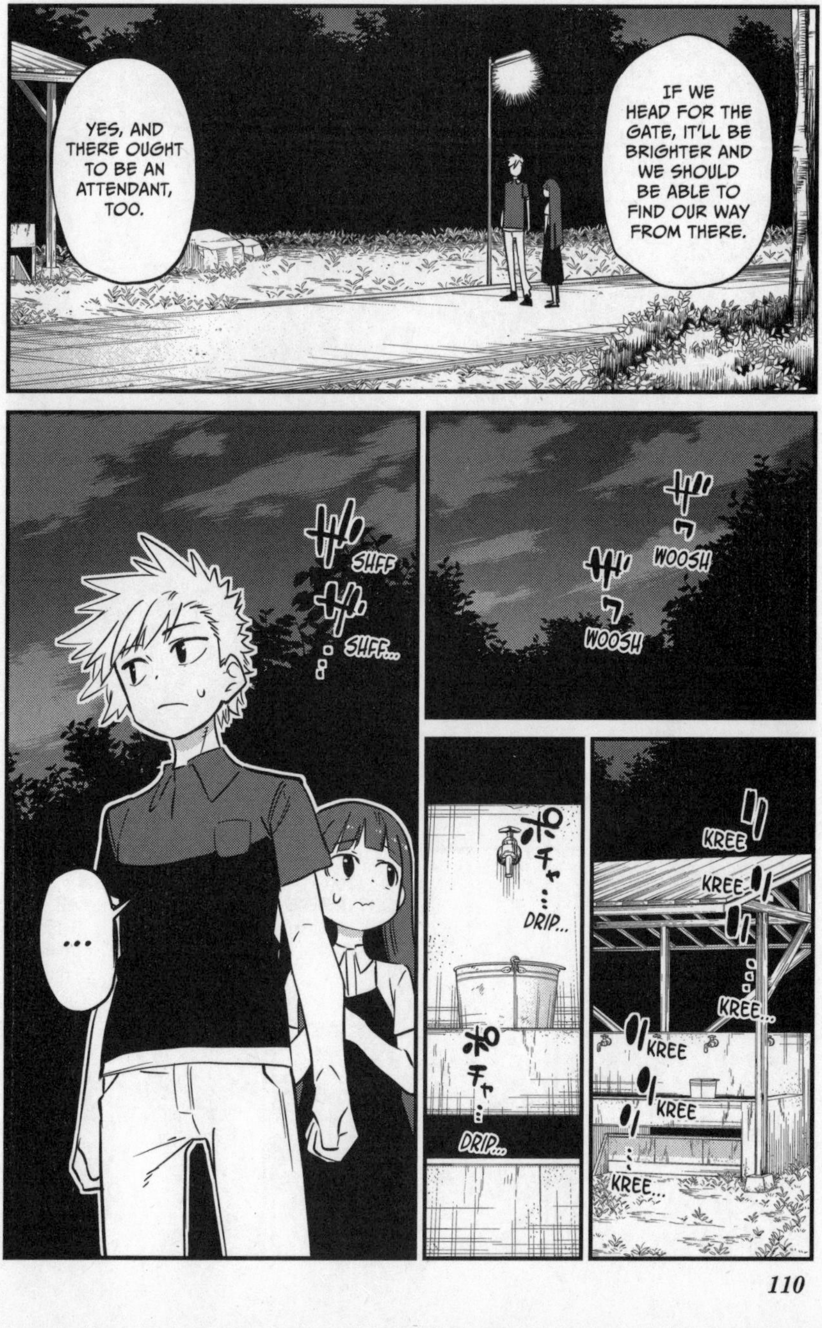
IF WE HEAD FOR THE GATE, IT'LL BE BRIGHTER AND WE SHOULD BE ABLE TO FIND OUR WAY FROM THERE.
YES, AND THERE OUGHT TO BE AN ATTENDANT, TOO.
ザワ WOOSH
ザワ WOOSH
KREE
KREE
KREE...
KREE
KREE
KREE...
ポチャ… DRIP...
ポチャ… DRIP...
SHFF
SHFF...
...

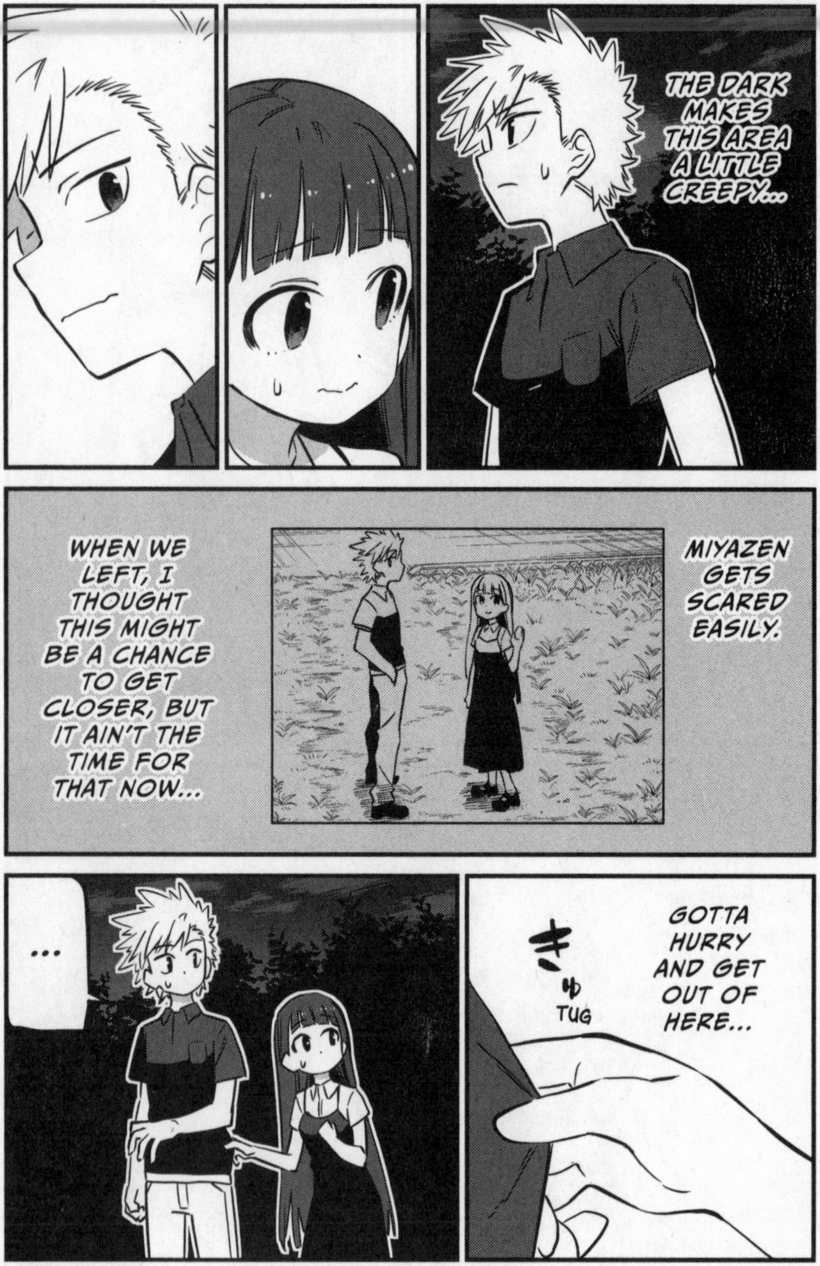
THE DARK MAKES THIS AREA A LITTLE CREEPY...
MIYAZEN GETS SCARED EASILY.
WHEN WE LEFT, I THOUGHT THIS MIGHT BE A CHANCE TO GET CLOSER, BUT IT AIN'T THE TIME FOR THAT NOW...
GOTTA HURRY AND GET OUT OF HERE...
きゅ
TUG
...

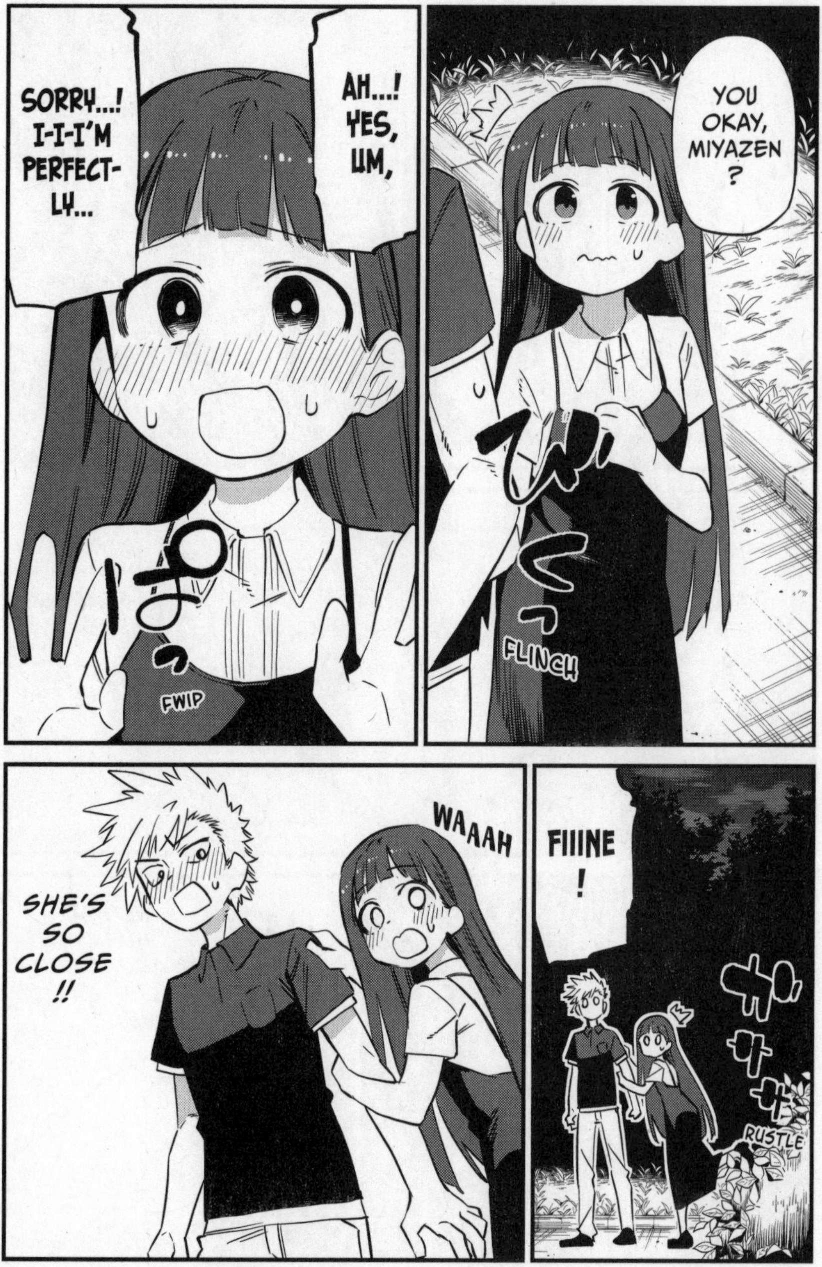
YOU OKAY, MIYAZEN?
びくっ
FLINCH
AH...! YES, UM,
SORRY...! I-I-I'M PERFECTLY...
ぱっ
FWIP
FIIINE!
ガサガサ
RUSTLE
WAAAH
SHE'S SO CLOSE!!

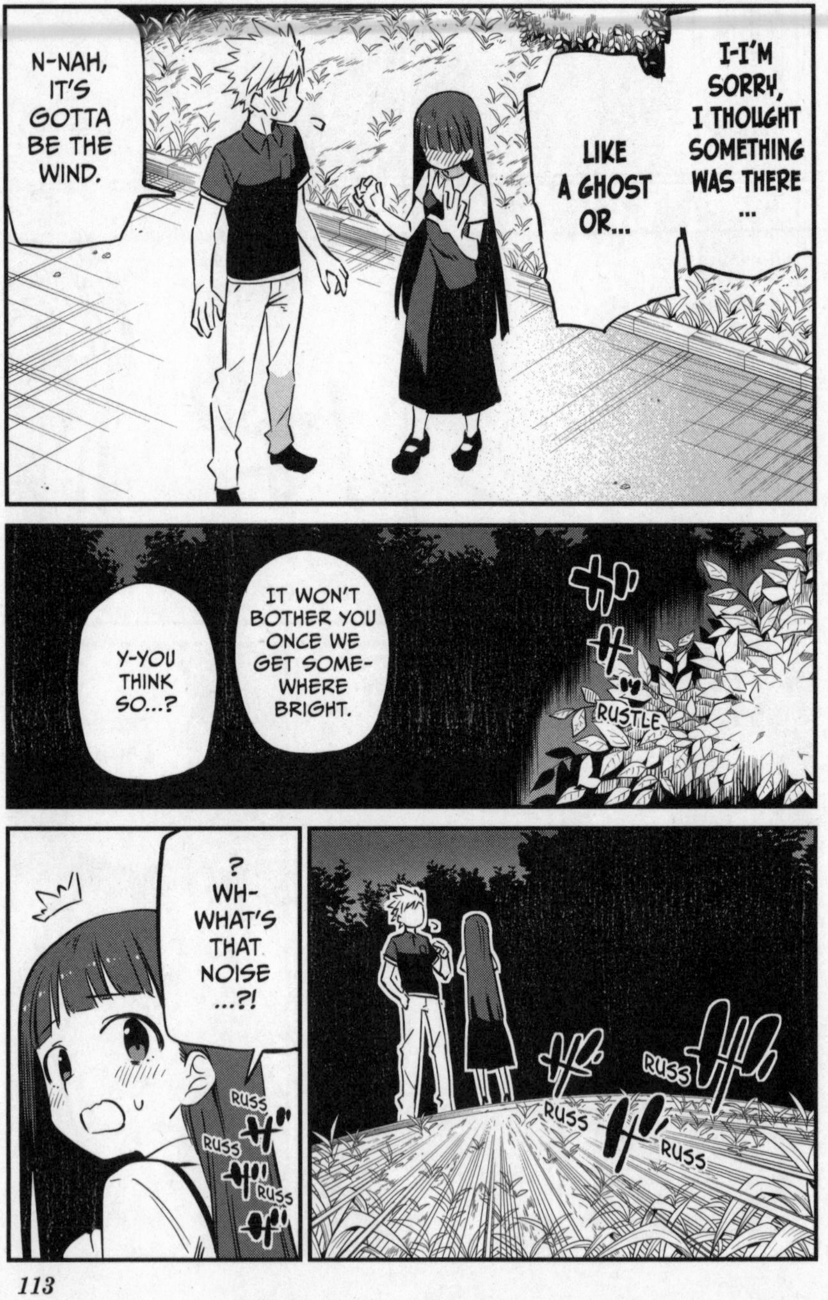
I-I'M SORRY, I THOUGHT SOMETHING WAS THERE ...
LIKE A GHOST OR...
N-NAH, IT'S GOTTA BE THE WIND.
RUSTLE
IT WON'T BOTHER YOU ONCE WE GET SOME-WHERE BRIGHT.
Y-YOU THINK SO...?
RUSS
RUSS
RUSS
? WH-WHAT'S THAT NOISE ...?!
RUSS
RUSS
RUSS

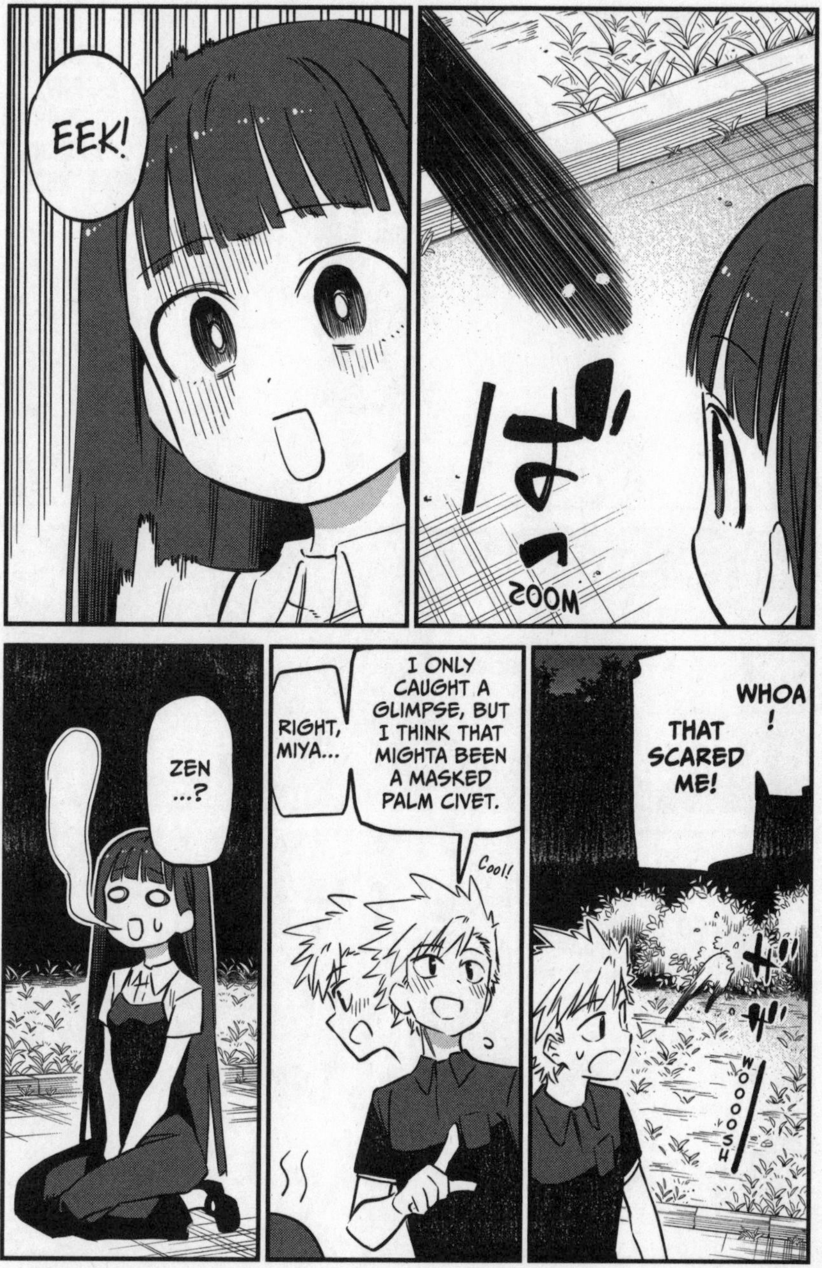
ばっ
ZOOM
EEK!
WHOA!
THAT SCARED ME!
WOOOOOSH
I ONLY CAUGHT A GLIMPSE, BUT I THINK THAT MIGHTA BEEN A MASKED PALM CIVET.
RIGHT, MIYA...
Cool!
ZEN ...?

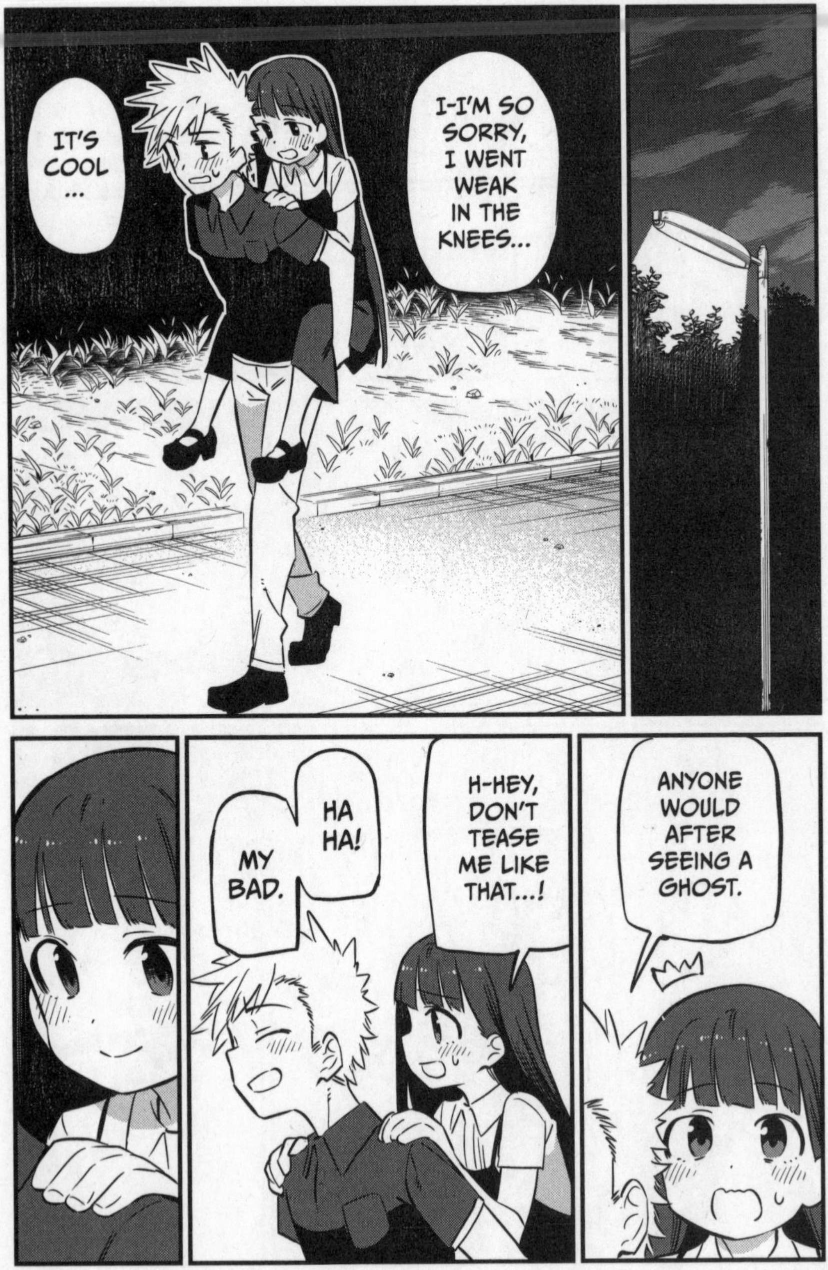
I-I'M SO SORRY, I WENT WEAK IN THE KNEES...
IT'S COOL ...
ANYONE WOULD AFTER SEEING A GHOST.
H-HEY, DON'T TEASE ME LIKE THAT...!
HA HA!
MY BAD.

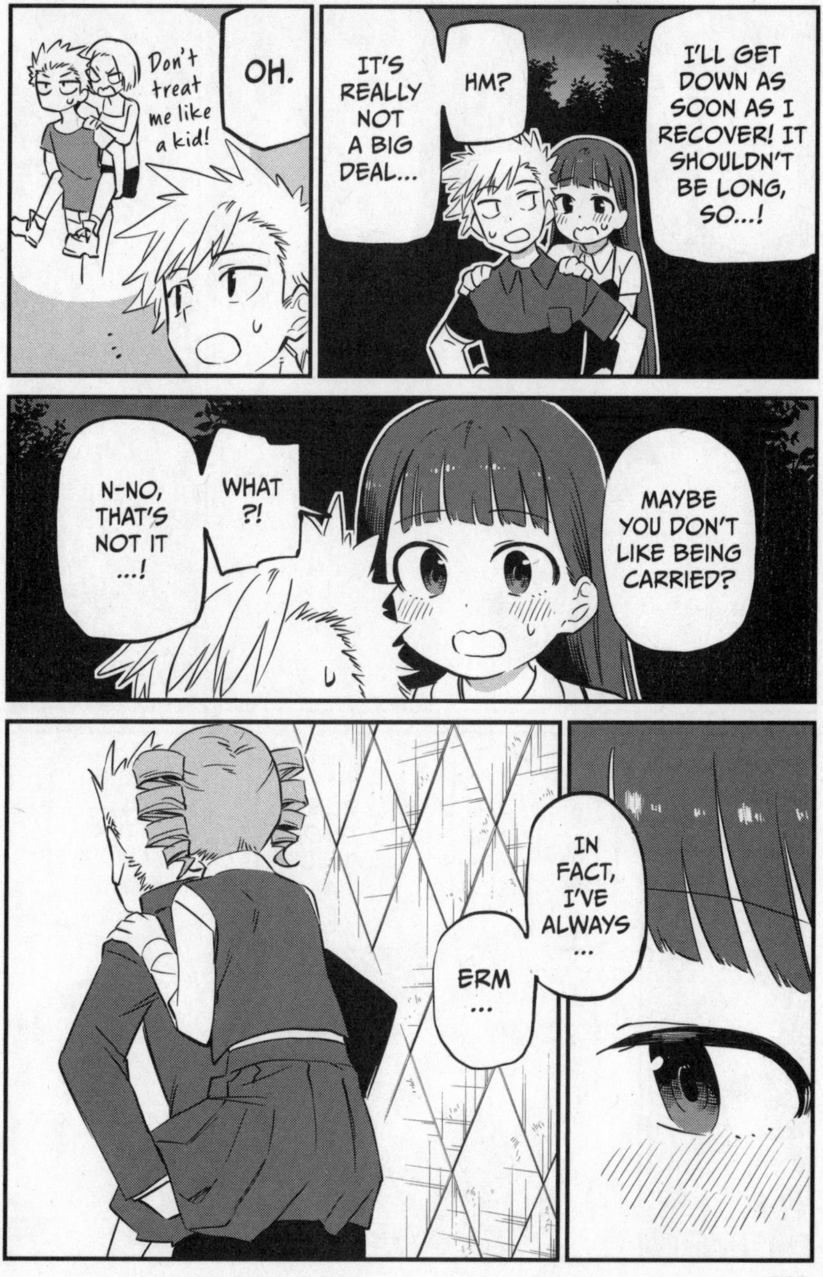
I'LL GET DOWN AS SOON AS I RECOVER! IT SHOULDN'T BE LONG, SO...!
HM?
IT'S REALLY NOT A BIG DEAL...
OH.
Don't treat me like a kid!
MAYBE YOU DON'T LIKE BEING CARRIED?
WHAT ?!
N-NO, THAT'S NOT IT ...!
IN FACT, I'VE ALWAYS ...
ERM ...

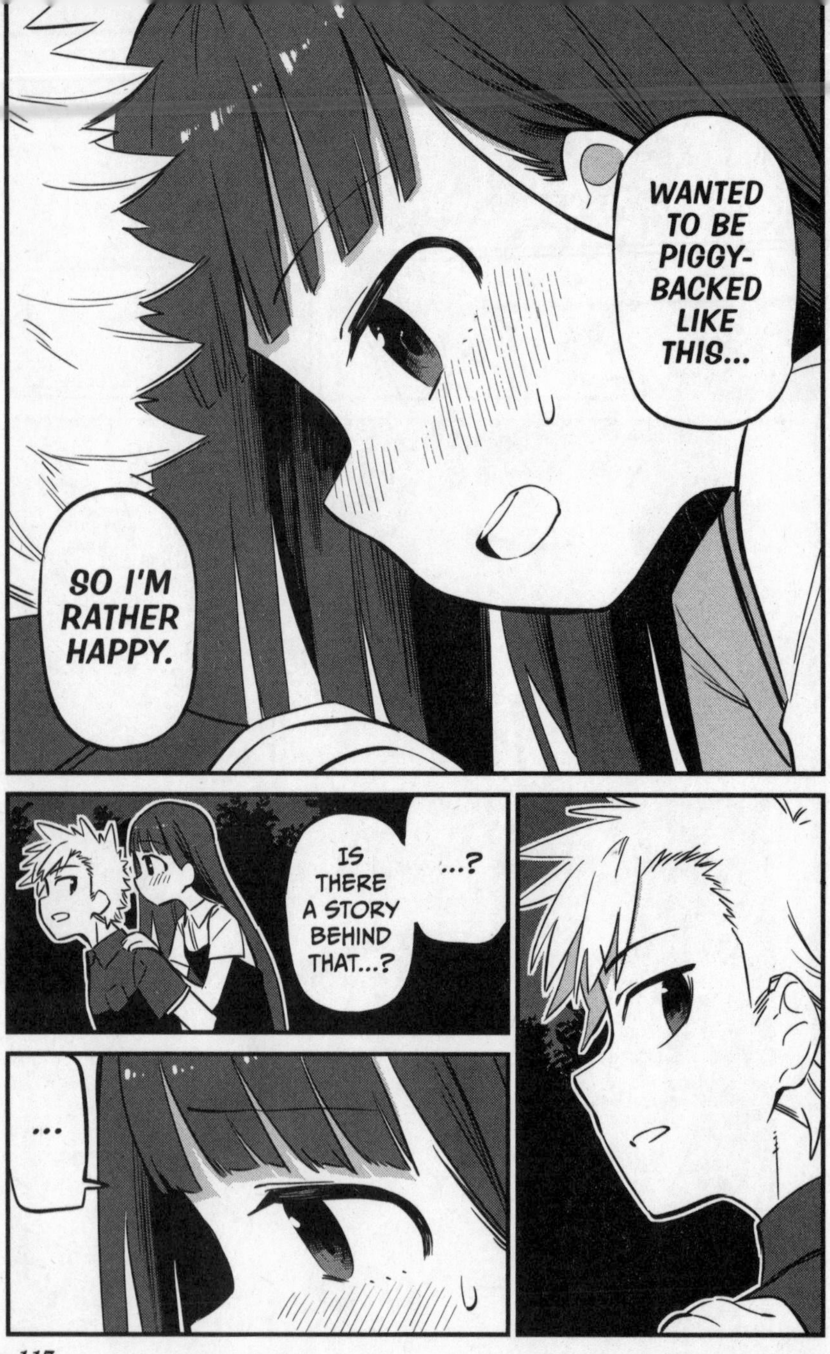
WANTED TO BE PIGGY-BACKED LIKE THIS...
SO I'M RATHER HAPPY.
...?
IS THERE A STORY BEHIND THAT...?
...

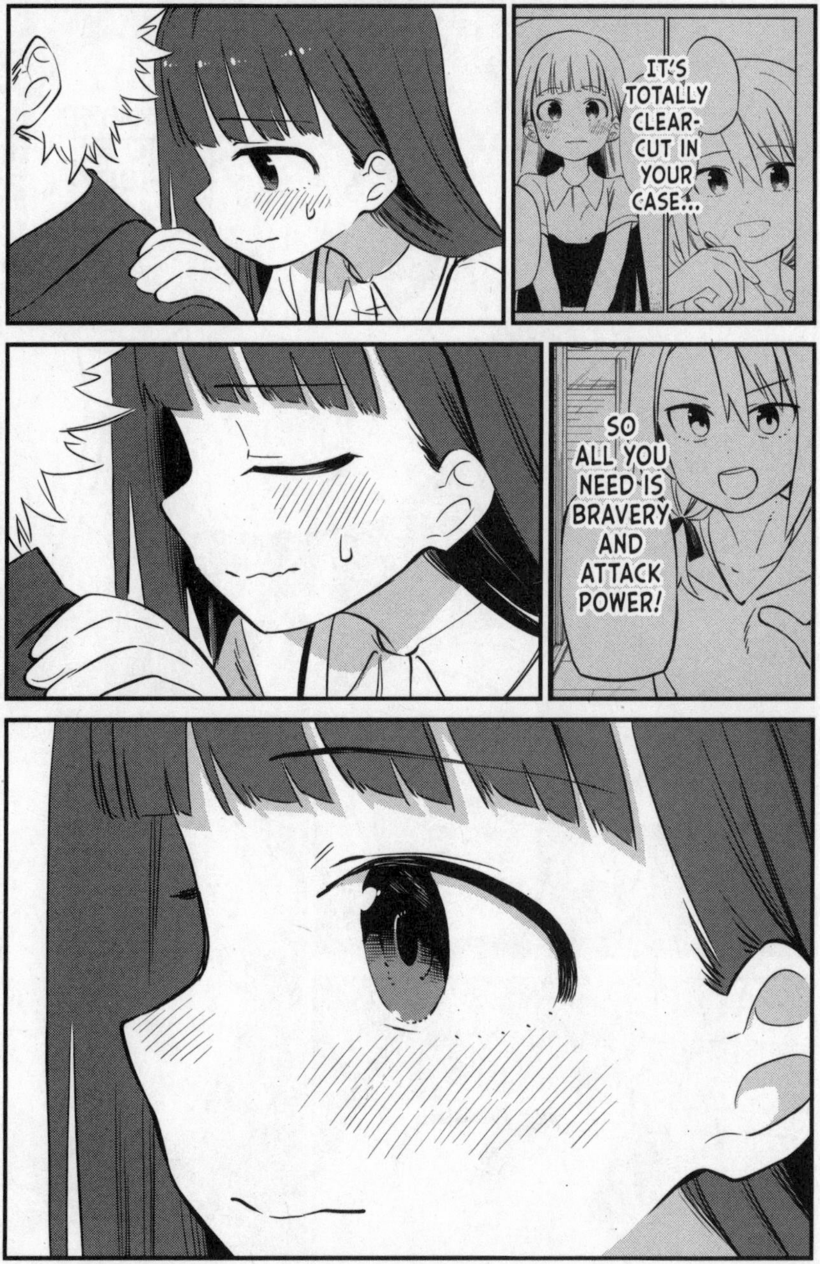
IT'S TOTALLY CLEAR-CUT IN YOUR CASE...
SO ALL YOU NEED IS BRAVERY AND ATTACK POWER!

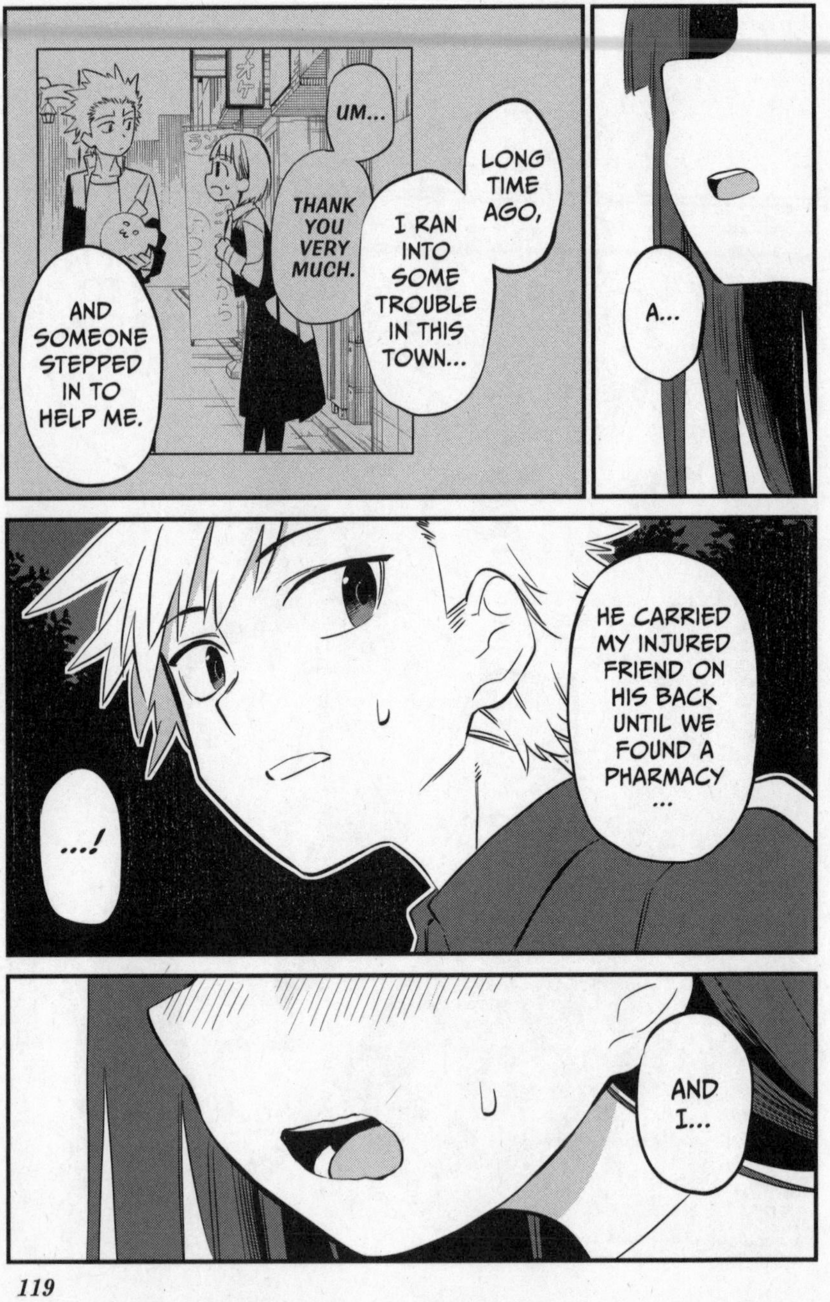
A...
LONG TIME AGO,
I RAN INTO SOME TROUBLE IN THIS TOWN...
UM...
THANK YOU VERY MUCH.
AND SOMEONE STEPPED IN TO HELP ME.
HE CARRIED MY INJURED FRIEND ON HIS BACK UNTIL WE FOUND A PHARMACY ...
...!
AND I...

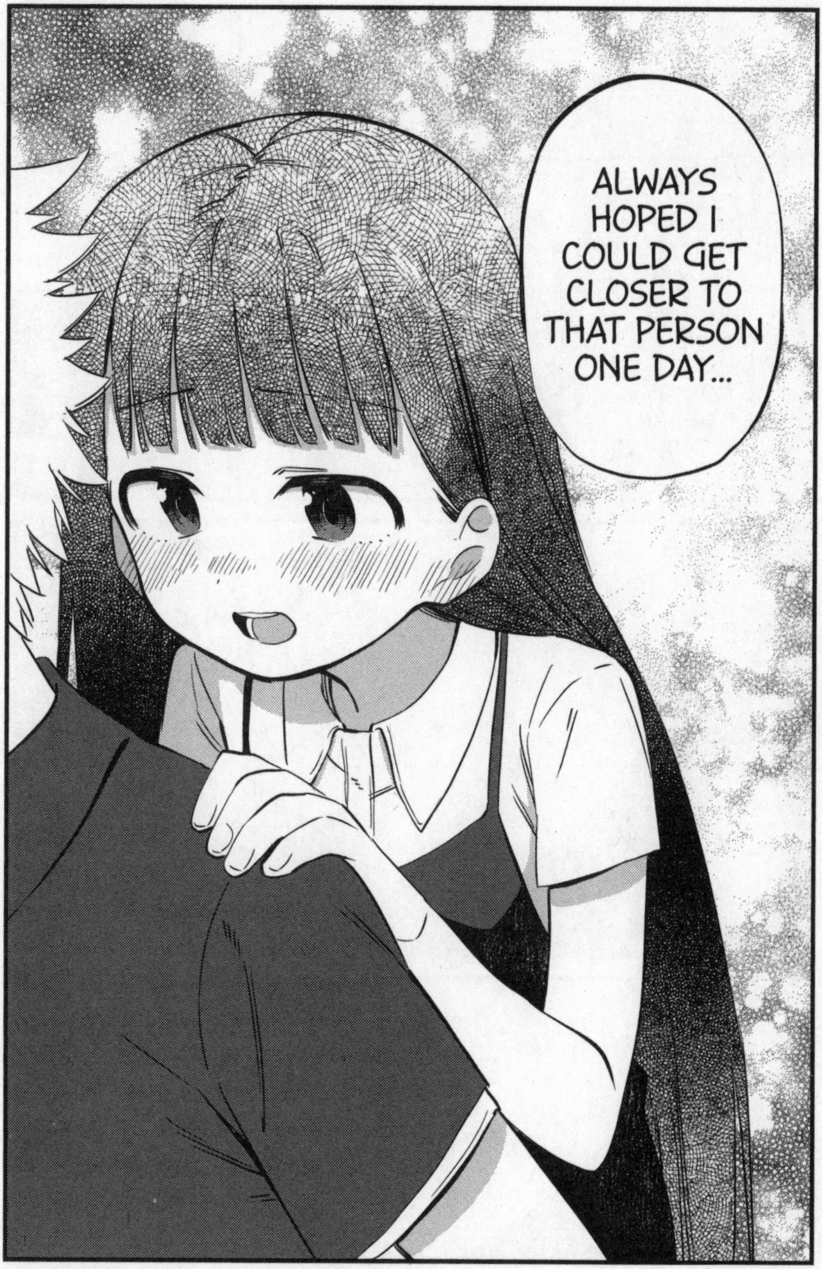
ALWAYS HOPED I COULD GET CLOSER TO THAT PERSON ONE DAY...

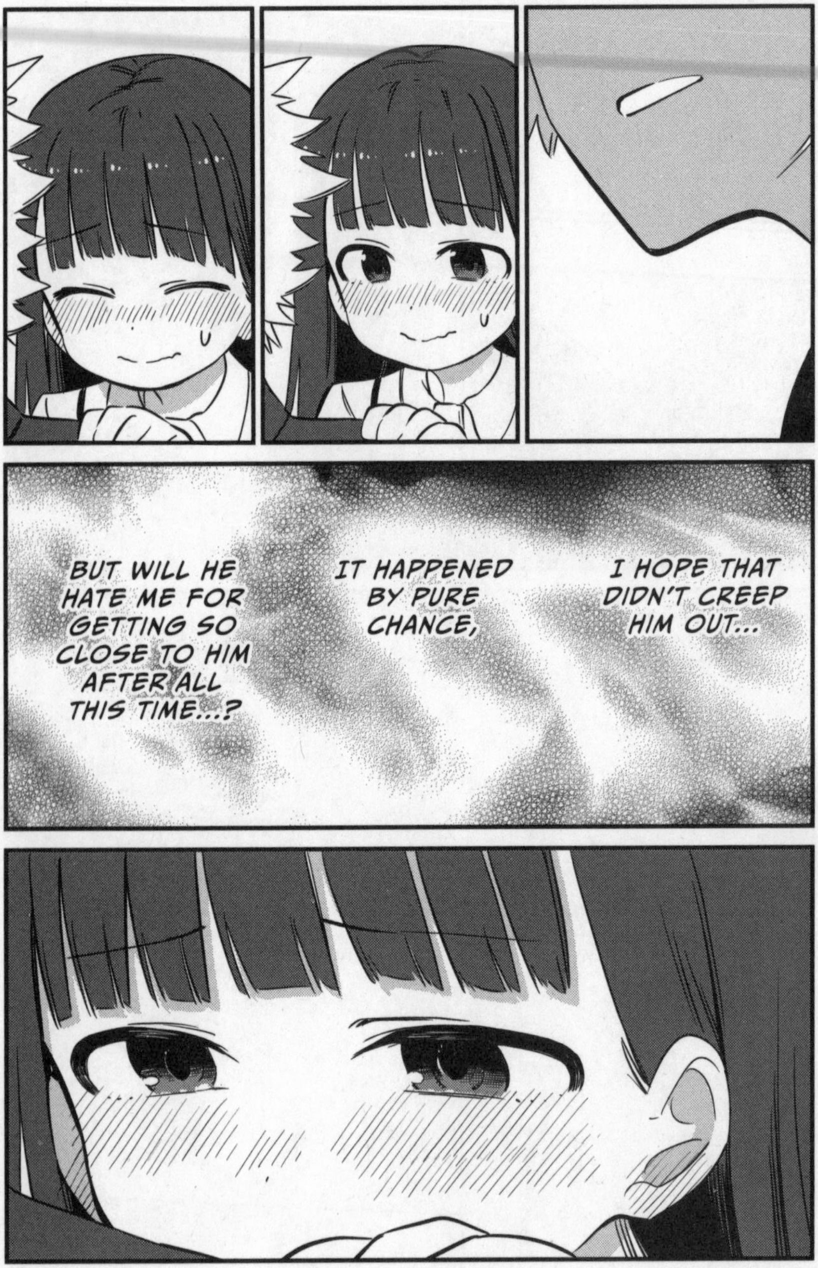
I HOPE THAT DIDN'T CREEP HIM OUT...
IT HAPPENED BY PURE CHANCE,
BUT WILL HE HATE ME FOR GETTING SO CLOSE TO HIM AFTER ALL THIS TIME...?

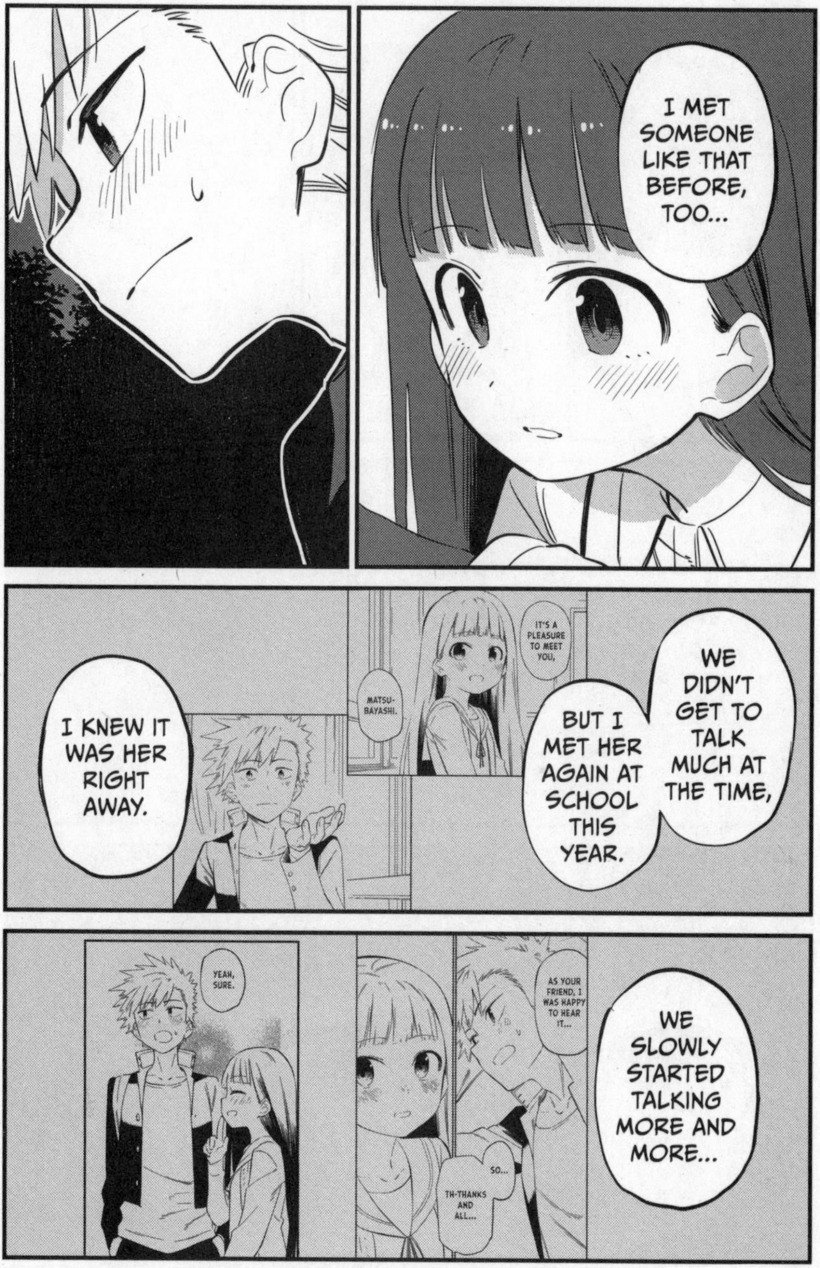
I MET SOMEONE LIKE THAT BEFORE, TOO...
WE DIDN'T GET TO TALK MUCH AT THE TIME,
BUT I MET HER AGAIN AT SCHOOL THIS YEAR.
IT'S A PLEASURE TO MEET YOU,
MATSU-BAYASHI.
I KNEW IT WAS HER RIGHT AWAY.
WE SLOWLY STARTED TALKING MORE AND MORE...
AS YOUR FRIEND, I WAS HAPPY TO HEAR IT...
SO...
TH-THANKS AND ALL...
YEAH, SURE.

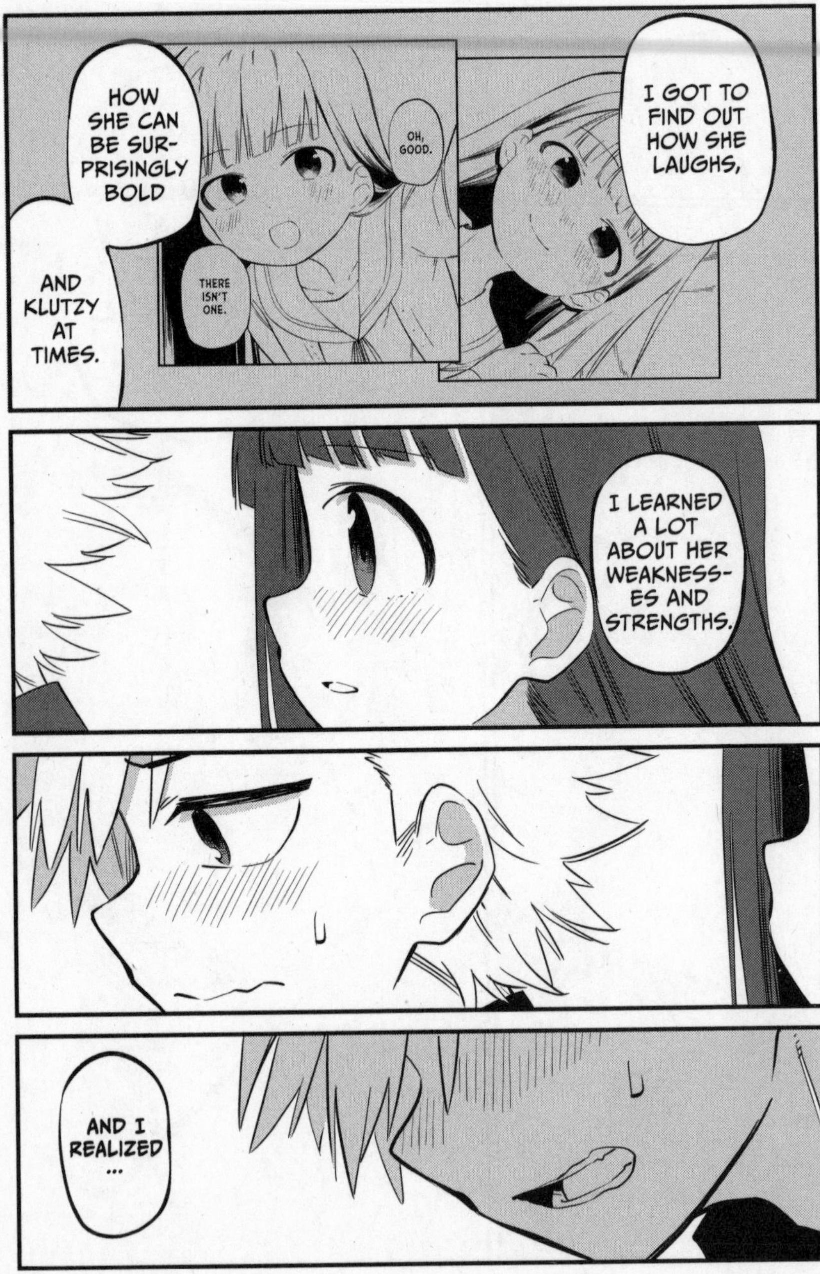
I GOT TO FIND OUT HOW SHE LAUGHS,
OH, GOOD.
HOW SHE CAN BE SURPRISINGLY BOLD
THERE ISN'T ONE.
AND KLUTZY AT TIMES.
I LEARNED A LOT ABOUT HER WEAKNESSES AND STRENGTHS.
AND I REALIZED ...

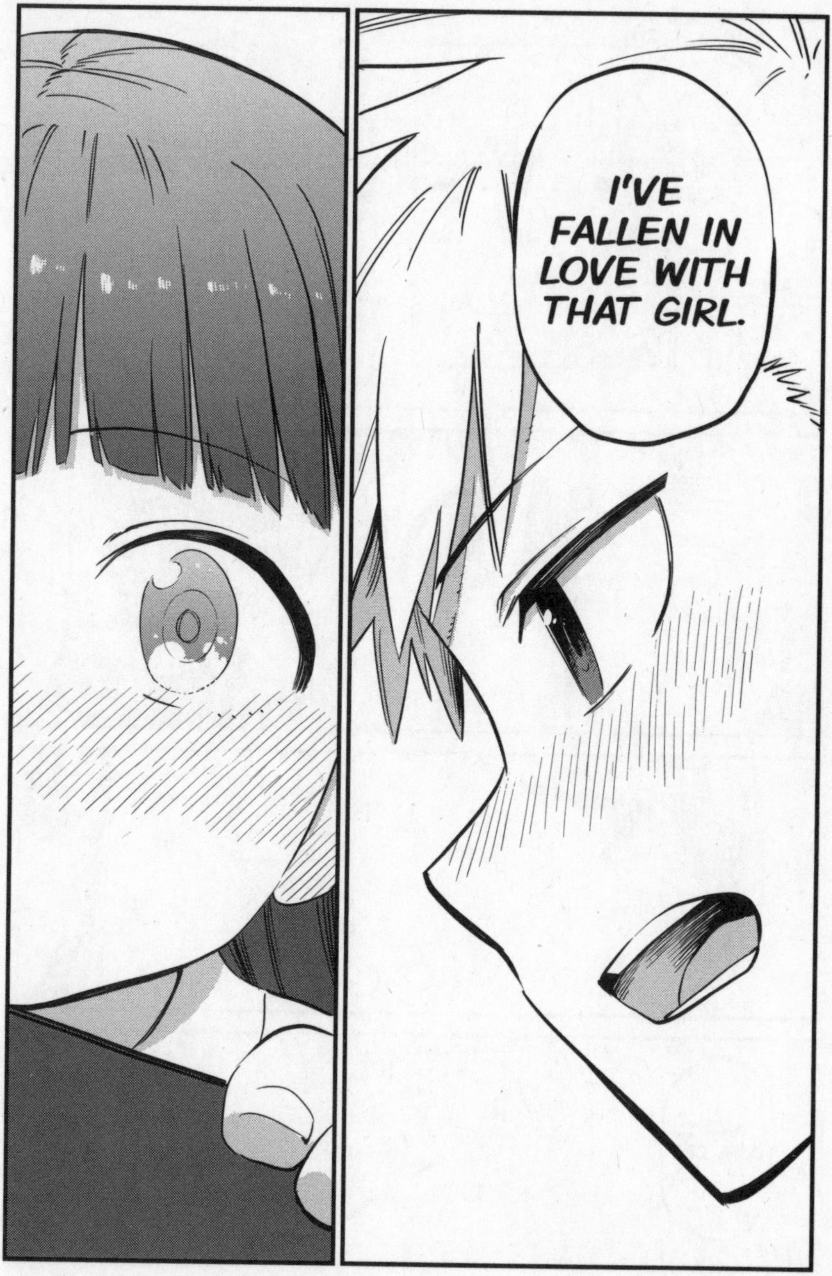
I'VE FALLEN IN LOVE WITH THAT GIRL.

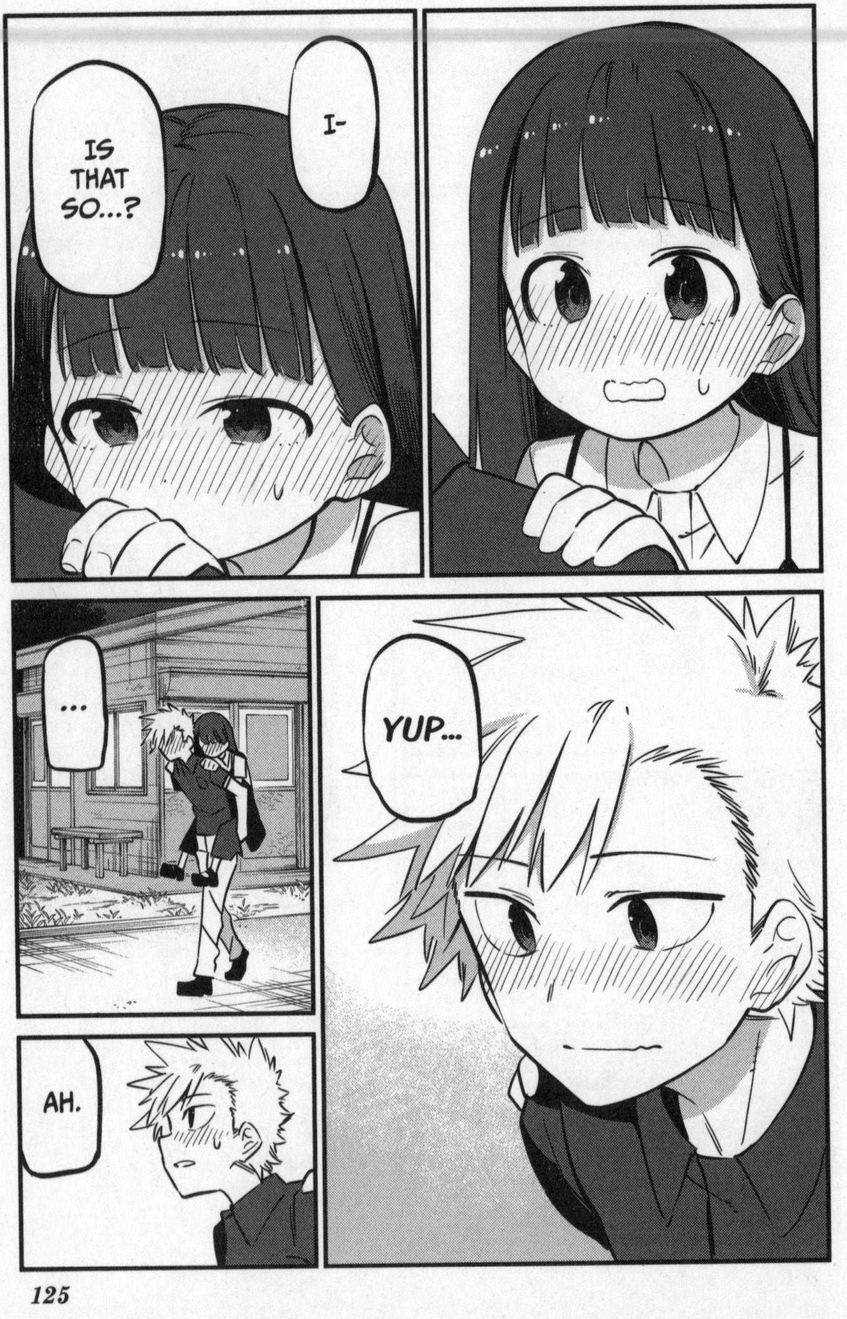
I-
IS THAT SO...?
YUP...
...
AH.

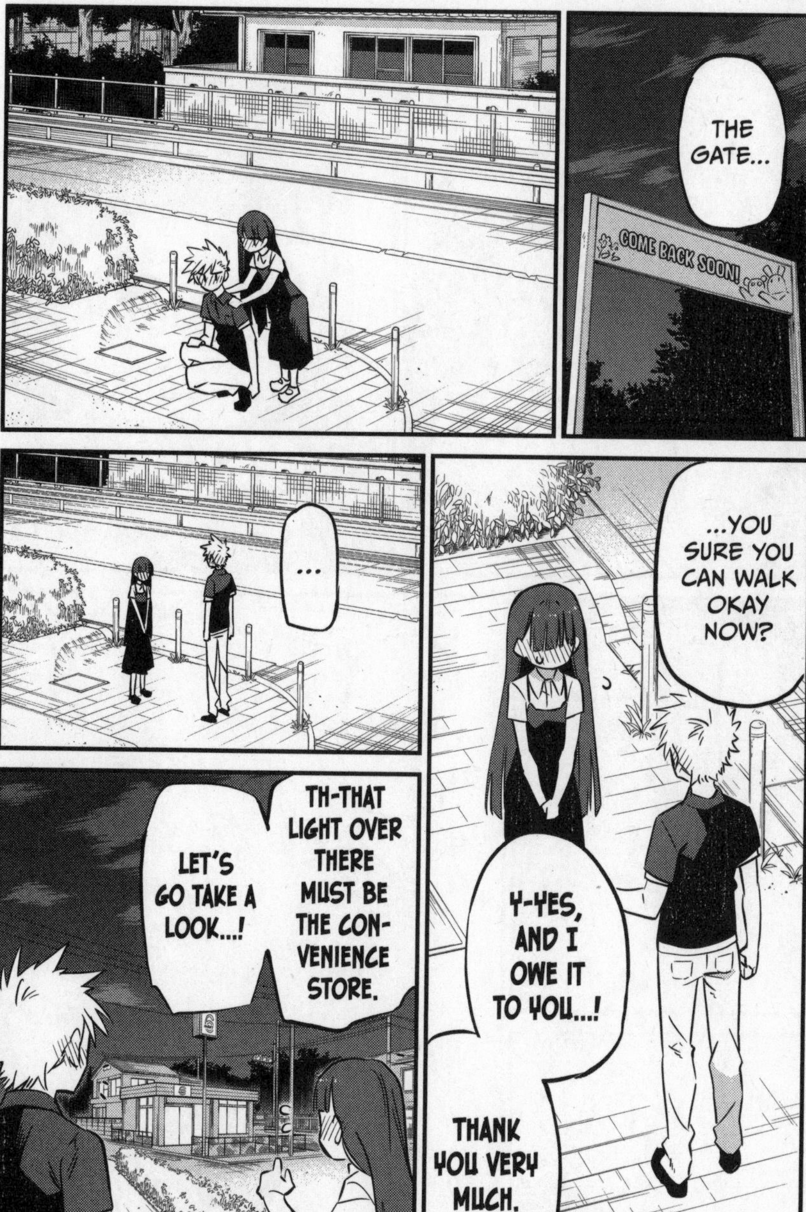
THE GATE...
COME BACK SOON!
...YOU SURE YOU CAN WALK OKAY NOW?
Y-YES, AND I OWE IT TO YOU...!
THANK YOU VERY MUCH.
...
TH-THAT LIGHT OVER THERE MUST BE THE CON-VENIENCE STORE.
LET'S GO TAKE A LOOK...!

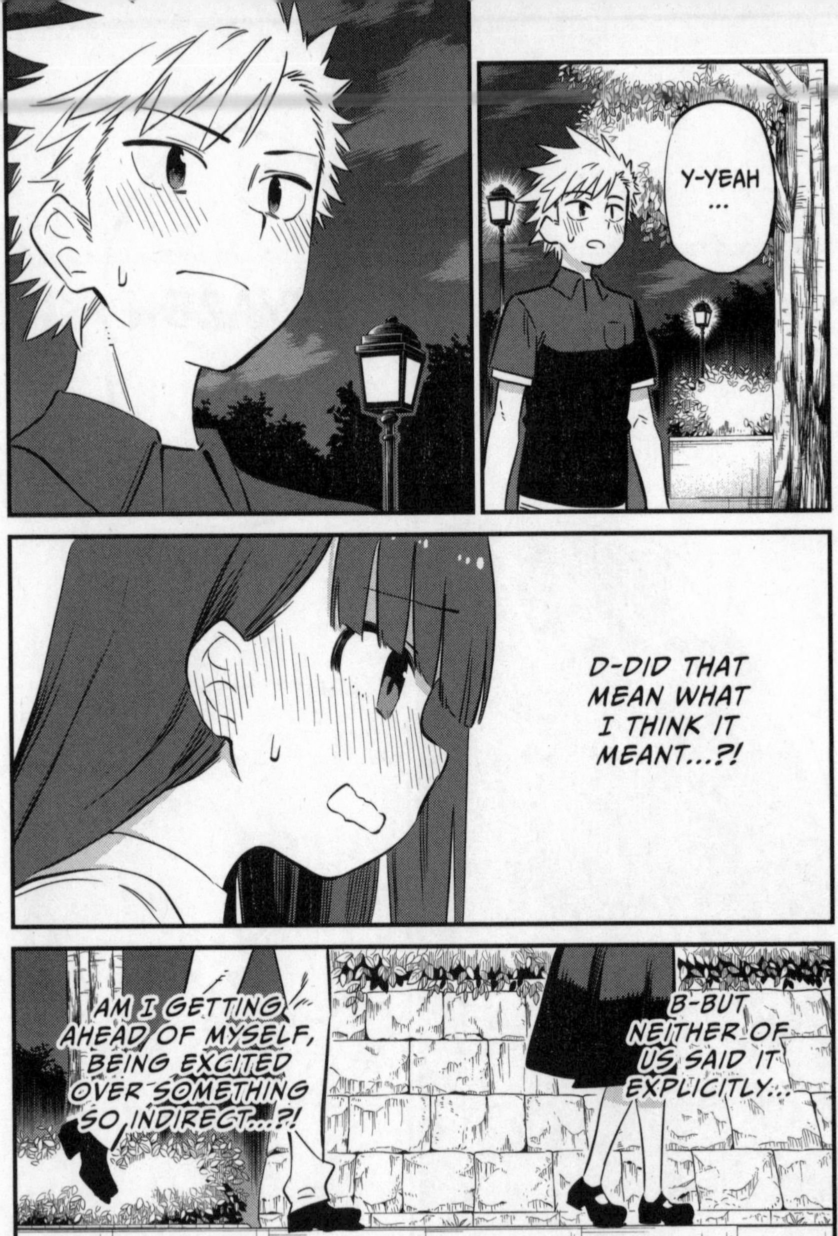
Y-YEAH ...
D-DID THAT MEAN WHAT I THINK IT MEANT...?!
B-BUT NEITHER OF US SAID IT EXPLICITLY...
AM I GETTING AHEAD OF MYSELF, BEING EXCITED OVER SOMETHING SO INDIRECT...?!

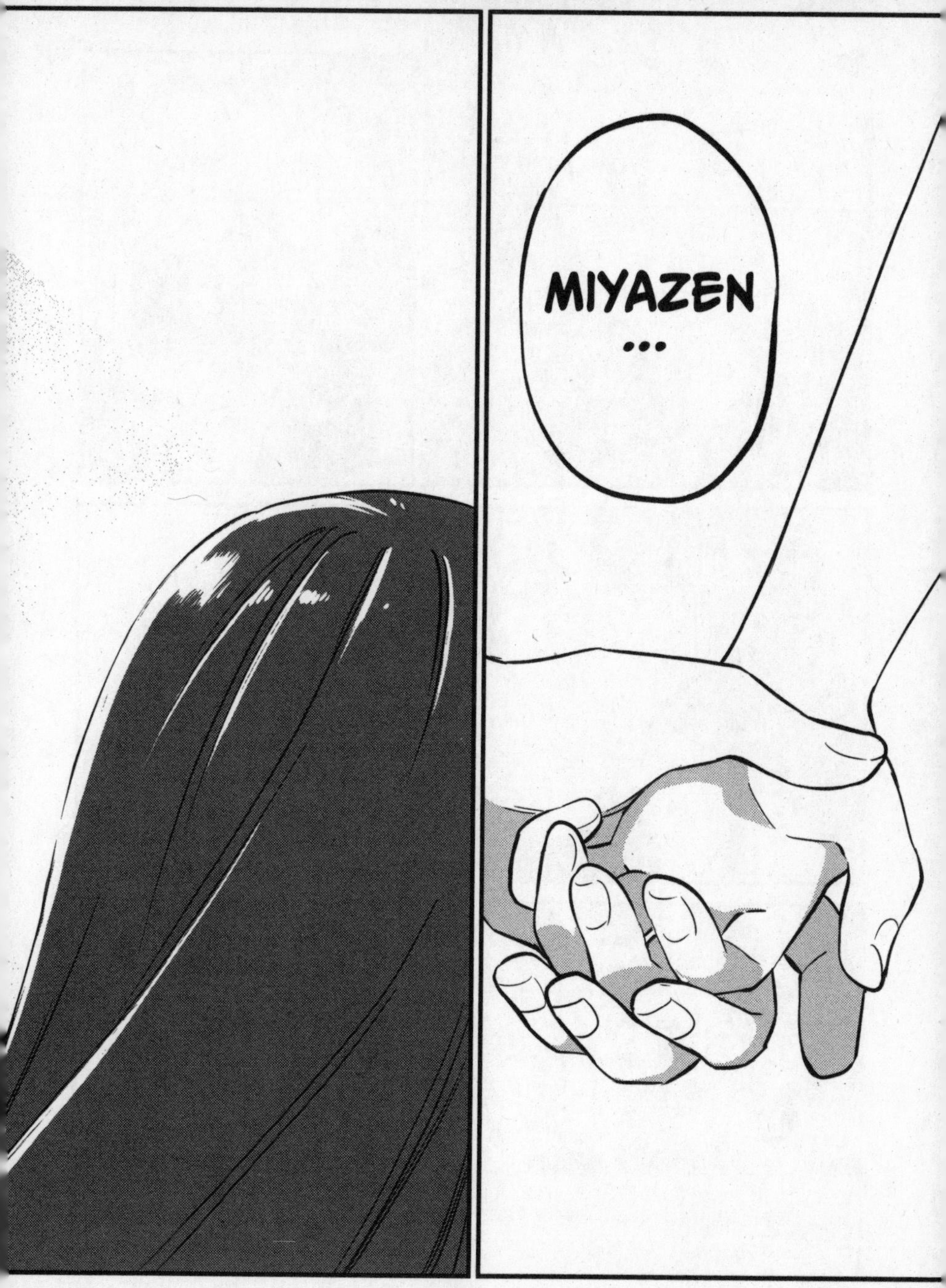
MIYAZEN
...

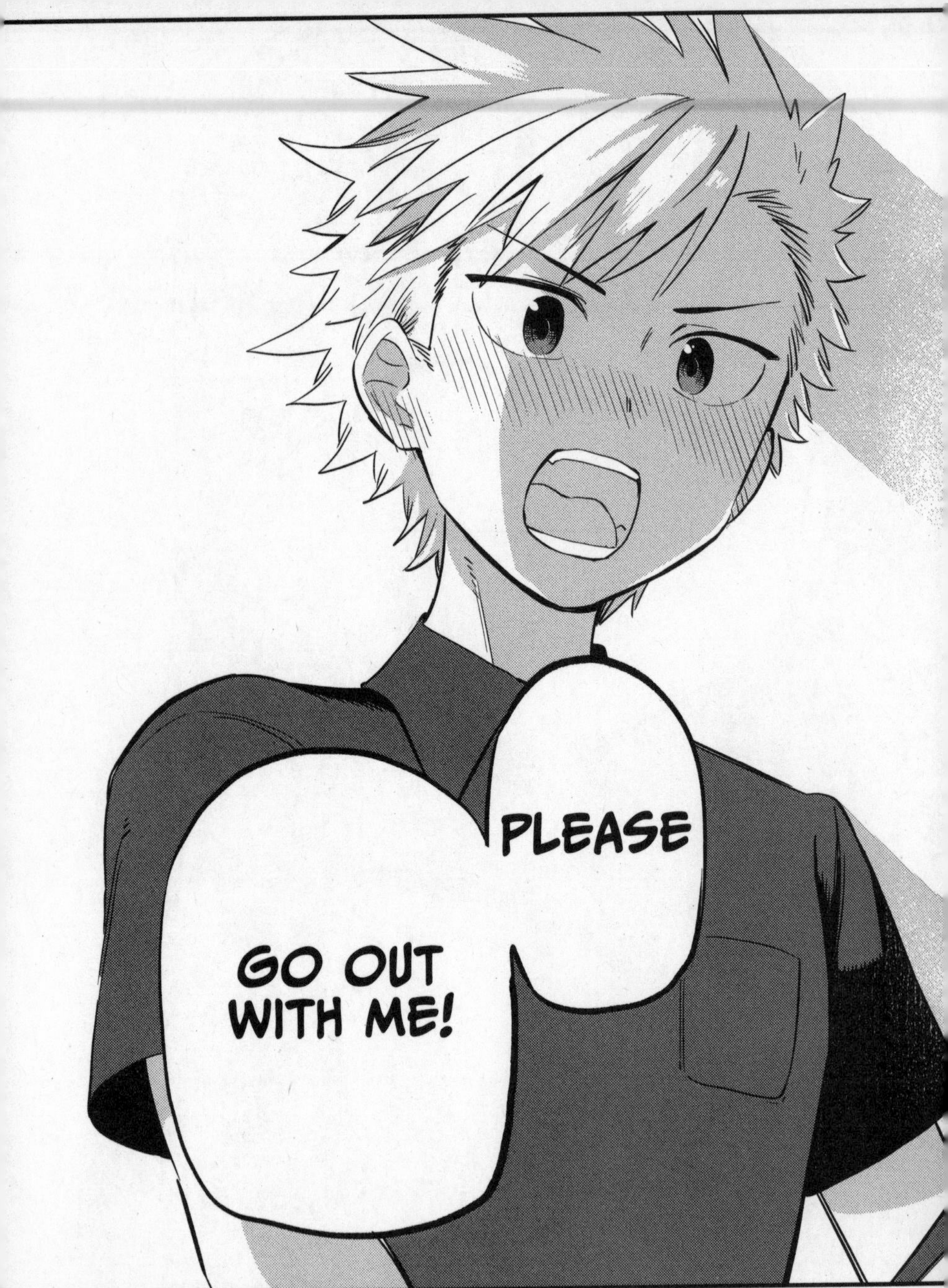
PLEASE
GO OUT WITH ME!

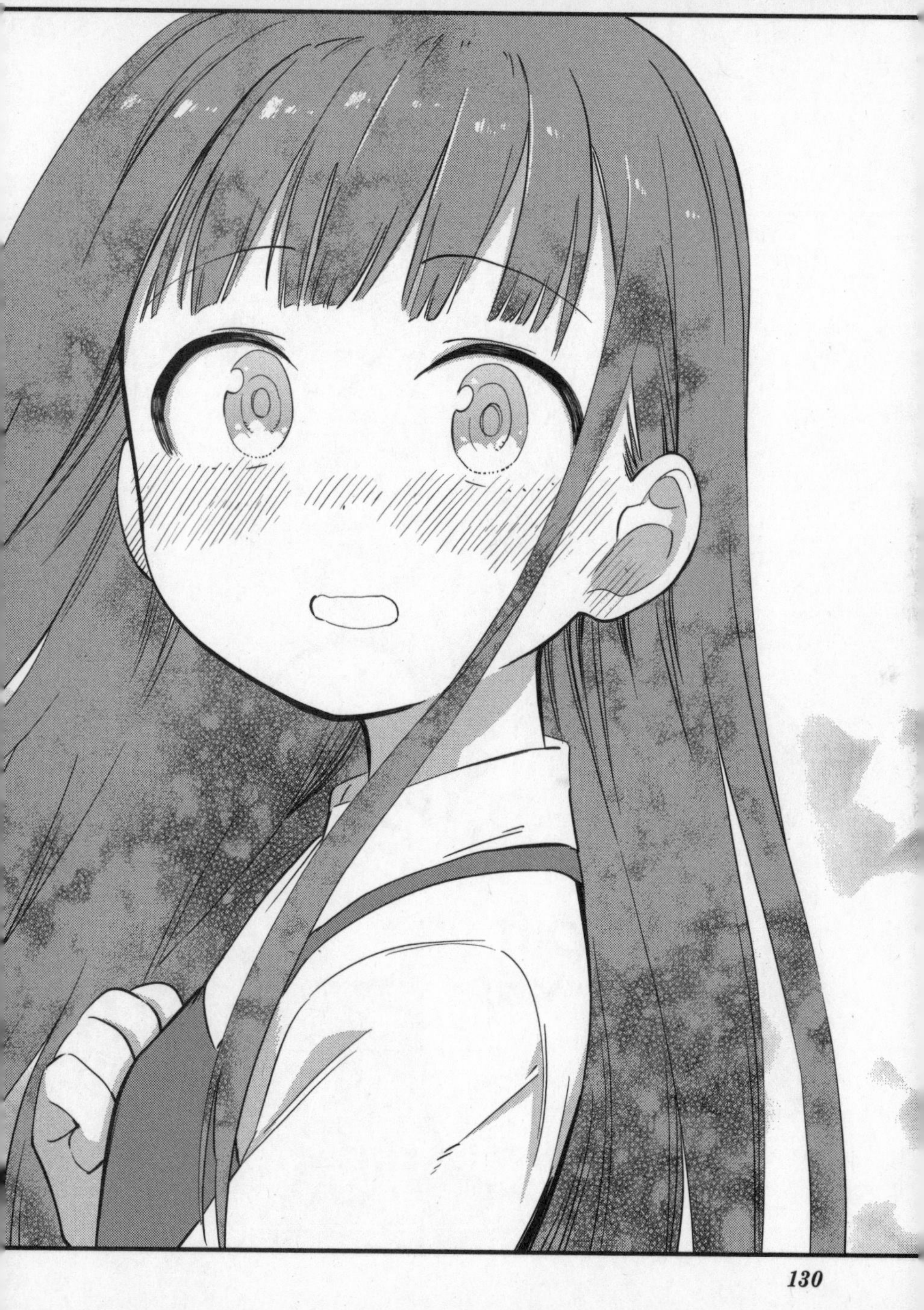

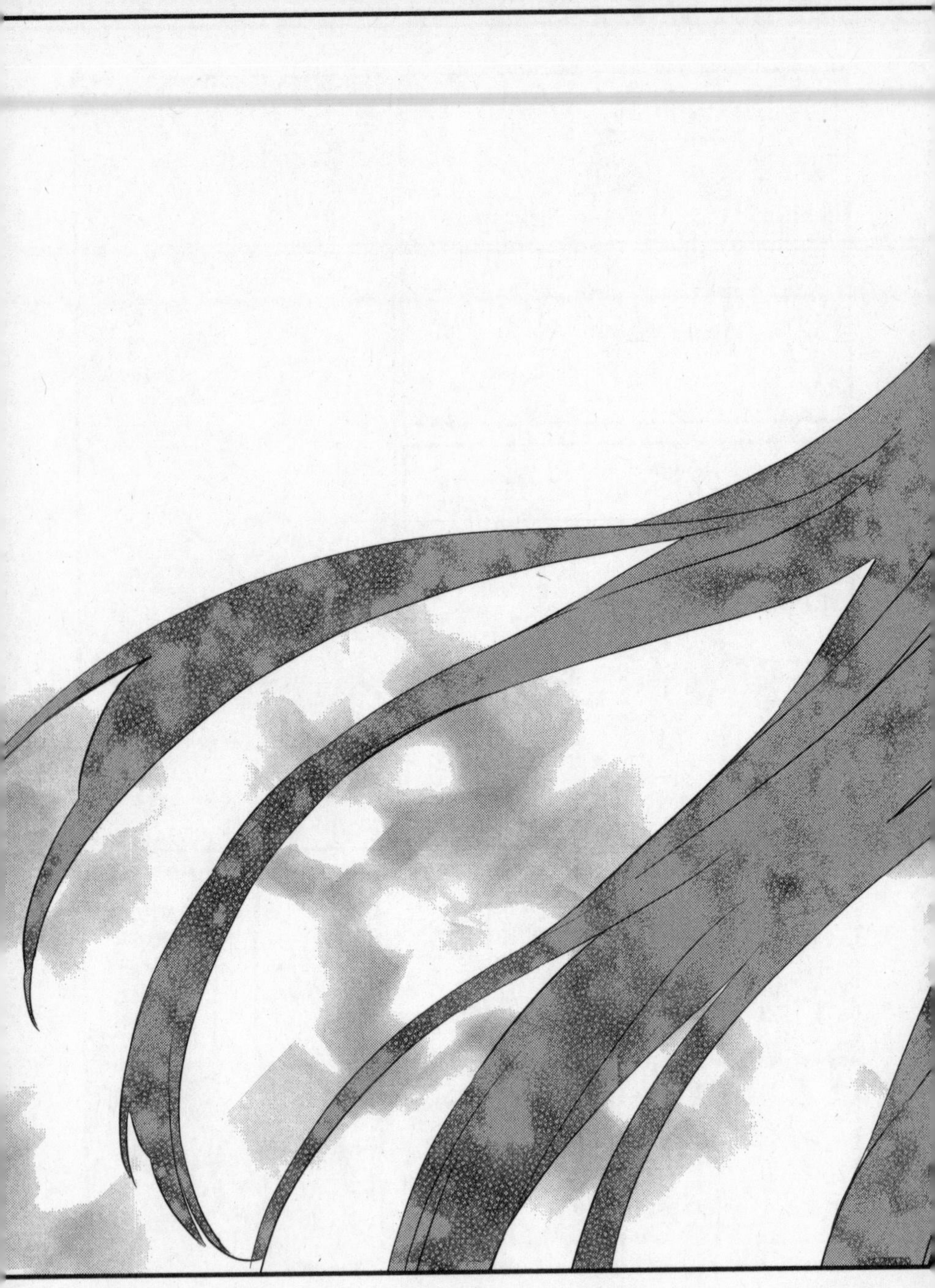

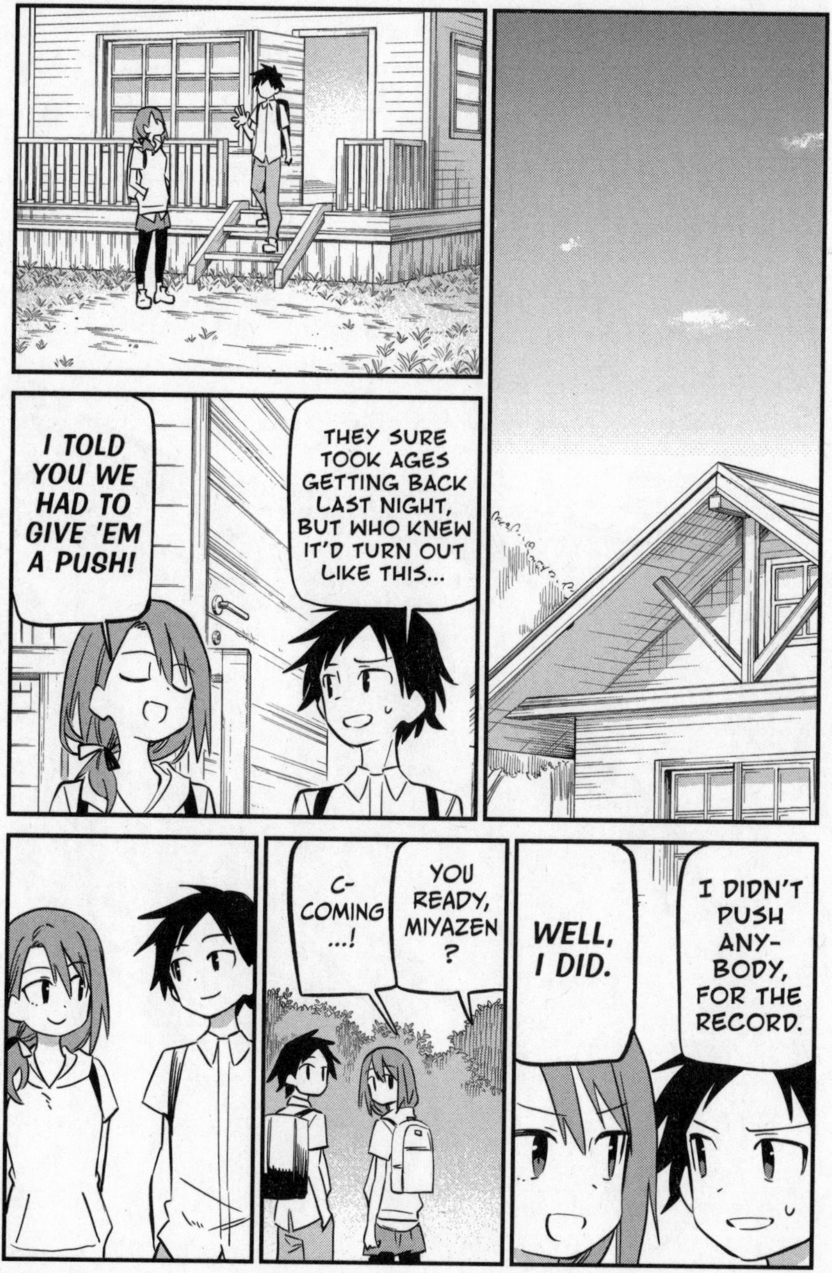
THEY SURE TOOK AGES GETTING BACK LAST NIGHT, BUT WHO KNEW IT'D TURN OUT LIKE THIS...
I TOLD YOU WE HAD TO GIVE 'EM A PUSH!
I DIDN'T PUSH ANYBODY, FOR THE RECORD.
WELL, I DID.
YOU READY, MIYAZEN?
C-COMING...!

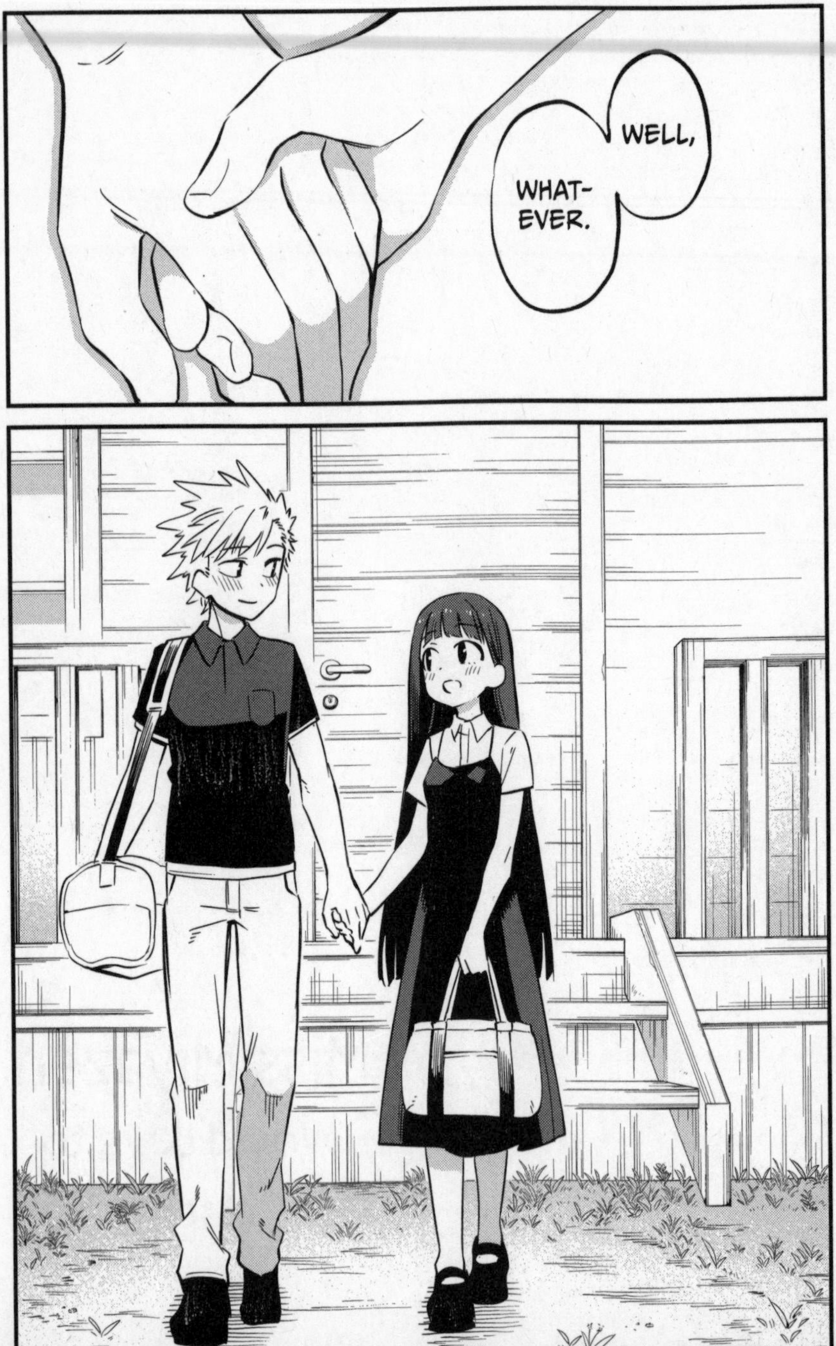
WELL,
WHAT-EVER.

Miss Miyazen
Would Love to
Get Closer to You

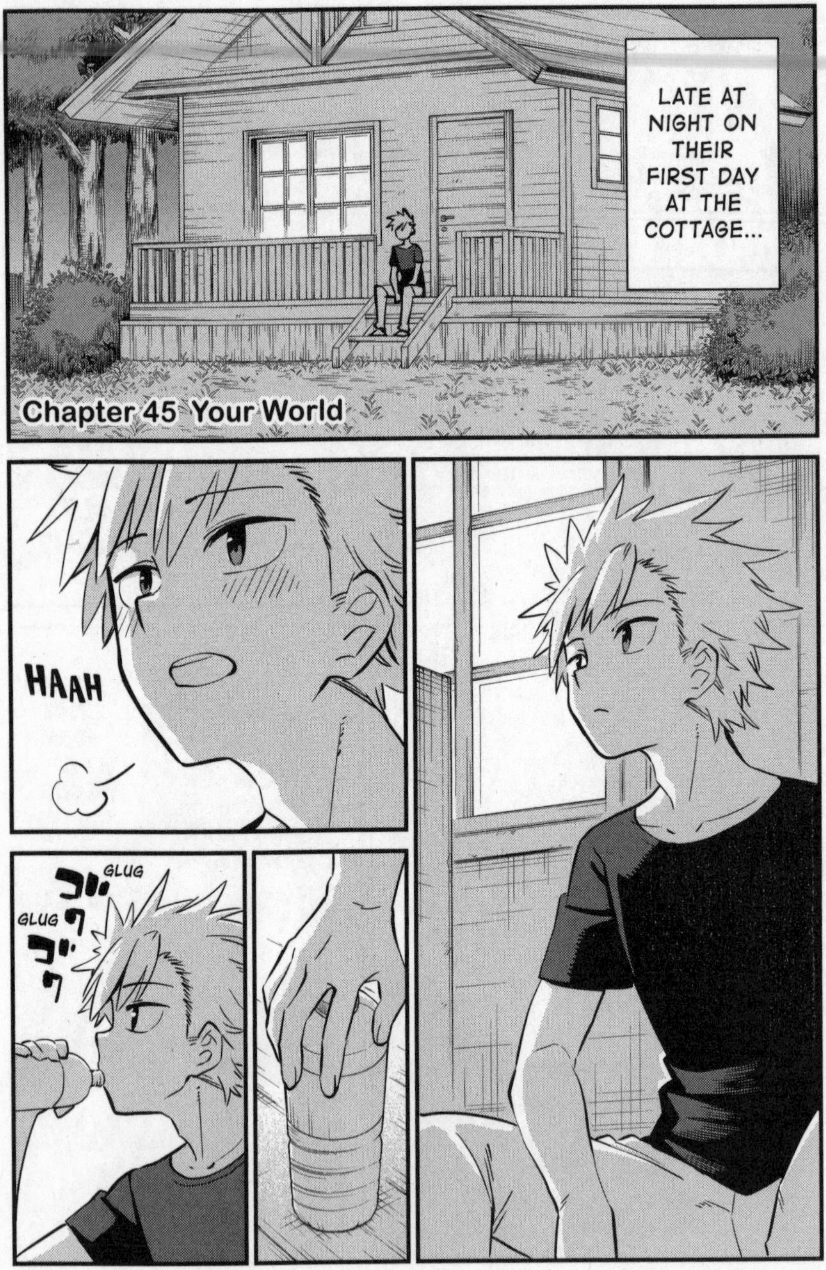
LATE AT NIGHT ON THEIR FIRST DAY AT THE COTTAGE...
Chapter 45 Your World
HAAH
GLUG
ゴク
GLUG
ゴク

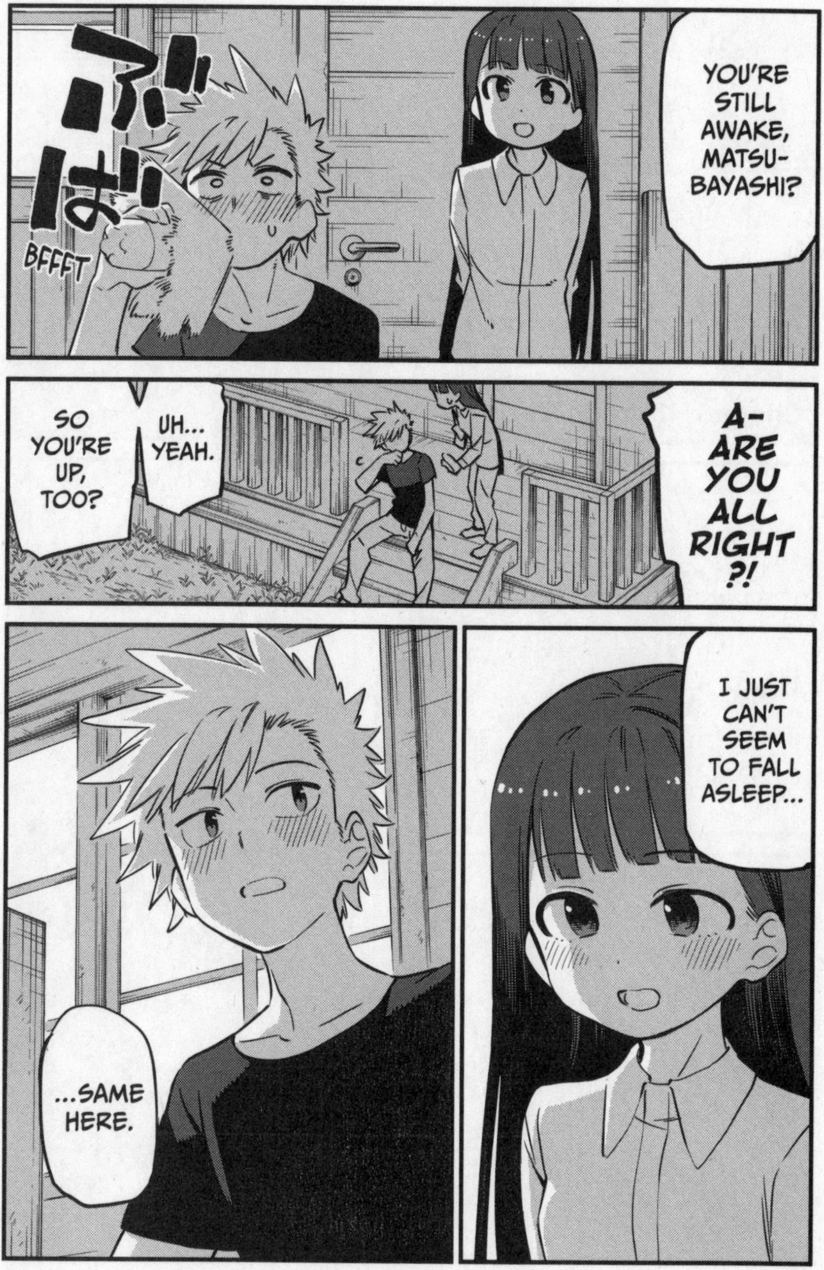
YOU'RE STILL AWAKE, MATSU-BAYASHI?
ぶばっ
BFFFT
A-ARE YOU ALL RIGHT?!
UH... YEAH.
SO YOU'RE UP, TOO?
I JUST CAN'T SEEM TO FALL ASLEEP...
...SAME HERE.

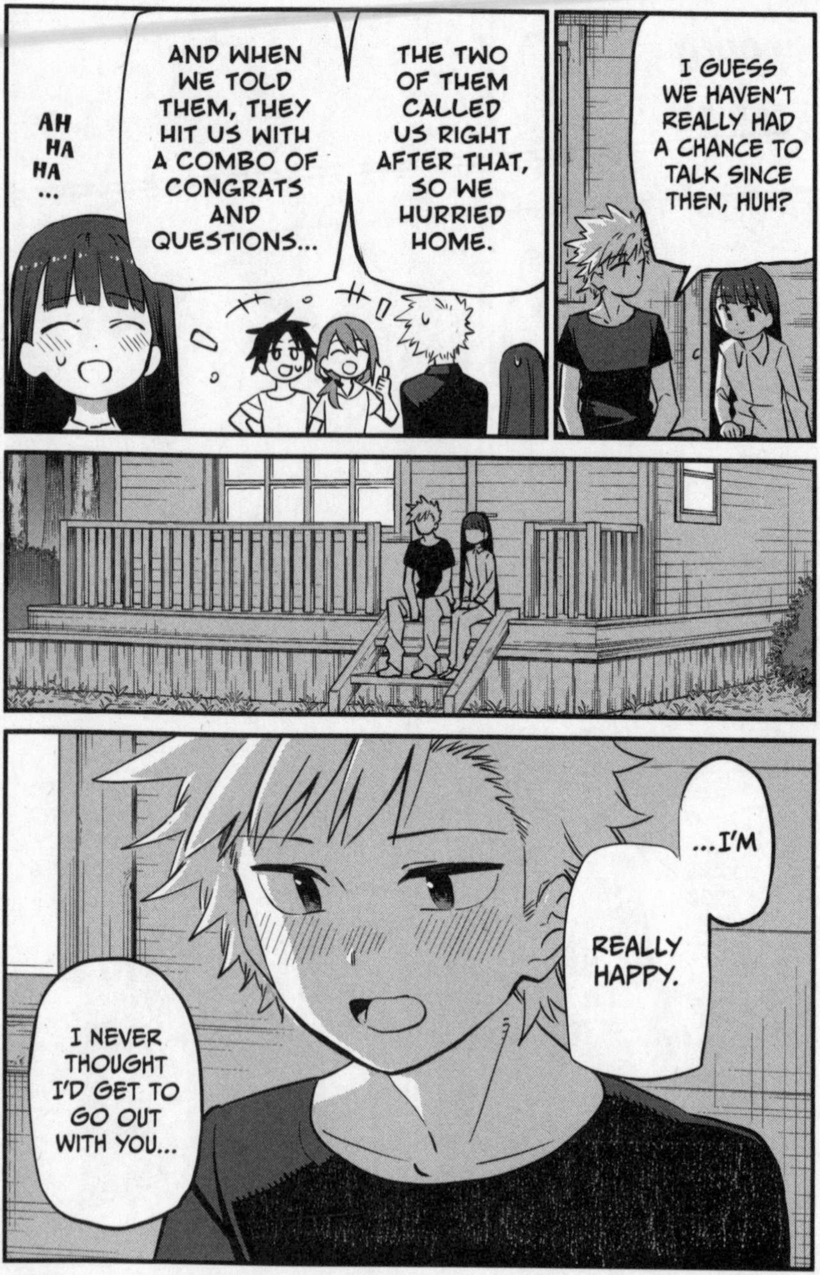
I GUESS WE HAVEN'T REALLY HAD A CHANCE TO TALK SINCE THEN, HUH?
THE TWO OF THEM CALLED US RIGHT AFTER THAT, SO WE HURRIED HOME.
AND WHEN WE TOLD THEM, THEY HIT US WITH A COMBO OF CONGRATS AND QUESTIONS...
AH HA HA ...
...I'M REALLY HAPPY.
I NEVER THOUGHT I'D GET TO GO OUT WITH YOU...

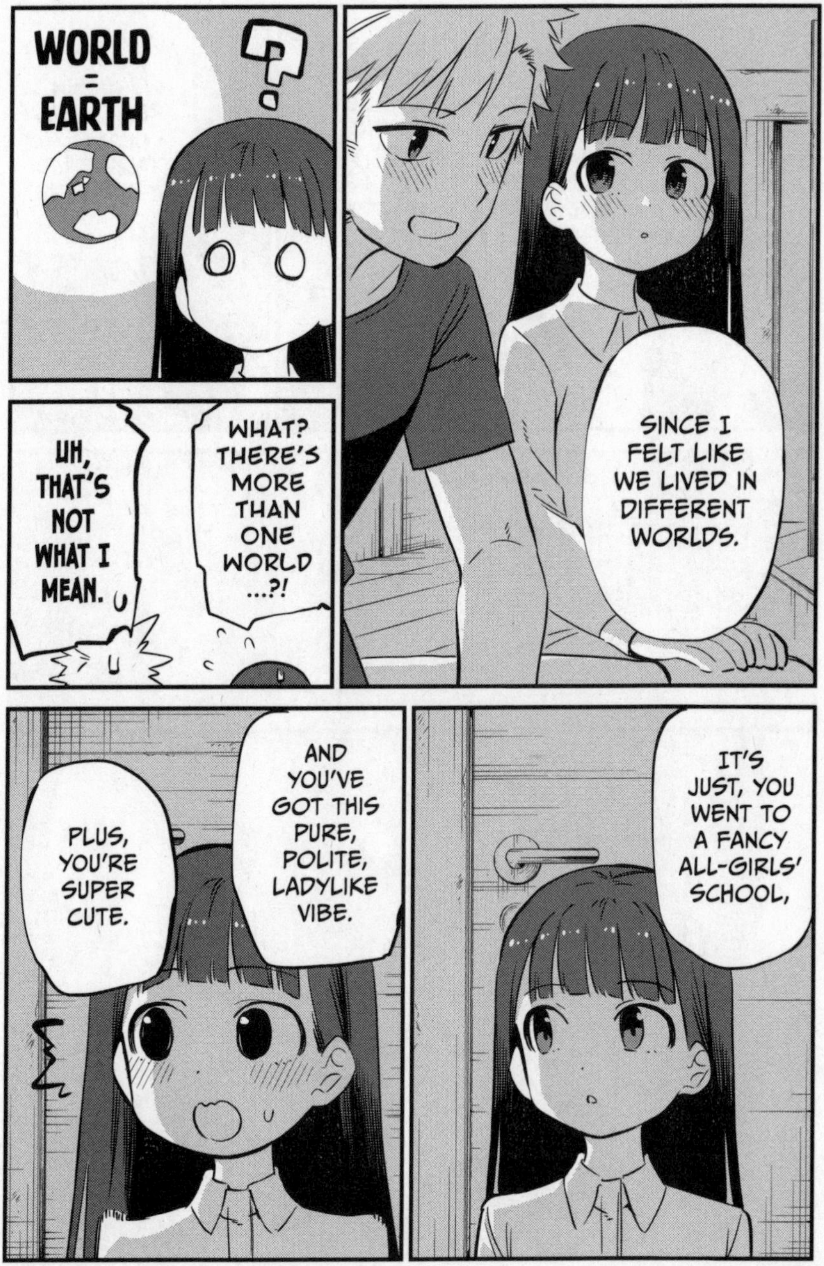
SINCE I FELT LIKE WE LIVED IN DIFFERENT WORLDS.
WORLD = EARTH
WHAT? THERE'S MORE THAN ONE WORLD ...?!
UH, THAT'S NOT WHAT I MEAN.
IT'S JUST, YOU WENT TO A FANCY ALL-GIRLS' SCHOOL,
AND YOU'VE GOT THIS PURE, POLITE, LADYLIKE VIBE.
PLUS, YOU'RE SUPER CUTE.

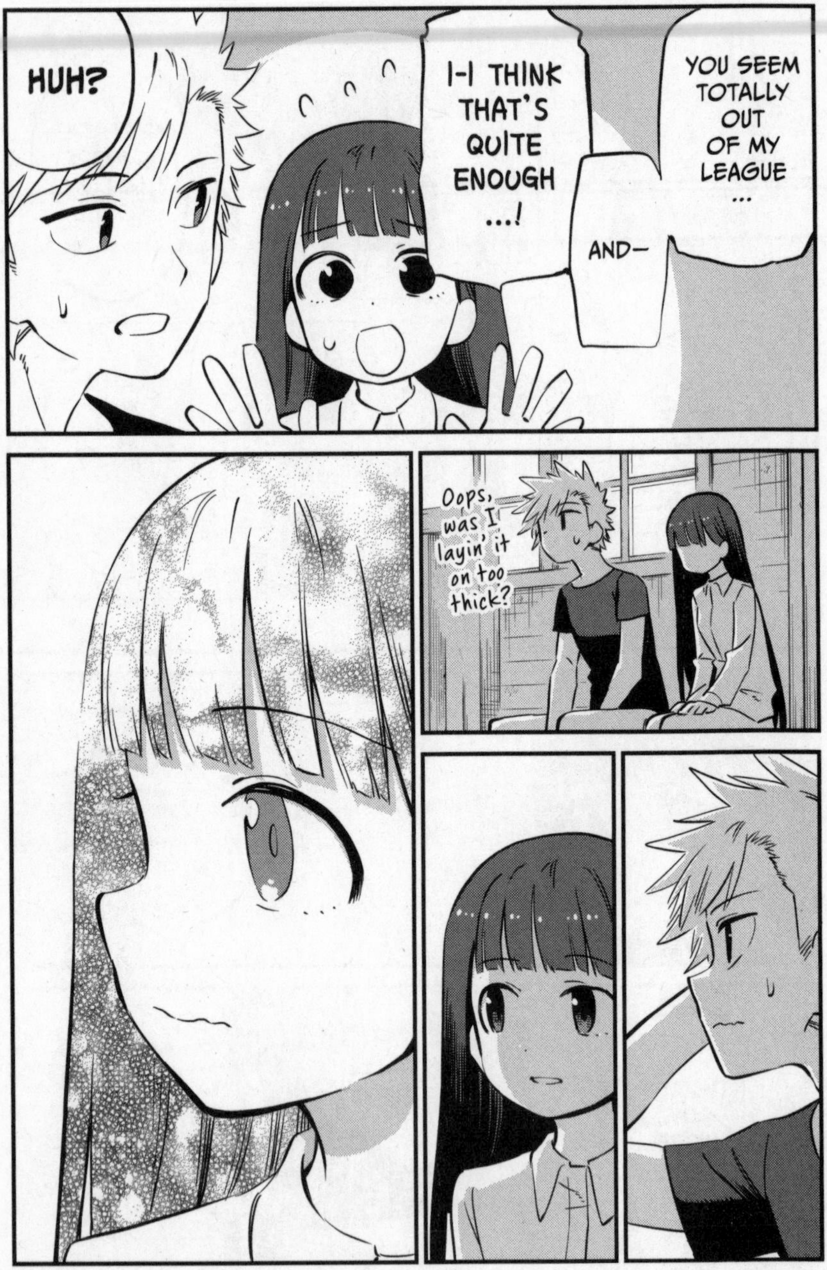
YOU SEEM TOTALLY OUT OF MY LEAGUE ...
AND—
I-I THINK THAT'S QUITE ENOUGH ...!
HUH?
Oops, was I layin' it on too thick?

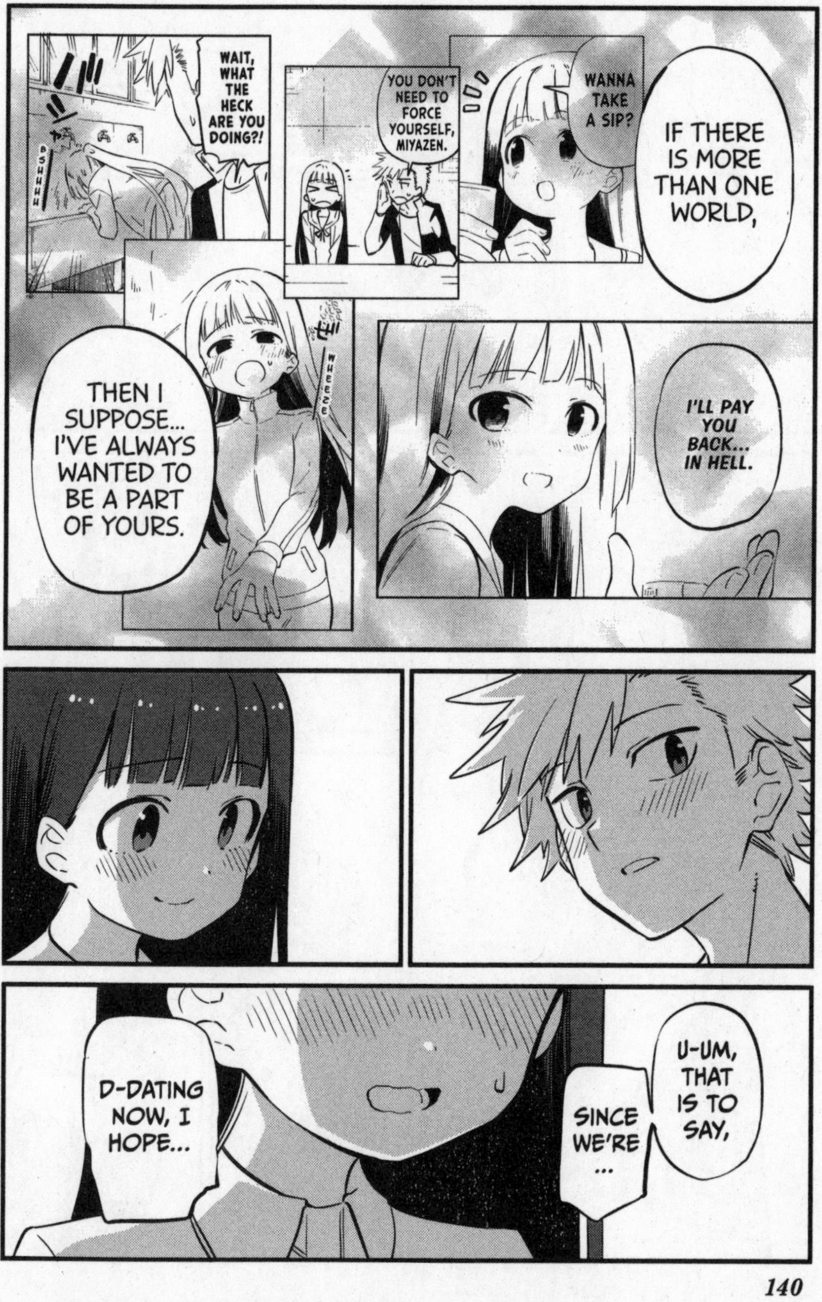
IF THERE IS MORE THAN ONE WORLD,
WANNA TAKE A SIP?
YOU DON'T NEED TO FORCE YOURSELF, MIYAZEN.
WAIT, WHAT THE HECK ARE YOU DOING?!
BSHHHH
I'LL PAY YOU BACK... IN HELL.
WHEEZE
THEN I SUPPOSE... I'VE ALWAYS WANTED TO BE A PART OF YOURS.
U-UM, THAT IS TO SAY,
SINCE WE'RE ...
D-DATING NOW, I HOPE...

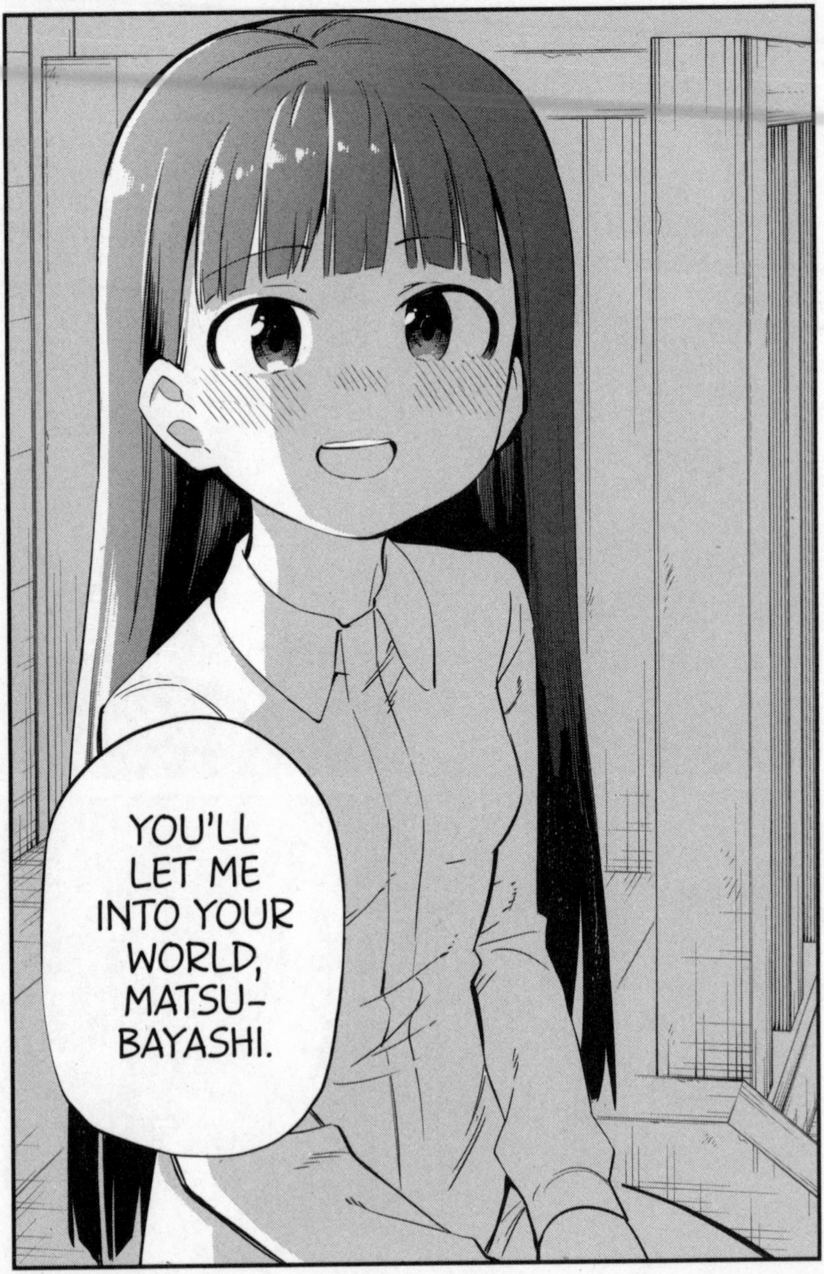
YOU'LL LET ME INTO YOUR WORLD, MATSU-BAYASHI.

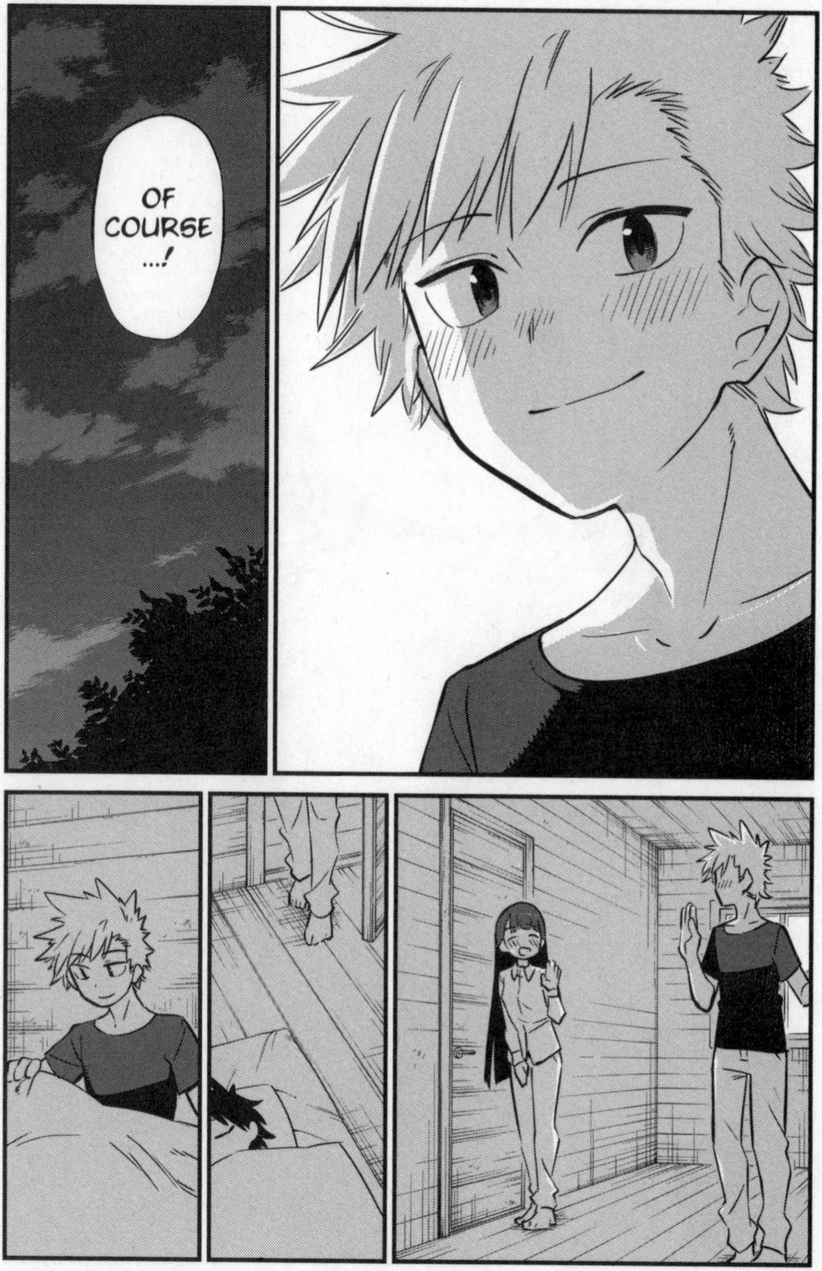
OF COURSE ...!

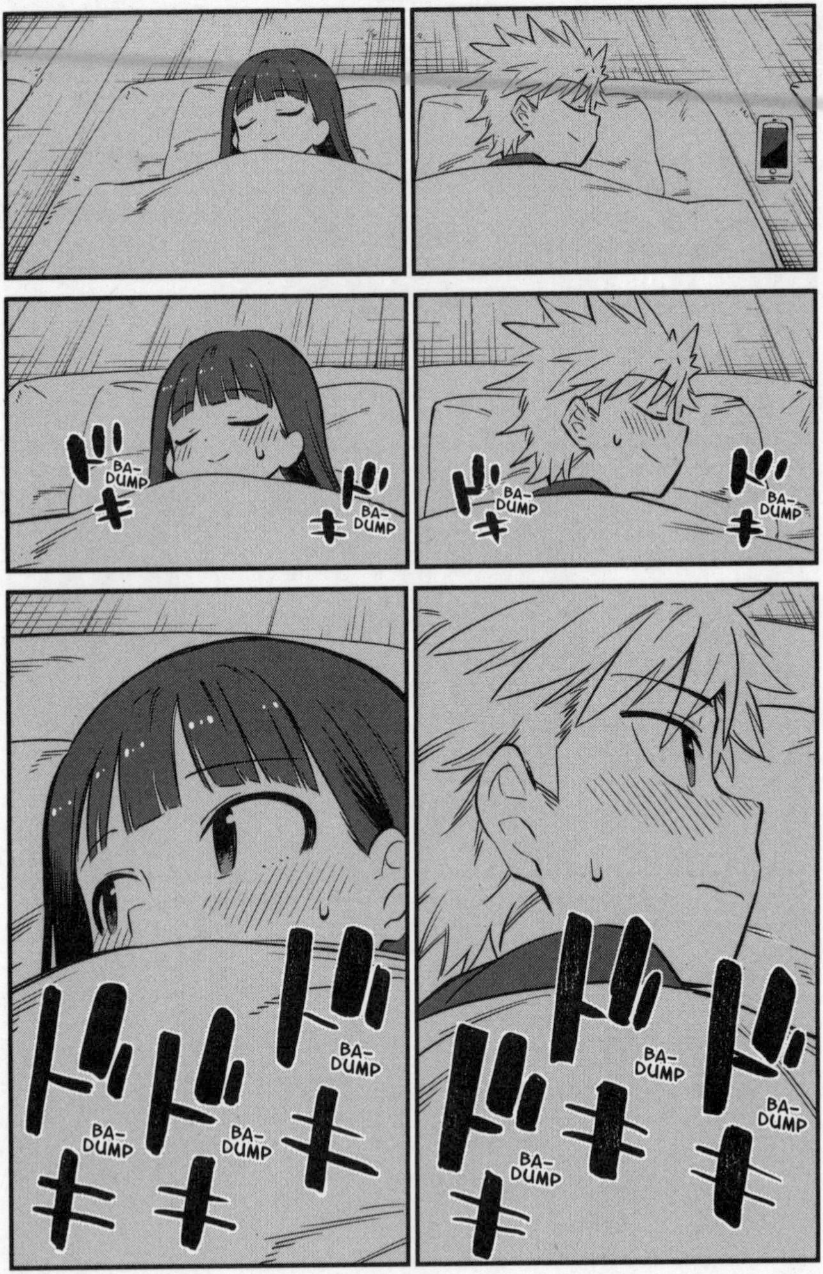
ドキ
BA-DUMP
ドキ
BA-DUMP
ドキ
BA-DUMP
ドキ
BA-DUMP
ドキ
BA-DUMP
ドキ
BA-DUMP
ドキ
BA-DUMP
ドキ
BA-DUMP
ドキ
BA-DUMP
ドキ
BA-DUMP

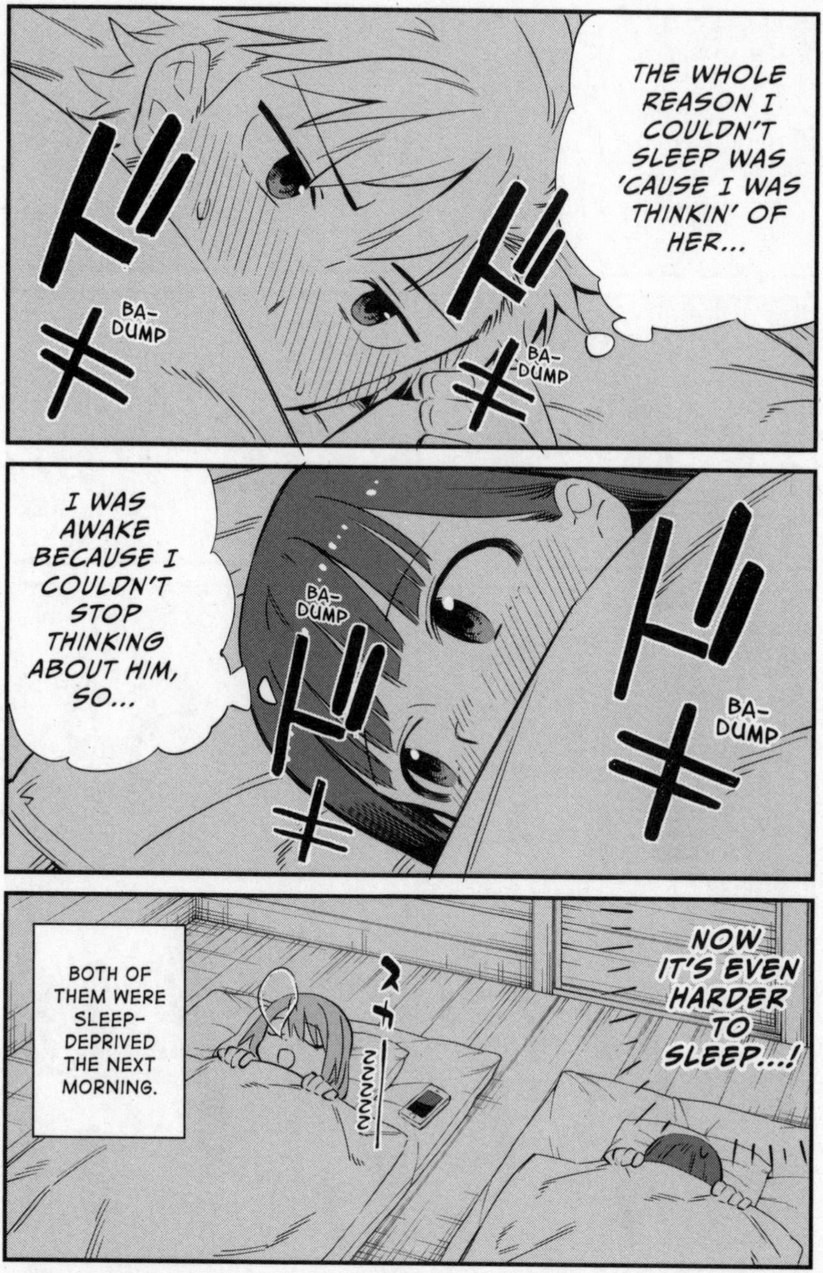
THE WHOLE REASON I COULDN'T SLEEP WAS 'CAUSE I WAS THINKIN' OF HER...
BA-DUMP
BA-DUMP
BA-DUMP
I WAS AWAKE BECAUSE I COULDN'T STOP THINKING ABOUT HIM, SO...
BA-DUMP
NOW IT'S EVEN HARDER TO SLEEP...!
BOTH OF THEM WERE SLEEP-DEPRIVED THE NEXT MORNING.

Miss Miyazen Would Love to Get Closer to You 3 / End

AFTERWORD

We've reached Volume 3 of *Miss Miyazen*.

The two of them have finally started dating, and they're much closer than when they could barely talk to each other. I hesitated over whether to have them go out during the series, but I wanted to see what they'd be like as a couple, so I decided to go with it.

I hope you'll continue to watch over them.

SPECIAL THANKS

Yuki Tabei
Hiroki Misaki
Hatsumaru Ugebeso

Editor Y-moto
Daimaru
All of my dear
readers

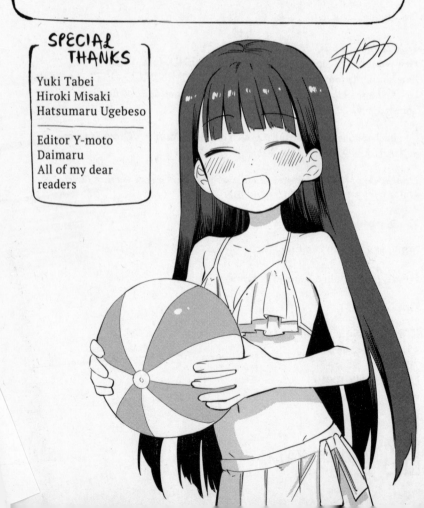

Miss Miyazen Would Love to Get Closer to You 3

A VERTICAL Book

Editor: Michelle Lin
Translation: Jenny McKeon
Production: Grace Lu
         Pei Ann Yeap
         Mercedes McGarry
Proofreading: Micah Q. Allen

Originally published in Japanese as *Ochikaduki ni Naritai Miyazen-san 3* by
SQUARE ENIX CO., LTD., 2021

Ochikaduki ni Naritai Miyazen-san first serialized in *Gekkan Gangan Joker*,
SQUARE ENIX CO., LTD., 2020-2021

This is a work of fiction.

ISBN: 978-1-64729-173-0

Printed in the United States of America

First Edition

Kodansha USA Publishing, LLC
451 Park Avenue South
7th Floor
New York, NY 10016
www.kodansha.us

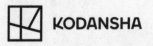